Underdevelopment and rural structures in Southeastern Turkey: the household economy in Gisgis and Kalhana

Underdevelopment and rural structures in Southeastern Turkey: the household economy in Gisgis and Kalhana

Zülküf Aydin

Published for
The Centre for Middle Eastern & Islamic Studies
University of Durham
by Ithaca Press London 1986

Durham Middle East Monographs No 2

First published in 1986 by
Ithaca Press 13 Southwark Street, London SE1,
for the Centre for Middle Eastern & Islamic Studies,
University of Durham

ISBN 0-86372-034-X

Printed in England by Biddles Ltd
Guildford & King's Lynn

Aydin, Zülküf
Underdevelopment and rural structures in southeastern Turkey: the household economy of Gisgis and Kalhana.
—— (Durham Middle East monographs; V2)
1. Rural development —— Turkey.
2. Turkey —— Economic conditions —— 1918
I. Title II. University of Durham. Centre for Middle Eastern and Islamic Studies III. Series
330.9566'702 HC492

ISBN 0-86372-034-X

Contents

List of Tables
List of Figures

CHAPTER ONE: INTRODUCTION 1
The Turkish Agrarian Debate 4
The Boratav thesis: the Fight for Socialism 5
The Erdost thesis: National Democratic Revolution 10
Historical Evolution of Landownership 13
Notes to Chapter One 18

CHAPTER TWO: REGIONAL UNDERDEVELOPMENT IN TURKEY 22
Theoretical Approaches 23
Cumulative causation 23
Internal colonialism 24
The Turkish Social Formation 30
The 1923-1929 period 31
1930-1939: Etatism 37
1940-1945: War Economy 39
Post-war period 40
Notes to Chapter Two 45

CHAPTER THREE: THE STRUCTURE OF SOUTHEASTERN ANATOLIA 50
Southeastern Anatolia 51
Population 51
Industry 53
Transportation and Communication 54
Education 54
Health 55
Agricultural inputs 56
State policies 56
Economic structure of Southeast Anatolia 59
Notes to Chapter Three 66

CHAPTER FOUR: PHYSICAL ENVIRONMENT, POPULATION AND AGRICULTURE 69
Physical Environment and Population in Gisgis and Kalhana 69
Gisgis: Physical Environment 70

Kalhana: Physical Environment 72
Population in Gisgis and Kalhana 76
Agriculture in Gisgis and Kalhana 88
Gisgis 89
Kalhana 95
Crop Production in Gisgis and Kalhana 99
The Productive Process in Gisgis and Kalhana 109
Gisgis 109
Kalhana 110
Notes to Chapter Four 112

CHAPTER FIVE: LAND AND STOCK OWNERSHIP 115
Landownership in Gisgis 115
Animal Ownership in Gisgis 118
Landownership in Kalhana 122
Animal Ownership in Kalhana 130
Notes to Chapter Five 135

CHAPTER SIX: RELATIONS OF PRODUCTION OUTSIDE THE HOUSEHOLD 137
Historical Evolution of the Relations of Production 138
Relations of Production outside the Household 144
Land use in Gisgis 145
Land use in Kalhana 149
Sharecropping in animal breeding and caretaking 156
Notes to Chapter Six 160

CHAPTER SEVEN: RELATIONS OF PRODUCTION WITHIN THE HOUSEHOLD 161
Division of Labour within the Household 161
Female Labour in Gisgis and Kalhana 166
Notes to Chapter Seven 188

CHAPTER EIGHT: CREDIT MECHANISMS 190
Organised Credits in Turkey 191
Unorganised Credits in Turkey 196
Organised Credits in Ergani 199
Unorganised Credits in Ergani 205
Notes to Chapter Eight 209

CHAPTER NINE: MARKETING STRUCTURES 211
Marketing Structures in Turkey 211
Marketing Structures in Diyarbakır 222
Marketing Structures in Gisgis and Kalhana 226
Notes to Chapter Nine 232

CHAPTER TEN: PATTERNS OF MIGRATION 233
Migration in Gisgis 234
Migration in Kalhana 243
Notes to Chapter Ten 252

CHAPTER ELEVEN: CONCLUSION 254
Notes to Chapter Eleven 262

BIBLIOGRAPHY 263

APPENDIX 282

INDEX 294

List of Tables

1. Population by age group and sex in Gisgis 78
2. Marital status of those over 14 in Gisgis 78
3. Population increase in Gisgis 78
4. Live births and infant mortality in Gisgis 81
5. Population by age group and sex in Kalhana 83
6. Marital status of those over 14 in Kalhana 83
7. Population increase in Kalhana 83
8. Landownership by primary job in Gisgis 90
9. Irrigated landownership in Gisgis 92
10. Unirrigated landownership in Gisgis 92
11. Land utilisation in Gisgis 92
12. Landownership by primary job in Kalhana 96
13. Land utilisation in Kalhana 96
14. Land under cultivation in Kalhana 100
15. Land under cultivation in Gisgis 100
16. Distribution of land among the inhabitants of Gisgis 116
17. Livestock ownership in Gisgis 119
18. Distribution of land among the inhabitants of Kalhana 128
19. Land fragmentation in big estates, Kalhana 128
20. Landownership within the village boundaries, Kalhana 128
21. Livestock ownership in Kalhana 131
22. Land use in Gisgis 145
23. Farming families by land owned, Gisgis 146
24. Landownership by sharecropping in Gisgis 148
25. Land use in Kalhana 149
26. Sharecroppers and sharecropped land in Kalhana 149
27. Number of selected household by land owned 171
28. Tasks performed by the members of a household 186
29. Credits received from the Agricultural Bank 199
30. Goods imported by Diyarbakır Province in 1969 223
31. Goods exported from Diyarbakır Province in 1969 224
32. Number of relatives living outside the village 235
33. Destinations of migrants from Gisgis 236
34. Reasons for leaving the village 238
35. Occupations of relations living outside the village 239

36. Unemployment in Gisgis 241
37. Seasonal labourers of Gisgis 242
38. Origins of household heads and their wives in Kalhana 245
39. Origins of household heads and their wives born outside Kalhana 245
40. Number of relatives living outside Kalhana 248
41. Destinations of migrants from Kalhana 250

List of Figures

1. Map of Turkey showing Southeastern Anatolia 52
2. Plan of typical village house 71
3. Map showing location of Gisgis and Kalhana 73
4. Sketch of Gisgis village 73
5. Sketch of Kalhana village 75
6. Efrahim's irrigation system 176
7. Design of a *Mişer* 176

1. Introduction

This is a study of two villages in the Southeast Anatolia region of Turkey and is concerned with the development of capitalism and capital accumulation. Turkey has long been an integrated part of the world capitalist system but, although the dominant mode of production is capitalist, peasant production plays an important role in the production of surplus. It is hoped that the present study of two villages in Southeast Anatolia will show the interaction between the peasant household economy and rural and urban capitalism in Turkey. As to the reason for choosing Gisgis and Kalhana villages, this is due to the fact that, despite their differences in terms of the size of landownership and of the nature of the organisation of production, the household economy plays an important role in both. Furthermore, the two villages adequately reflect the rural structure of Southeast Anatolia. That is, they highlight the two types of landholdings and the two sets of production relations which coexist in this region.

The two types of landholdings, which are the outcome of historical conditions specific to the region, are those of large estates and small peasant holdings. Large landowners can and do own all the land in some villages, while small peasant holdings characterise other villages. It is for this reason, for example, that some sociologists have categorised villages in terms of whether or not the whole village is owned by a landlord or by the village residents. (1)

As to the two types of production relations, these are due to the fact that, although large estates become more and more mechanised and capitalist oriented, since the 1950s the peasant household units have also survived and continued to play an important role in the production of surplus.

The peasantry and rural structures have constituted the subject of many studies in a variety of disciplines, including anthropology, sociology, economics, politics and others. Especially in underdeveloped countries where the agricultural sector is predominant, analysis of the peasantry and rural structures becomes vital for understanding the dynamics of the society and the mechanisms at work.

Attempts were made by both Marxists and non-Marxists to try to understand the nature and future of the peasantry. While modernisation theorists like Redfield, Wolf or Shanin (2) have attempted to formulate a 'general type' of peasantry, much of Marxist literature has concerned itself with the nature and future of the peasantry under capitalism. (3)

An important limitation of the modernisation approach, (4) which attempts to produce a general definition of the peasantry, is that it fails to differentiate between various types of cultivators who have existed in different historical periods in different types of societies. A general descriptive definition of the peasantry is ahistorical. Furthermore, the agglomeration of rural producers under the term 'peasant' tends to ignore the differentiation of peasants in class terms and treats them as a homogenous group. Various interpretations of the peasantry from the modernisation standpoint contain an inherent evolutionist bias, since they place the peasants somewhere on the unilinear development scheme of civilisation as exemplified by Redfield's concept of the folk-urban continuum. Modernisation not only assumes that a unilinear development is possible but also claims that the western model of development is the ideal type to be followed by the peasant societies of the underdeveloped world; once the inherent internal obstacles to development are removed, peasant societies of the underdeveloped world can develop along the western path. By emphasising the internal structure of underdeveloped countries, the modernisation theory ignores the colonialist and imperialist exploitation of the third world.

Classical Marxist analysis (5) of rural development, on the other hand, tends to overemphasise the destructive nature of capitalism in agriculture which would eventually bring about two conflicting classes: the rural proletariat and the rural capitalists. Kautsky and Lenin's writings on the peasantry espouse this liquidation of the peasantry. In underdeveloped countries, Lenin's analysis of the peasantry and his Development of Capitalism in Russia have been extremely influential. Uncritical application of Lenin's method in analysing the rural structures of the Third World by some sections of the left has tended to underplay the vitality of the peasantry under capitalism and to ignore the diversified nature of the incorporation of the peasantry into capitalist development. This is mostly due to the acceptance of a specific and limited conception that identifies capitalism with wage labour. Therefore, the quantification of wage labour relation becomes a defining point of the existence or non-existence of capitalism in a production unit, region or country. Non-existence or limited existence of wage labour relations is considered sufficient to label a country or a region as pre-capitalist, feudal or semi-feudal. This, as suggested, misses out many of the ways and mechanisms of capitalist penetration of the countryside.

On the other hand, Chayanov's concept of the peasant economy, derived from the analysis of the Russian countryside, is not very helpful either in understanding the historical process of rural transformation, simply because what it poses is a static and ideal behavioural model of a peasant household. (6)

A clear understanding of rural structures, together with a sound theoretical analysis of the peasantry is very crucial, not only as an academic exercise, but also for its political connotations. A misunderstanding of rural structures or a mechanical application of certain theories in political practices can lead to disastrous consequences, as exemplified in the debate around the agrarian question in Turkey.

The Turkish Agrarian Debate

Political developments among the Turkish left in the late 1960s and early 1970s were very closely related to the debate on the Turkish Agrarian Question. The debate was important in two senses. First of all it contributed to the understanding, or misunderstanding, of the nature of the transformation undergone by the Turkish countryside. Secondly, its theoretical conclusions were used in an uncritical fashion in the construction of political strategies by various sections of the Turkish left, which believed in the unity of theory and practice. Believing in the correctness of their theory, and that the time was ripe, thousands of students poured into the streets demonstrating and agitating for a revolution. Some went into the rural areas to organise the ostensible allies of the working class, the peasants, in a National Democratic Revolution. But the peasants' response was to report them to the authorities. The turbulence which resulted brought about a right-wing military intervention in 1971 rather than a National Democratic Revolution or a Socialist Revolution, and renewed turbulence led to a right-wing military takeover again in 1980.

In the following pages we shall attempt to show that the arguments put forward in the debate were theoretically unsound and empirically unfounded; the positions taken in the debate were based on a misunderstanding of the concept of the mode of production, and the political strategies drawn from these positions were responsible for the 'Tragedy of the Turkish Left' in the 1970s and 1980s.

The Boratav thesis : the fight for socialism

Although there were numerous minor contributions to the debate, the two major contributions came from Korkut Boratav and Muzaffer Erdost. (7) In a short article published in Emek, the journal of the Turkish Workers' Party, Korkut Boratav summarised the arguments published in more detail in his book Income Distribution. (8) He argued that three distinctive relations of production could be observed in Turkish agriculture: petty (simple) commodity production, of which the most widespread was simple commodity production, which is subject to the exploitation of merchant and usurer capital. Boratav considered the relations of exploitation between simple (petty) commodity production and merchant and usurer capital as primitive forms of capitalist exploitation. The fact that the largest part of agriculture is under the influence of primitive capitalist relations leads one to the conclusion that a primitive capitalist mode of production is dominant in Turkey. In Income Distribution, Boratav tries to show the insignificance of feudal and semi-feudal relations in Turkey by the use of statistical data. In his view, it is possible to say that feudal and semi-feudal relations of exploitation, which occur either in sharecropping form or in more pure and rigid forms, are intensified in the cases where an ağa (landlord) owns one or more villages. According to the Village Inventory Surveys carried out by the Ministry of Village Affairs and covering 22,047 villages in 43 provinces, the number of villages totally owned by a landlord, family or dynasty is 71, constituting only 0.32 per cent of the total. This ratio is higher in Eastern provinces but still does not exceed 11 per cent of the total number of villages in the provinces of Tunceli, Ağrı, Hatay, Mardin, Erzurum, Diyarbakır, Siirt, Urfa and Gaziantep. A conclusion may be drawn from this criterion: that feudal and semi-feudal relations are extremely limited, and only cover more than 10 per cent of villages in some of the Eastern provinces.

Another criterion put forward by Boratav to show the limits of feudal and semi-feudal relations is the number of landless peasants working as sharecroppers. The Village

Inventory Surveys for 43 provinces show that landless sharecroppers constitute only 2.6 per cent of total farming families. If the number of small landowners who also work as sharecroppers is added to this percentage, the figure increases considerably. The 1963 Agricultural Census states that sharecropping families are 15 per cent of all farming families. But, in order to be considered as a semi-feudal relationship, sharecropping will have to be in the form of small holdings. If the number of peasants working as sharecroppers for small landowners is excluded from the calculation, the number of peasants sharecropping for landlords who own 500 *dönüms* or more land would be about 90,000 (2.6 per cent of total farming families). (9) Boratav maintains that, if the boundaries of ağadom were to be extended to 200 *dönüms* of land, then only 3.3 per cent of farming families could be classified as sharecroppers.

It is clearly evident that Boratav uses these three criteria to denote the nature and extent of feudal and semi-feudal relations of production: the number of landless families, the number of sharecropping families working for a large landowner, and the number of villages whose lands belong to an individual, a family or a dynasty. From this he arrives at the conclusion that feudal and semi-feudal relations of distribution constitute only an insignificant part - a mere 2.6 to 3.3 per cent - of Turkish agriculture. However, Turkish agriculture is not purely capitalist either: since only 10 per cent of farming families work as wage labourers, this relation of production cannot be considered dominant in the Turkish countryside. The most common or predominant relation (of production) is based on small ownership, which embraces 75-80 per cent of the rural population. (10) Since in Turkey small producers lose their surplus product not to the feudal element but to merchant and usurer capital, Boratav argues that a backward capitalism is dominant in Turkey.

Boratav may be right to argue that the type of capitalism existent in Turkey is not a fully developed capitalism but his method of identifying the backward nature of capitalism in Turkey is extremely dubious. Boratav's use of the size of land holding as a criterion in identifying capitalism and feudalism is quite erroneous. The identification of sharecropping arrangements with semi-feudal relations of production is not very convincing either. Quite a number of recent Latin American studies have shown that the use of sharecropping arrangements by large landlords is not a sign of feudalism but a result of profitability calculations made by the landlords. (11) Our own research in Southeastern Anatolia, where landlord-sharecropper relations are most widespread, has also revealed the fact that it is much more beneficial, both economically and politically, for the landlords to use sharecroppers rather than wage labourers in certain cases. Capital accumulation is one of the basic features of capitalism, and the landlords' decision-making is affected by their concern for capital accumulation.

In deciding whether capitalism or feudalism is dominant in a particular country it is extremely misleading to look at the relations of production or the immediate process of production in single units of production. Boratav has made the mistake of confusing a mode of production with the immediate process of production and relations of exploitation. It is wrong to identify sharecropping with semi-feudalism and wage labour with capitalism. Boratav's empiricist method leads him to a static definition of modes of production. His concept of mode of production is read off from relations of production and his definition of relations of production is read off from statistical data (the validity of which is doubtful).

Lenin warned against too stereotyped an understanding of capitalism in rural areas in his Development of Capitalism in Russia. (12) Kautsky also argued that the development of capitalism in agriculture does not have to follow the same path as in industry. Peculiarities of agriculture present certain obstacles to the separation of direct producers from their means of production:

> To study the agrarian question according to Marx's method, we should not confine ourselves to the question of the future of small-scale farming; on the contrary, we should look at all the changes which agriculture experiences under the domination

> of capitalist production. We should ask: is capital, and in what ways is capital taking hold of agriculture, revolutionizing it, smashing the old forms of production and poverty and establishing the new forms which must succeed. (13)

In order to be able to talk about capitalist domination in agriculture we should, then, ask Boratav: is it really necessary to have predominance of the wage labour relation, which could be counted empirically? Taking capitalism as a world system, Wallerstein argues that wage labour is not a necessary labour form but only one of the possible labour forms to be used in capitalism. (14)

In his explanation of the nature of Turkish capitalism, Boratav comes very close to the concept of the articulations of modes of production, without using the concept. He argues that within a social formation there exist various relations of production side by side or inside each other. However, one of these relations of production is dominant, while others are subordinate. The relations of production which are congruent with the superstructure of the society are the dominant relations of production. (15) Boratav confuses relations of production with modes of production and, in most of his writings, uses them interchangeably. We already know how Boratav uses statistical data to identify the existence of certain relations of production (and modes of production). The dominance of one mode of production over others within a social formation does not mean, in Boratav's writings, that they are subordinate to the laws of motion of the dominant mode of production. The way he treats the statistical data suggests that the dominance of one mode of production is tantamount to its percentage being predominant compared with the ratio of other modes of production (or relations of production). Therefore the capitalist mode of production based on wage labour constitutes 10 per cent of the social formation, feudal and semi-feudal relations of production based on sharecropping constitute about 5-10 per cent, and simple commodity production based on small holdings constitutes 75-80 per cent. (16) Even if the statistical definition of modes of production provided by Boratav were acceptable, there is no dominant mode of production in the articulationist sense; there is rather a co-existence of several modes of production, one of which happens to be the most widespread. This kind of approach has been criticised by Banaji, who argues that individual enterprises in an economy can show different relations of exploitation of labour. The important point is that these enterprises are subject to the laws of motion of that economy. For Banaji, to identify the mode of production with the form of exploitation of labour is to engage in vulgar Marxism. He maintains that relations of exploitation such as wage labour, sharecropping, etc. are simple categories since they can occur in different modes (epochs) of production. The concept 'mode of production' cannot be deduced from the survival and reproduction of different forms of exploitation in individual enterprises or branches of the economy. In an economy where capitalism is dominant, 'pre-capitalist enterprises, contrary to formal appearances, are in essence capitalist since they are subordinated to capitalist laws of motion'. (17) In the same vein, Bernstein argues that capitalism has become universal and has destroyed the conditions of reproduction of other modes, even when forms of subjugation of labour units of production typical of these modes have only been partially transformed. (18)

As stated earlier, Boratav's contention that a backward, primitive capitalism is dominant in Turkey may be right; however, his statistical formulations and empiricist definitions do not warrant such a conclusion. The nature of agrarian structure cannot be understood by focusing solely on the number of wage labourers, on the amount of land owned or by studying agriculture in isolation, independently of the whole mechanism of social production.

Boratav's analysis was adopted by the Turkish Workers' Party (TWP) in sketching out their tactics and political strategies. In the journal of the TWP, several writers reiterated Boratav's argument that a kind of capitalism was dominant in Turkey and that, therefore, the revolutionary struggle should be channelled into the fight for socialism. (19)

For them, both in industry and in agriculture a working class who could lead a struggle for socialism had emerged. The development of capitalist relations had proved detrimental to small and middle peasants and pushed them to unite with the working class, giving them a revolutionary potential. Therefore, conditions for a fight for socialism were now ripe.

The Erdost thesis : national democratic revolution

The appearance of Boratav's article in Emek No.6 attracted severe criticism from those who believed in the dominance of feudal and semi-feudal modes of production in Turkey. The most aggressive criticism came from Erdost, who attacked Boratav's interpretations of statistical data and his theoretical position. (20) Erdost criticised Boratav for using unreliable statistics in arriving at the conclusion that the extent of feudal relations was 5 per cent of the total rural structure. Erdost's criticism could have been accepted had it not been for the fact that he calculated the extent of feudalism and semi-feudalism as constituting 46 per cent of the total structure. (21) In doing so, Erdost in fact falls into the same trap as Boratav by using the amount of land as a sufficient criterion for a definition of feudalism or semi-feudalism. Secondly, it is not possible to identify a mode of production with the relations of production within a single unit of production. Agrarian structure cannot be identified as feudal, semi-feudal or capitalist by focusing solely on a household or a village, or even a region in isolation from the context of larger structures like a social formation or the capitalist world system. The number of workers or sharecroppers in these units, or the amount of land owned, cannot be used as the only criterion for the identification of a mode of production.

Erdost differentiates between patriarchal, semi-feudal, feudal and capitalist production very categorically. Among the 9 million production units in Turkey only 600,000 employ wage labour and therefore the capitalist mode of production, he argues, cannot be considered a dominant mode of production. He admits that capitalist relations do exist in Turkish agriculture, but they are in no way dominant. He maintains that, in a country like Turkey, where small peasant holdings are predominant, one cannot speak of the dominance of capitalism. On the contrary, one can hold that pre-capitalist relations of production are dominant in agriculture. (22) One of the most crucial denominators used by Erdost to show the dominance of pre-capitalist relations of production in the Turkish countryside is the extent of the production of commodities. Simple commodity production should be separated from capitalist production. Production of commodities for the market in order to be able to buy some necessities such as salt does not aim at a profit. Indeed, it is absolutely different from the production of commodities for profit. If the producer produces commodities by the use of wage labour in accordance with the formula m-c-m, then there is a capitalist commodity production. Since small peasant holders do not sell most of their products in the market, the exploitation of small producers can be measured by the amount of commodities offered for sale in the market. This does not exceed 10 per cent of the total wheat crop, which is the largest crop produced by small producers. (23) The logical conclusion of Erdost's argument is that capitalist relations of production constitute 10 per cent of total agrarian relations.

This is highly misleading, because 'once commodity relations are incorporated in the cycle of the peasant household as an economic necessity', as Bernstein argues, 'the question of how much of its resources are devoted to the production of use-valued and of commodities is secondary, though still important'. (24) Today, capitalism has acquired a universal character; the pre-capitalist appearance of the family farm should not lead us to believe that this constitutes a mode of production. Capital controls the conditions of reproduction of the peasant family farm. The problem should be posed not in terms of whether or not capitalism exists in the countryside, but in terms of how capital comes into relations with the household and through which mechanism does capital exercise its dominance over the household. In doing so we must avoid determinism and functionalism. By this we mean that the household should not be considered a passive receiver unit, whose way of organisation is determined by the requirement of capitalism in its relationship with the outside world. Instead, the household should be treated as a unit constantly interacting with the outside world, doing its best to reproduce itself and its unity. Once this is accepted, we will have avoided one of the major difficulties of contemporary Marxism in trying to conceptualise small producers who own their means of production and use family labour in production as the main labour force. Moving on from the propositions that capitalism destroys all pre-capitalist modes of production wherever it goes and that capital accumulates in the hands of a few while the majority of the small producers lose their means of production, or in other words, become proletarianised, and therefore two distinct classes come into being, some Marxists find it difficult to conceptualise the peasantries of the Third World. This is because they do not fit into the definition of proletariat, simply because they own their means of production and use family labour. Marxists such as Amin, Banaji and Bernstein try to fit these peasantries into their scheme through claiming that peasants of the Third World are disguised proletarians, concealed wage labourers. (25) The argument put forward by Bernstein is that, through the control of the conditions of household production, capital is able to extract the surplus product produced by the household by means of family labour; therefore that part of the product remaining within the family is a concealed wage and the household labourers are disguised proletarians.

This type of explanation is confined to the problematic of capital accumulation and does not explain why capitalism does not proletarianise small producers but, in order to be consistent with the premise that capitalism eliminates small producers, this approach simply qualifies them as disguised proletarians. It takes the household as a passive unit of production and consumption open to all the impositions of capitalism. If this is the case, if capitalism can impose its will upon the household, then why does it not proletarianise them? Two possible answers come to mind: either capitalism is not able to destroy the household; or the relationship between capitalism and the household is a two-way relationship. To accept the first explanation is tantamount to denying the logic of capitalism, that it destroys other modes of production in its development. So we are left with the second alternative, that there is an interaction between capital and the household. While capital is trying to expropriate more and more surplus, the household tries to survive and reproduce itself.

However, capital, being unable to get rid of the household, tries to internalise the mode of calculation of the household into its circuit in order to benefit from this mode of labour usage as much as it can. It is no longer a wonder that, in so many places, peasants refuse to accept innovations introduced by governments in order to improve production. Peasants feel threatened by the introduction of new varieties of crops and seeds, artificial fertilisers and such like, which raise their production costs and make them more and more dependent on the market.

While we suggest that the interaction between the household and capital should be analysed, we do not by any means claim that household (peasant) production constitutes a mode of production <u>sui generis</u>. It is our contention that the relations of production, distribution and exchange at village level can best be analysed if the local structures and processes are treated as part of larger structures of the social formation and the world economy. The mechanisms which ensure the articulation of the local structures with the larger structures have to be specified, and there is therefore a constant attempt to illuminate the role of merchant capital, of the State, of marketing structures, and of migration as the mechanisms of articulation.

Historical Evolution of Landownership

In a region where agriculture is the predominant economic activity, the control of the land as an important means of production can be considered one of the most significant factors affecting the relations of production, class structure, landlord-peasant relations, and the mechanisms of the articulation of the local structures with the larger structures. Therefore it seems necessary to give a brief account of the historical development of the landownership patterns in Eastern and Southeastern Anatolia in this introduction, before embarking on the analysis both of the region and of Gisgis and Kalhana. This should not only provide the necessary historical background against which to evaluate the present landowning structure, but also permit us to highlight the important differences which characterise the land system in Eastern Anatolia as compared to other parts of Turkey.

In a context where the Islamic State was the absolute owner of all land, these lands being called miri, (26) the basis of the Ottoman land system was the dirlik (27) and its fundamental element was the tımar. (28) This mode of organisation provided the centralised authority with control over production, and was also suitable to the military structure of the state. Tımars of three different magnitudes were granted in the Ottoman Empire to those whose loyalty or service to the state and sultan was recognised, or to those who provided the sultan with cavalry and loyal service in war. The income of certain designated tımars extracted by different tımar holders was of three kinds:

(i) Has : not less than 100,000 akçe (Ottoman currency)
(ii) Zeamet: between 20,000 and 99,999 akçe
(iii) Tımar between 3,000 and 19,999 akçe (29)

The holders of tımars, sipahis, were not the owners of the land but representatives of the state, whose duty it was to collect taxes from the reaya (peasants) who had the usufructory rights in the land. The reaya's right of usufruct was inheritable, provided that the land was not left uncultivated for three successive years or more. (30) The peasant cultivated the land with his own implements, and each year gave a part of his harvest, the amount of which varied between one tenth and one half of the crop according to the fertility of the land and common usage, to the sipahi. (31) Furthermore, the peasants' freedom of mobility was restricted by the state to certain designated locations. (32) As for the sipahi, he was only a government official who collected taxes from the producers and provided soldiers for the state when required to do so. The sipahi's right of possession in dirlik could be taken away from him by the state if necessary.

The state-owned land system, miri, began to decline from the second half of the sixteenth century onwards, due to the weakening of the centralised authority. It is beyond the scope of this chapter to deal with the reasons behind this decline, which have been examined in several scholarly contributions. (33) It is important, however, to note that, from the sixteenth century onwards, parallel with the weakening of the centralised authority, the miri land system was replaced by the iltizam (34) system. In this system, in order to increase the income of the state the collection of the öşr (35) was sold to mültezims (tax farmers) who would organise and undertake the tax collection. The reayas (peasants) were left at the mercy of the mültezims as to how much tax was to be levied from them. As a result, in some provinces strong notables (ayans) and tax farmers (mültezims) gained strong positions and by 1808 the state was constrained to confirm their positions. These local notables and tax farmers acted as the owners of the lands and forced the peasants to pay more and more taxes, first in kind, then later in cash. We may call this trend 'a feudalisation of the miri system'. (36)

However, miri lands were not the only form of land within the boundaries of the empire. In different parts of the empire other types of landownership can be observed. In Eastern Anatolia, for example, there were some sancaks (administrative unit in the Ottoman Empire) where the dominant form of landownership was serbest mir-i miranlık, yurtluk/ocaklık and mir-aşiretliği.

Serbest mir-i miranlıks were those sancaks which were also called hükumet (37) such as Cizre, Genç, Bitlis, Imadiye, Mahmudiya. In these cases, ownership of the land rested with the holders, but they nevertheless recognised the higher sovereignty of the Ottoman state. Tımar and zeamet did not exist in these serbest mir-i miranlık, and the sancaks were virtually the property of their holders, beys who paid a certain amount of tax and provided soldiers to the state if necessary. (38) Furthermore, local tribal leaders, beys, were given large estates in return for their support of Sultan Selim against Shah Ismail of Iran in 1514 and the following years. The sancaks of these local beys were called yurtluk/ocaklık and were inherited by their children. The state could not dismiss the local bey, nor could it appoint a new bey to a sancak. In Diyarbakır province, for example, the number of yurtluk/ocaklık sancaks was eight: Sokman, Kulub, Tercil, Mihrani, Itah, Pertek, Çapakçur and Çermik. (39) There were also about four hundred mir aşiretliği (tribal leaderships) in Diyarbakır, Van and Sehrizar. The leaders of these tribal groups held the ownership of the land, and on their death their children would inherit their lands. (40)

As we can see, the lands given as property (mülk) under the names of serbest mir-i miranlık, yurtluk/ocaklık and mir aşiretliği were the basis of a different structure, whose remnants are still in existence in Eastern Anatolia. This difference was to achieve importance after the sixteenth century when the centralised Ottoman State gradually lost its control over the land. The inability of the central authority to control its provinces led to the consolidation of the power of local notables (ayans) vis-à-vis the reaya who actually worked the land. In the case of the eastern notables, who had had a different status from ordinary tımar holders anyway, they were able to enjoy almost total private ownership in land.

Furthermore, with the acceptance of private property in land in 1926, following the establishment of the Turkish Republic in 1923, eastern notables, tribal leaders and big land holders who were de facto owners of large lands became de jure owners. Therefore it would not be misleading to suggest that the roots of the unequal land distribution in Eastern Anatolia lie in the historical background. Today's large estates and small peasant holdings have been structured by this specific historical development of landownership in the region. _Yurtluk/ocaklık_ and _serbest mir-i miranlık_ lands constitute the basis of today's large estates, whereas the lands tax-farmed out to _mültezims_ and worked by _reayas_ (peasant families) constitute the basis of small peasant holdings. For the _reayas_ became the owners of the land over which they had had only usufructory rights before the Republic.

Admittedly, in addition to the above indicated historical aspects, other factors such as the commercialisation of Turkish agriculture have also contributed to the determination of the present landowning structure in Gisgis and Kalhana. However, as these are factors that will be discussed in later chapters it suffices to point out here that, in Eastern and Southeastern Anatolia, two land systems coexisted: the _yurtluk/ocaklik_ and _serbest mir-i miranlık_ etc., which were the basis for large estates, and the state lands worked by _reayas_ (peasant families). These _reayas_ had the right of possession over the land and paid taxes that were collected by _sipahis_ and later by _mültezims_. With the acceptance of private property in land in 1926, however, those _reayas_ who produced the official document proving that they were the users of the land became the real owners of the land to which previously they had only had the right of possession.

The fieldwork of this study was collected in Gisgis and Kalhana villages of Ergani district of Diyarbakır province, in the Southeast Anatolia region of Turkey. The aim of the fieldwork was to collect material to show the importance of the household economy for the developing Turkish capitalism. The Southeast, together with the Eastern region, is the most underdeveloped part of Turkey. Limited industrialisation, low level of development of the productive forces, and dominance of rural production are some of the features of this underdevelopment. The transfer of the surplus produced in the region to the developed western part of Turkey is the prime reason behind this underdevelopment, and the household economic unit, as the producer of this surplus, is the main bearer of the burden of capital accumulation in Turkey. Before going into the details of the ways in which this surplus is appropriated from the household, we shall try to show the structures (regional and national) within which the household economy exists. Chapter two, therefore, attempts to explain how the underdevelopment of Eastern Anatolia (including Southeast Anatolia) is the result of the region's integration into the capitalist economy. Capitalism develops unevenly: while bringing about development in one part, it causes underdevelopment in another part.

We shall also give an account of the recent economic and political history of the Turkish formation, emphasising that, in its efforts to develop a Turkish capitalism, the Turkish State played the part of a buffer mechanism in the underdevelopment of the region and in the transfer of the surplus produced by the household economy in the region.

Notes to Chapter One

1. See, for example: Yasa, 1970, 71-76; Besikçi, 1969, 65-67; also Tütengil, 1975, 135-139
2. See: Shanin, 1971a, 1971b, 1973-74; Redfield, 1956; Wolf, 1955, 1956; Kroeber, 1948
3. For a recent review of literature on the Marxist interpretation of rural development see: Glavanis and Glavanis, 1983. See also: Ennew, Hirst and Tribe, 1977; Bernstein, 1976, 1979
4. For a concise treatment of the modernisation approach to rural development, see: Long, 1977
5. Lenin, 1964; Banaji, 1976
6. Chayanov, 1966. For critiques of Chayanov, see: Littlejohn, 1977; Harrison, 1977; Patnaik, 1979
7. Some of the contributions to the debate appear in: Boratav 1969a, 1969b, 1970a, 1970b; Erdost 1969a, 1969b, 1969c, 1969d, 1970; Kardam, 1970; Kutlay, 1970a, 1970b
8. Boratav, 1969a, 1969b
9. Boratav, 1969a, 108-110 (page numbers refer to the third edition, 1976)
10. Boratav, 1969a, 112-113
11. See Martinez-Alier, 1977

12. Lenin, 1964
13. Banaji, 1976
14. Wallerstein, 1974
15. Boratav, 1970a, 178-180
16. Boratav, 1970a, 211 and 1969a, 113
17. Banaji, 1977b
18. Bernstein, 1977
19. See _Emek_, June 1969 and April 1970, especially articles by Selik (June 1969) and Çulhaoğlu (April 1970); also Kutlay, 1970a, 1970b
20. Erdost, 1969c
21. Erdost, 1969c, 39-40
22. Erdost, 1969c, 40 and Erdost in _Türk Solu_ No. 80
23. Erdost, 1969c, 44-46
24. Bernstein, 1979, 426
25. See: Chapter Two 'Capitalism and Ground Rent' of Amin, 1977, especially 59-60; Banaji, 1977a, 34; Bernstein, 1976
26. In the Islamic Ottoman State, all lands belonged to the state, and were therefore called _miri_ (crown) lands. For a detailed explanation, see: Barkan, 1937a, 1938, 1943
27. The term _dirlik_, in its most general sense, is used in the history of the Ottoman state organisation to denote all kinds of sources of income assigned to those who serve the state. However, the term is used here in its strict sense. What we wish to denote by the term _dirlik_ is virtually equal to the _timar_ system, according to which the agricultural surplus is controlled and used, and _dirlik_ therefore means the agricultural source of income of a certain class in the Ottoman Empire. For more detailed information, see Akdağ, 1971, 251-260
28. Despite the fact that the term _tımar_ is used to denote the Ottoman land system as a whole, larger _tımars_ were specifically called _has_ and _zeamet_, and the smallest _tımar_ was itself called _tımar_.
29. _Koçi Bey Risalesi_ (Koçi Bey's Essay) (1939), p. 112, gives these divisions, for the three different categories which are described as follows:

Has are those dirliks whose yearly income is over 100,000 akçe and which belong to viziers and sultans. See Sencer, n.d., 251

Zeamets are given to the people of high rank, state officials and successful warriors. The holders of has and zeamet dirliks have to provide the state with one cebellu (cavalryman) for every 5,000 akçe of their income; Ayni Ali Efendi, 1964, 54

Tımars whose value are between 3,000 and 20,000 akçe are those dirliks whose holders have to provide the state with one cavalryman for every 3,000 akçe of their income after the first 3,000 akçe, in the case of a war; see Berki, 1960, 67

30. Barkan, 1943, 7
31. Barkan, 1940, 322
32. Barkan, 1937b, 106
33. See, for instance, Inalcık, 1955, especially 224, Lewis, 1968, 21-40; Keyder, 1976; Islamoğlu and Keyder, 1977; Akdağ, 1945
34. In order to raise the drastically declined state revenues, from the seventeenth century onwards the Ottoman state started to rent out miri lands to mültezims, who were contractor intermediaries between the central authority and the peasants. This farming out of miri lands to the highest bidder was called iltizam farming (tax farming). According to this system, the mültezim collected the traditional agricultural tax of öşr from the peasants in the name of the state. A certain amount of the öşr collected from the peasants was given to the state as rent. For a detailed description of the nature and the extent of tax farming in the Ottoman Empire see Genc, 1975; and for the effects of tax farming see Inalcık, 1964
35. Öşr was a tax in kind, equal to one-tenth of the annual product; see Inalcık, 1959 for an extensive description of Ottoman taxes
36. For a similar argument, see Tezel, 1971. See also Keyder,

1976, 179. Keyder calls this process the 'feudalised transformation of the AMP' (Asiatic Mode of Production)

37. *Hükumet* means 'government' in the Turkish language in general, but the administrative units under the control of local notables were called *hükumet* in the Ottoman Empire.
38. Uzunçarşılı , 1964, 580
39. Uzunçarşılı , 1964, 581
40. Ayni Ali Efendi, 1964, 58; Uzunçarşılı , 1964, 581

2. Regional Underdevelopment In Turkey

Regional underdevelopment is a central concern of much of the literature that attempts to grasp the socio-economic and political reality of the Eastern and Southeastern regions of Turkey. Some of the literature confines itself to showing the differences between regions in terms of the level of infrastructure, average per capita income, number of hospitals, doctors, schools, etc. Other contributions approach the phenomenon of regional differentiation in the light of 'ethnic' differences, while others situate this disparity in a political economy of the Turkish State. As an introduction to this chapter, we shall outline two of these approaches to regional underdevelopment in Turkey. This will then be followed by an evaluation of the Turkish social formation in a manner that indicates the type of general theoretical framework within which this book is being written. In other words, we shall be outlining the framework within which we shall later examine the household economy in the villages of Gisgis and Kalhana.

Theoretical Approaches

Cumulative causation

Ruşen Keleş (1) argues that the advantages provided by the economic and physical geography of a region are 'the most important factor in the development of that region'. (2) Borrowing from Myrdal, he refers to this as an 'historical coincidence' where, once disparities are created between regions, they show a certain regularity under free market conditions. The relations and interactions between the developed and underdeveloped regions are summarised by Keleş in terms of two types of effects: 'backwash' and 'spread' effects. Both the capital and labour flow from the backward to the developed region are considered to be 'backwash' effects, while the increased demand in the developed region induces, to a certain extent, investment in the backward regions, which represents one of the 'spread' effects of the developed regions. Another 'spread' effect, highlighted by Keleş, and of particular relevance to this study, is the migration of disguised unemployed labour from underdeveloped to developed regions, which he suggests renders possible an increase in the marginal productivity of labour in underdeveloped regions. Nevertheless, Keleş emphasises the fact that, as a result of the 'backwash' effects, demand increases in the developed region and this demand induces investment which, in turn, increases incomes, and the increased incomes in turn increase demand. The capital requirements of new investments, of course, are partly met through the capital flow from the backward regions: the 'backwash' effect. Together with Myrdal, Keleş suggests that, as a result of this cumulative causal relation, 'poverty becomes its own cause' and richness leads to further richness and therefore a poor region cannot accumulate capital in order to achieve a cumulative development. (3)

It is Keleş's failure to analyse the historical process of regional underdevelopment in the light of the 'cumulative causation' theory which constitutes the major limitation of this approach; a limitation which is, of course, embedded in Myrdal's own work. The 'cumulative causation' theory (4) seriously questions the notion of equilibrium and is diametrically opposed to that of neo-classical economics, which claims that the free play of the market will reduce regional inequalities. Instead, it argues that the working of the market forces, especially capital and labour movements, increase the existing regional inequalities rather than decreasing them. Nevertheless, although Myrdal is able to show ever-increasing regional inequalities empirically, he fails to situate them in the very process of capital accumulation. It is this failure which is exemplified in his analogy between regional inequalities and the ever-increasing gap between developed and underdeveloped countries, which leads to an ahistorical analysis that cannot account for exploitation, domination, or unequal and combined development.

Internal colonialism

Unlike that of Myrdal, the 'internal colonialism' approach emphasises the exploitative nature of the relations between the regions. In its Turkish version, the 'internal colonialism' model takes an ethnic and nationalistic character where the exploitation of the Kurdish East by the Turkish West becomes the major focus of the approach. Such a focus only partially reflects the socio-historical reality of the region (East and Southeast Turkey). (5)

The 'Internal Colonialism' model argues that the very existence of underdevelopment in Eastern Turkey is the direct result of an international policy employed by the Turkish State against Kurdish people, ever since the establishment of the State in 1923. This seems to be an oversimplification of the question. How far can ethnicity be held responsible for economic development? How far can we go in identifying ethnic relations with class relations? It is such questions as these which constitute the major limitations of the 'internal colonialism' approach.

An example of such an approach is the work of one of the most prominent advocates of Kurdish nationalism, Ismail Beşikçi.

Beşikçi argues against the view of the Türkiye Işçi Partisi (Turkish Workers' Party), exemplified by Behice Boran in her book Türkiye ve Sosyalizm Sorunları (Turkey and the Problems of Socialism), (6) in which she contends that the inequalities between the developed West and the underdeveloped East in Turkey are due to the law of uneven development of capitalism. (7) According to Beşikçi, the fact that capitalism creates uneven development does not apply to the Turkish case because the Kurds are not Turks. (8) 'The law of uneven development of capitalism can explain regional inequalities only under the conditions that all the people living within the state boundaries are of the same nation (sic).' (9)

Beşikçi contends that the most important reason for the underdevelopment of Eastern Anatolia is the fact that there is a national contradiction between the Turkish dominant and admininstrative classes and the Kurdish nation. An important limitation is his attempt to examine exploitation in purely ethnic terms - Turks exploiting Kurds - rather than in class terms. Ethnic groups, however, are not undifferentiated homogenerous groups, they are differentiated in class terms within themselves. Capitalists are interested in accumulating capital; they are not concerned with the ethnicity of the people whose surplus product they appropriate. They will co-operate with the dominant elements of other ethnic groups as long as this co-operation is to their advantage. In fact it can be shown that dominant classes in Eastern Anatolia have benefited from their incorporation into the state apparatus in Turkey.

Landlords (ağas), tribal leaders and sheikhs are very effective in the politics of the Eastern and Southeastern regions. The introduction of the multi-party system in 1945 strengthened the position of the ağas, tribal leaders and sheikhs, whose social functions had gradually been eroded during the previous thirty years or so. Owing to their economic and ideological superiority, the ağa, sheikh and tribal leader trio has been able to manipulate the distribution of votes among the political parties. Knowing the ability of ağas, sheikhs and tribal leaders to direct peasants, mürits (members of religious sects) and the tribal people respectively in these regions, the political parties have favoured them immensely. The authority of this trio had been weakened due to factors which had brought about the opening up of rural communities, such as mechanisation and capitalisation of agriculture, improvement in transportation and communication, migration from rural to urban areas, education, rapid population increase, etc. Nevertheless, with the advent of the multi-party system they discovered not only the possibility of translating their influence over the masses into material interest, but also the possibility of intensifying their control over the people through their increasing influence on the state apparatus under the multi-party system. (10)

It should be emphasised that the question of development and underdevelopment is of an economic rather than an ethnic nature. Ethnicity might be related to the problem but can not explain it. What we are saying is simply that it is wrong to conclude that Eastern Anatolia is underdeveloped because the Kurds live there. There must be something more than ethnicity as the main cause of the regional underdevelopment in Eastern and Southeast Anatolia. Bettelheim's criticism of the notion that the exploitation of one nation by another is colonialism can be applied to Beşikçi's thesis that the Turkish nation exploits the Kurdish nation. Bettelheim writes:

> Because the concept of exploitation expresses a production relation - production of surplus labour and expropriation of this by a social class - it necessarily relates to class relations (and a relation between 'countries' is not and can not be a relation between classes. (11)

Beşikçi does not offer any rigorous analysis of the regional inequalities; his explanations remain mainly at the level of rhetoric. He does not try to bring together ethnicity and the features of the working of capitalism in explaining regional inequalities, as H. Wolpe (12) does in the case of South Africa.

The conceptualisation of class relations does not exist in Beşikçi's explanations of the underdevelopment of Eastern Anatolia. Instead, domination, exploitation and oppression are treated as taking place between national and ethnic groups. Beşikçi's theory is unable to answer two questions raised by Wolpe:

> First, what is the relationship between the system of class exploitation and domination and the relations of racial, ethnic, cultural or national exploitation and domination characteristic of internal colonialism? Second, in what way does internal colonial exploitation differ from class exploitation? (13)

Despite his persistent reference to national oppression and exploitation of one ethnic group by another, Beşikçi makes no attempt to link these to the system of class exploitation, nor does he specify these oppressive and exploitative relations, apart from stating over and over again the fact that Kemalist governments have been denying the existence of the Kurdish nation. (14)

Such an attempt has been made by Wolpe in the case of South Africa. Wolpe argues that the 'internal colonialism' thesis used by the South African Communist Party is extremely vague because it fails 'to distinguish between forms of colonial, political, ideological and cultural domination and modes of imperialist economic exploitation'. (15) Capitalism, once established as a dominant mode of production, tends either to consolidate or to dissolve pre-capitalist modes of production with which it coexists in an articulated way in a social formation. South African capitalism benefits from the reservation of non-capitalist relations of production because in this way the capitalist sector reduces its cost of production and therefore raises the rate of surplus value by way of employing labourers, part of whose subsistence needs is met by their kin groups in labour reserves. (16) Since what is preserved is the tribal groups themselves, the ideologies and political policies focus on the segregation, conservation and control of

African 'tribal' societies. (17) Therefore it is the logic of capital accumulation which is responsible for the underdevelopment of the labour reserve areas, not the racist policies or ideologies which try to justify the segregation.

The importance of Wolpe's work comes from its attempt to show that the relations of production and class relations lie behind the apartheid ideology and the underdevelopment of black labour reserves in South Africa. No such attempts is made by Beşikçi to show the relationship between the development of capitalism in Turkey and the underdevelopment of Southeastern and Eastern Anatolia. Of further interest for this thesis is the work of Mandel, who argues that development and underdevelopment are the basic features of capitalism, and regional uneven development is the spatial juxtaposition of these two features of capitalism. (18) Regional underdevelopment is an inevitable outcome of a capitalist economy, the aim of which is to grow continually through investments in the areas where the highest rate of profit is possible. Investments are unequally distributed because the factors determining the rate of profit are unequally distributed within the country and therefore the growth of the economy will be uneven. The bourgeois state, by creating the national market, ensures the flow of labour and capital from the underdeveloped to the developed regions. Underdeveloped regions are not only a source of labour for the developed regions; they are also a very important market for the products of the developed regions. (19)

Although Mandel's theory is a very useful framework in the analysis of regional underdevelopment, it does not take into consideration the specific conditions under which regional underdevelopment occurs, and therefore it remains very general. However, I think that, despite its generality, Mandel's theory, with a few additional points, will serve as a useful framework for understanding regional underdevelopment in Turkey. One of the points to add is that the development of capitalism in Turkey is not of an autocentric nature. Capitalism did not develop in Turkey as a result of the internal dynamics of Turkish society.

Capitalism first used Turkey as a market, then as a place

for investment. However, the first investments in Turkey by capitalism were made in order to improve the infrastructure, so that marketing of the commodities produced by the West would be easier. (20) These investments included railway networks, ports, water-works, electricity grids, etc. Western Anatolia (Marmara and Aegean regions), being close to the sea routes and to Europe and, in addition, being the heart of the Ottoman Empire, as well as being the area, together with the Çukurova region, for the production of raw materials (cotton and tobacco) for Western capitalism, enjoyed the lion's share of foreign investments. At the end of the War of Independence in the 1920s, the Kemalist regime inherited a country with almost no industry and a very limited infrastructure. The existing infrastructural establishment and manufacturing workshops were mainly concentrated in the West. Kemalists, who aimed at creating a Turkish capitalism, (21) implemented a state capitalism policy, giving priority to the areas where the existing infrastructure rendered possible the most rapid and profitable returns on investments. The accumulation needs of emerging Turkish capitalism necessitated deliberate neglect of some areas in terms of investments. The deliberateness of the Kemalist policy stemmed from the profit logic of capital, not from the fact that Eastern Anatolia was Kurdish, as Kurdish nationalists would have us believe. In order to take advantage of the labour reserves in Eastern Anatolia in the years of _étatist_ policy, railways were built to connect the remote East with the developing West. For instance, the Haydarpaşa (Istanbul) to Kurtalan (Siirt) railway line was completed in 1935, cutting across Turkey from the northwest to the southeast. In this way Turkish capitalism took advantage of a labour force produced and reproduced within a non-capitalist mode of production without taking on the burden of the reproduction costs of the labourers. Today, not only Turkish capitalism but also international capitalism takes advantage of this situation. The Turkish workers in Western Europe, mainly in West Germany, are a good example of this.

The result of such processes and state policies was the underdevelopment of this region _vis-à-vis_ other parts of Turkey.

In order to grasp the nature and magnitude of this underdevelopment, it is necessary to examine the larger structure in some detail.

The Turkish Social Formation

The Ottoman Empire was incorporated into the world capitalist system as a supplier of food and raw materials and as an open market for cheaply produced European manufactured goods. (22) The 1838 Commercial treaty with Britain which rendered possible the opening up of Ottoman Turkey as a market for European goods has been widely accepted as the beginning of the development of underdevelopment in Turkey. (23) As a result of this free trade, Ottoman manufacturing industry collapsed and Ottoman Turkey became integrated into the world system through trade. (24) In the international division of labour, Turkey played the role of an exporter of agricultural products like cotton, tobacco and grains and an importer of manufactured goods. Local Christian minorities gained ascendancy by becoming the representatives of foreign companies and engaging in import and export business. The predominance of merchant capital in Turkey prevented the development of an industrial bourgeoisie.

Specific historical conditions created by Turkey's entry into the First World War and by subsequent events: the Greek invasion of Western Anatolia and the War of Independence (1918-1922), strengthened the power basis of the local nobility (eşraf), merchants and tribal and religious leaders who mobilised the masses for the war.

After the War of Independence (1918-1922) fought against the Greek Army, which had invaded Anatolia during the First World War, the predominance of non-Muslim merchants was brought to an end and their Turkish counterparts took their place and their role in the integration of Turkey with the world system.

The First World War and the ensuing War of Independence mostly benefited the merchant bourgeoisie, who took advantage of the war economy, characterized by scarcity and inflation, by engaging in speculation and black marketeering. During the two wars a considerable accumulation of merchant capital was witnessed.

Before the First World War the level of production in Anatolia was low, production techniques in agriculture were very primitive, and industry was virtually non-existent. (25)

The 1923 – 1929 period

The newly established Republic (1923) faced the problem of reconstructing the economy, which was almost completely ruined. (26) Owing to the wars, the integration of Turkey into the World economy had been interrupted. This process of integration was restarted by the new Republic. Between 1923 and 1929, the levels of production and exports were increased. (27)

At the end of the War of Independence, the class dominance of merchants and landlords had not changed its nature; the only important change was that Muslim merchants took the place of non-Muslims and powerful landlords managed to gain the control of lands left by expatriated Greeks. In other words, the merchant bourgeoisie and landowning classes came out of the wars stronger.

The influence of merchants and landowners on the State apparatus is quite evident in the policies followed between the establishment of the Republic in 1923 and the Great Depression of 1930. Since the economy had been characterised by the export of agricultural products and the import of manufactured goods ever since 1838, agriculture was the 'primary channel of integration into the world economy'. (28) Merchants and landowners had large stakes in policies aimed at increasing agricultural productivity. For this reason, attempts were made to increase the amount of land under cultivation, to mechanize agriculture, to subsidise the purchase of agricultural machinery, to improve transportation facilities, to introduce private ownership in land and to abolish the traditional *aşar* tax (tithe). (29) One thing must be remembered: all these measures taken to increase agricultural production and speed up the commercialisation of agriculture contributed to the impoverishment of the small peasantry to the benefit of big landowners, merchants and usurers. The producers of marketable crops such as cotton, tobacco and vegetables were under the exploitation of merchant and usurers' capital. The interest on the usurers' loans varied, according to the 1931 Agricultural Congress reports, between 50 per cent and 600 per cent. (30)

Measures taken to commercialise agriculture

In the 1920s, the political power took the following measures to speed up the process of commercialisation in agriculture. First, with the adoption of the Swiss Civil Code in 1926, which recognised the private ownership of land, the unequal distribution of land was consolidated. Although we do not have exact data relating to land distribution in the 1920s, the figures from 1913 will give an idea of how land was distributed. Five per cent of the farmers had 65 per cent of the agricultural land, and 87 per cent of the farmers had 35 per cent of agricultural land, leaving 8 per cent of the peasants landless. (31) The 1923 constitution guaranteed that, in the case of any expropriation, the money was to be paid in cash immediately, and so both the constitution and the civil code secured the big landlords against any land reform. The recognition of private property prepared the basis for land to become a commodity and, furthermore, cadastral surveys, which started in 1925, are worth mentioning as a factor in hastening the development of capitalism in agriculture.

As early as 1923, it was decided, through legislation, that agricultural machinery was to be imported by the Agricultural Bank and distributed to farmers without duty. (32) Another law in the same year recognised that the importation of animals should be exempted from duty. However, these exemptions were unable to bring about any rapid mechanisation in agriculture, owing to the lack of money needed for the importation of the machinery. Another implementation was that of agricultural credits, which increased at a great rate in the first years of the Republic, rising from TL928,000 in 1922 to TL16,214,000 in 1926 (33) and TL36,000,000 in 1930. (34) According to

Hershlag, 'The increase was uneven and not yet adjusted to the real needs of the peasantry. Additional sources of credit were needed in order to avoid the farmer's heavy dependence on the usurer'. (35) In 1934, I.H. Tökin, talking about credit co-operatives, noted:

> It is hard to say that the credit co-operatives established by the Agricultural Bank are useful for peasants, simply because, being members of the administrative council of the co-operatives, usurers and middlemen have been using the co-operatives as a means towards their own interests. Peasants pay their debts to usurers, who are members of the administrative committee, with the credit they get. A considerable number of co-operatives have become virtually an organisation of usurers. With regard to the situations where town merchants are members of the co-operative, peasants are using their credits to buy their consumption needs in the towns and this money accrues to the merchants in the towns. Town merchants, thanks to the credit co-operatives, have gained a sort of organized market. (36)

The credit policy rendered possible an accumulation of money in the hands of a few and the pauperisation of the masses. (37)

Another important factor in the commercialisation of agriculture was the abolition, in 1925, of the _aşar_ (tax in kind) which in theory was one tenth of the product but in practice had been much higher. (38) It is possible to imagine that, with the abolition of _aşar_, small producers might have increased their surplus product and the home market might have been developed. However, as the _aşar_ was lifted a land tax which had to be paid in cash was introduced, and this forced big producers to produce for a market. The _aşar_ constituted more than half of the state's income in the first years of the Republic and the lifting of it possibly alleviated the exploitation of peasants by landlords, usurers and merchants but, in order to increase the reduced state income, the prices of some essential goods, such as salt, sugar, paraffin, etc., were raised. (39)

The taxes paid by the peasants, however, were not confined to the aşar. Besides indirect taxes, the peasants used to pay several other taxes such as road tax, education-share tax, animal tax and so on. The road tax seems to have been very important. In accordance with the law of 21st February 1921, each person aged between 18 and 60 was to pay an amount equal to four days' wages, fixed according to the local wage level. This tax burden was increased in February 1925 by raising the number of days to between six and twelve; the exact number was to be decided by the provincial councils. Those who were not able to pay this tax were to work in the area for six to twelve days instead. Taking into consideration the fact that most of the peasants were not involved in a money economy, it is easy to see which form the road tax took in practice. The peasants paid their taxes either as corvée or by borrowing from usurers under unfavourable conditions. Of course, in the latter case the amount of tax increased in proportion with the rate of the usurer's interest. I.H. Tonguç gives a concrete example of how this tax affected the peasants: 'If there are three people in a peasant family liable to pay the road tax of TL6, in order to pay the total amount of TL18 they have to sell two calves or a cow'. (40)

Industry

The fact that integration into the world capitalist system results in the de-industrialisation of the periphery does not mean that all handicraft industry would be completely wiped out. Traditional small-scale production had survived in Turkey in the 1970s, despite a considerable degree of commercial integration into the world economy. (41) However, the most important feature of industrial development in Turkey in the 1920s was that foreign capital came to Turkey to invest in larger scale manufacturing industry in collaboration with Turkish capital. (42) To facilitate the activities of foreign capital, a law was passed in 1924 allowing foreigners to obtain private property in Turkey. In a move to improve industrial production, some institutional measures were introduced to encourage small savings and to finance domestic industry and participation in private enterprises the Iş Bankası (Work Bank) was established in 1924 (43) and the Bank for Mining and Industry (Sanayi ve Maadin Bankası in 1925. (44) In principle, the latter aimed at governing the state-owned industrial establishments inherited from the Ottomans. In actual fact, the function of the bank was to encourage the industrial investments of the private sector and to transfer the profits to private companies while taking all the risks. (45)

Another important measure was the Law for the Encouragement of Industry in May 1927, whereby the government guaranteed financial support to private enterprises if they were good enough to be recognised by the Ministry of Commerce. The recognised enterprises were to be exempt from many taxes, such as immovable property tax, land tax, profit tax, surtaxes on all previous taxes due to provinces and municipalities, supplementary personal tax and licence fees due to municipalities for construction, steam engines, motors and so on. They were also provided with free land on which to establish their enterprise, with the installation of telephones free of charge, etc. (46) However, one should not imagine that industrialisation was encouraged and supported by the state in order to loosen its dependence on, and integration with the world economy. On the contrary, these measures were taken as a result of Turkey's integration with the world system. Not only was foreign investment encouraged, but also small scale production which was directly linked with foreign investment. 'The law for the Encouragement of Industry neglected the government's wish to implement its own declarations and the resolutions of the congress of Izmir concerning the encouragement of private initiative, government intervention being restricted to those cases where private activity had ceased.' (47)

The state apparatus was thus used for the enrichment of the private sector. Another tool was the monopolies, most of which, inherited from the Ottomans, were engaged in the importation, production and selling of certain commodities. The implementation of monopolisation in Turkey does not bear any resemblance to Western monopoly capitalism, which resulted from the break-up of the mechanism of competition in favour of a financial oligarchy which merged financial capital with industrial capital, and the emergence of the state apparatus as a means towards this oligarchy. In Turkey, monopolism originates from the non-development of capitalism and has been used as a means to develop capitalism.

The government declared that some sectors of the national economy should monopolise not only in terms of production but also in terms of administration and sales, and then these rights of monopolies were to be protected in order to secure high profits easily without any competition. In this economic system the state was in the position of distributing wealth. In practice this meant that the decisions rendering possible the enrichment of a handful of people were to be taken by highly ranked bureaucrats. Apologist of the time, Yakup Kadri Karaosmanoğlu, noted, forty years later, 'In those days the cadre of yesterday's national struggles, today's progressives, had the nature of a profit and interest company ... Some of these were after land speculations, some after membership in administrations of big companies, while some were chasing commissions'. (48)

The monopoly for matches and flints was given first to a Belgian and then to an American company. Among the founders of the Turkish Match Monopoly joint corporation with the Belgian company in 1925 were (General) Ismet Pasha, M. Celal and Y. Nadi. The monopoly of spirits and alcoholic drinks was given to a Turkish-Polish joint company in 1926. The monopoly of gunpowder and explosives was given to a French company in 1927. The export-import monopoly of oil was given to the American Standard Oil Company. In addition, the working of the harbours of Istanbul, Izmir, Trabzon and Mersin was monopolised and handed over to joint companies. (49)

The enrichment of a handful of people (merchants, landlords and bureaucrats) took place parallel with the weakening of the treasury. The burden of this tendency was carried by the social categories who were not given shares from the plundering by means of taxes, most of which were of an indirect nature. The production, importation, and exportation of primary consumption goods (salt, sugar, spirits, oil, matches, etc.) were under state monopoly, and all these goods were subject to indirect taxes which comprised two-thirds of state income. In 1925, state income derived from salt was TL10,180,000, whereas the income tax collected from merchants, traders and wage earners amounted to TL4,233,000. (50) In short, most of the state income was derived from the peasants and workers by means of indirect taxes levied on essential consumption goods, and this income was distributed to the merchants and landlords through the state apparatus in which merchants, landlords and bureaucrats held the power.

Foreign Capital

Some have claimed that foreign capital did not play any important role in Turkey after the 1920s. This is a fallacy, because these people were evaluating foreign capital as directly invested capital, but we know that, in the period under consideration, both Turkish politicians and Turkish capitalists were ready to accept and encourage foreign capital on condition that it worked in collaboration with Turkish capital and organised itself with Turkish companies. (51) From the above it may be concluded that, until 1930, the Turkish government and Turkish bourgeoisie were not in favour of breaking the ties between imperialism and Turkey; rather, they were in favour of strengthening them. The Turkish leading cadres were not against imperialism, but against the direct invasion and rule of imperialism, namely direct colonialism. (52)

1930 – 1939 : étatism

During the 1920s, considerable growth in agricultural production was achieved but the development of industry was very limited since the dominance of merchant capital was not conducive to such development. (53) However, while the total agricultural product was increased through favourable state policies, the inequalities between small peasants and large landowners also increased. (54)

The impact of the Great Depression, as in many countries, was deeply felt in Turkey, where the economy was based on the export of agricultural products, the prices of which declined drastically. (55) The volume of exports and imports decreased too, leaving not only merchant capital, but also the reproduction of society as a whole in a crisis situation, since Turkey depended on the import of basic necessities like flour, sugar, textiles, etc. Therefore the Great Depression necessitated an industrialisation of at least an import substitution type to alleviate the negative impacts of depression by creating a market for traditional export products and substituting the traditional import products. (56) However, since there was no industrial bourgeoisie in Turkey to carry out this industrialisation, the State assumed this role and it is for this reason that the capital accumulation policies carried out by the State in the absence of an industrial bourgeoisie were widely called étatism. (57) The State investments were aimed not at supplementing private enterprise but rather at complementing them. (58) The State directly entered into the sphere of production, and accumulation of capital was secured through direct and indirect taxes, through the control of foreign trade and by control of the price mechanism. (59)

The burden of capital accumulation of an internally financed industrialisation was shouldered by the masses. The tax policy of the state and the development of the income of the state monopolies reveal the class base of the attempts to industrialise the country. The income of the state budget largely depended on indirect taxes, of which the burden was mostly carried by wage earners and the poorer classes. Not only were the agricultural incomes of the big farmers exempt from income tax, but also the income tax paid by merchants and industrialists was of little account in the total income of the state treasury. For instance, income tax collected between 1929 and 1935 was approximately 12 million Turkish lira per year, 60 per cent of which was paid by workers, civil servants etc. In this period aggregate income tax paid by merchants and industrialists per year was TL4,800,000, which was little more than two per cent of the total tax income of the state. (60) This figure indicates which classes carried the burden of state capitalism.

State capitalism was not implemented against the interests of the private sector. On the contrary, it was in accordance with their interests. What was understood by étatism was state activism in the fields where private enterprise failed or was not strong enough; in other words, in those areas where it was impossible for private enterprise to be realised, such as the building of infrastructural establishments, main industrial institutions, electrical power stations, railway networks and an iron and steel industry, all of which were handled by the state. Moreover, the state left to the private sector areas like agriculture, commerce and services etc., which were traditionally operated by that sector. (61)

1940 - 1945 : war economy

During the 1930s, some significant industrial development took place in Turkey. The first textile and sugar factories were established during these years. In foreign trade, a protectionist quota and clearing systems were introduced. However, by 1935, when the depression years were coming to an end, Turkey's foreign terms of trade improved and the speed of étatism decreased. The 1940-1945 period was a war period, during which time the nation was kept in a state of mobilisation. A considerable part of the working population was recruited for the army, and most of the state income was devoted to military expenditure. Imports fell from \$120 million in 1938 to \$50.55 in 1940-41. The level of productivity fell as a result of the extraction of the working population from the production sphere, and the reduction in imported production inputs. The output of wheat fell from 4.2 million tonnes in 1939 to 2.2 million in 1945. (62) The volume of foreign trade also dropped sharply, the smallest volumes being recorded in 1940, when imports were TL19 million and exports TL111 million. (63)

The feeding of the army and the populations of the big

cities constituted a serious problem, and inflation was inevitable. Between 1939 and 1948, prices rose by 434 per cent, an average of 48 per cent per year. (64) The burden of the war economy was shouldered again by the masses, while a few groups of merchants and big farmers, taking advantage of the situation, made incredible profits. A part of the bureaucracy also had a continuous share of these profits. (65)

The laws passed in this period seem to be important. First, the Wealth Tax (Varlık Vergisi) Law of 1942. This was a tax to be collected once only from those who made great profits during the war years. The amount of the tax was fixed arbitrarily by commissions, which desired to levy heavy taxes on the minorities and the commercial bourgeoisie of Istanbul. Second, the Soil Products Tax, which was collected from big and small farmers. By not differentiating between big and small farmers this tax caused quite a lot of difficulty for the small farmers who produced for home consumption and whose productivity had fallen greatly due to the conditions brought about by the war. In short, the war conditions coupled with state policies allowed the merchant bourgeoisie and landlords to accumulate considerable wealth and capital through speculation, black marketing and plunder. (66)

Post – war period

Following the Second World War, the world economy was restructured under the dominance of the U.S.A. The class structure of Turkey necessitated the resumption of her pre-depression role within this new international division of labour. Turkey willingly took on the role of food and raw materials supplier for the West. Turkey's several appeals to be included in the Marshall Aid plan were accepted on the conditions that Turkey would develop her agriculture with the aid she was to receive and would buy industrial goods from the West. The United States and international institutions under the control of the United States directed Turkey's economic policy. Thornburg's 1950 report is an example of American intervention in Turkish policy making. In this report, entitled 'A Criticism of Today's

Economic Situation in Turkey' (Türkiye'nin Bugünkü Ekonomik Durumunun Tenkidi), Thornburg noted that Turkey was an agricultural country and should be content with simple agricultural equipment and that Turkey did not need artificial fertiliser, so that the establishment of a fertiliser factory would be unnecessary. The Karabük Iron and Steel Plant should be liquidated, and the government should take measures to encourage foreign capital to invest in Turkey. (67)

The World Bank Committee, invited by the Turkish government to examine the conditions which would help determine the economic policy of the government, prepared a report which was considered very valuable, as was the Thornburg report. The World Bank report, known also as the Barker Report, suggested that étatism should be abolished, that comprehensive planning was not necessary at all, that priority in development should be given to agriculture and the production of raw materials. The whole sphere of the economy should be opened to private enterprise and the existing regulations preventing foreign capital from coming into Turkey should be revised because foreign capital must be brought into the country. (68) Turkey was accepted into the OEEC in 1948, following the preparation of the 1947 Economic Development Plan, which gave priority to development in agriculture, transportation and communication and relied heavily on external finance. (69) As a result, in the early 1950s a significant amount of American Aid poured into the country as credit to be used in financing agricultural mechanisation and state enterprises in infrastructure. (70) While mechanisation led to a very significant increase in the area under cultivation, cheap credits were extended to farmers and the prices of agricultural products were supported. For instance, land under cultivation between 1950 and 1960 increased from 9,868,000 hectares to 15,305,000 hectares. A similar trend was witnessed in agricultural credits, which rose from TL780 million in 1950 to TL2,602 million in 1955. (71)

The number of tractors also rose, from 1,750 in 1948 to 16,585 in 1950, 37,743 in 1954 and 40,000 in 1955. (72) However, in 1953 only about one per cent of farming families were benefiting from this mechanisation of agriculture. (73) Under the conditions prepared by the government, rich farmers enlarged their lands through the liquidation of their sharecroppers and tenants, through cultivation of previously unused lands, renting and buying of new land, and appropriation of pasture lands. (74) Capitalist production in agriculture became more and more evident in large holdings. (75)

Industry

The years 1950-1954 were a period of liberalisation in Turkey, during which the United States and Canada were stocking their grain because of the Korean War. This made it possible for Turkey to increase her national income through the exportation of grain. However, the economy entered a crisis after 1955, owing to the fact that the reclamation of cultivable lands had reached its limit and, with the end of the Korean War, the United States and Canada had begun to market their grain. As a result, decreasing exports and increasing imports created a foreign currency problem which signalled the end of import liberalisation. From 1954 onwards, custom duties and import quotas were reintroduced. (76) Under crisis conditions this would have resulted in the shrinking of the markets of metropolitan capital. However, the 1950s were a period of expansion of world capitalism. This expansion is characterized by the internationalisation of capital. In other words metropolitan capital indirectly recaptures the markets in has lost, by way of establishing production units in the country. Foreign capital came to Turkey to invest, in co-operation with Turkish capital, in luxury consumption goods. The highly profitable and protected domestic market contributed to the development of an assembly industry in Turkey. In accordance with the rise in the importance of the internal market, the private sector moved into the industrial sector, while the state sector was concentrated in the production of intermediate commodities as inputs for the private sector. (77) International organisations like the IMF, OECD and IBRD gave their approval and support to Turkey's import substitution industrialisation during the 1960s, aimed at the internal market. (78) It must be noted, however, that the import substitution industry, from the 1930s to the 1950s, concentrated on consumption goods like textiles and food processing, while the trend from the late 1950s onwards has been one of concentration on durable consumer goods like cars, refrigerators etc. The import substitution industry exacerbated Turkey's dependence on developing countries, since this type of industrialisation necessitates the transfer of technology, intermediate goods and investment goods. This dependence was further intensified through Turkey's integration with the Western military pacts, such as NATO (1952) and CENTO, both of which forced Turkey to undertake large-scale military expenditure, thereby hindering her general development.

Import substitution industrialisation (ISI) continued during the first half of the 1970s, relying on the existence of a large domestic market. The limitations of a domestic market-oriented industrialisation became very evident once the market was saturated. ISI policies led to the neglect of the traditional sector which accounted for a large part of foreign exchange earnings. Constant deficits of balance of payments were met by external credits until 1977. But from this date the rate of development came to a halt. The only way out of this crisis seemed to lie in a structural transformation of the economy. A leap forward from domestic-oriented industrialisation to an export-promotion economy was seen as the only solution. Priority was given to export-oriented industries using domestic inputs in the Measures of 25th January 1980. These Measures were introduced after a long period of negotiation between Turkey and international agencies, especially the IMF and OECD. As a result, wages were dramatically reduced in real terms but prices were freed, the domestic economy was open to international competition, anti-inflationary monetarist policies and the encouragement of foreign capital. The military intervention of 12th September 1980 ensured the institutional framework for the implementation of these Measures, which proved to be disastrous by 1984. Nokta magazine reported, in August 1984 that, during the previous eight months, inflation and unemployment had increased drastically while exports had decreased and the deficit in the balance of payments further increased. (79) However, these Measures ensured further integration of Turkey into the world capitalist system.

Agriculture

In spite of all the efforts of the state, industry has not been able to become the most important sector in terms of employment. The agricultural working population still accounted for 60.4 per cent of the active population in 1980, while the figure was 16.3 per cent for industry and 23.3 per cent for the service sector. (8 Although the share of agriculture in the GNP is gradually decreasing, the export of agricultural goods still plays a very important role in meeting the foreign currency requirements of industrial development. Agricultural production is carried out in a rural structure, where the most important means of production is unevenly distributed. Among the active population in agriculture, landless families constitute 30 per cent on average, while this percentage increases to 45 per cent in eastern provinces. (81) In 1980, while 40.7 per cent of holdings controlled 79.9 per cent of the total land, 26 per cent of holdings controlled only 3.8 per cent of the land. The pervasive small family farms do not yield enough for the subsistence of the holding.

During the planned period since 1963, it has been expected that agriculture should produce large surpluses to finance industrial development. For this purpose measures have been taken to decrease fallow lands and lands under grain cultivation, and to increase the production of commercial crops, pulses, garden crops and animal fodder. In the development plans, a transformation to capital-intensive agriculture was envisaged. To speed up the technological development in agriculture, the use of modern equipment and inputs has been encouraged and the provision of chemical fertilisers, fuel, insecticides and pesticides, improved seeds, etc. has been subsidised. Although some increase in production has been witnessed, it has not met expectations. (82) Given the inequalities in the distribution of resources in agriculture, it can be argued that subsidies to agriculture have widened the gap between small peasants and large landowners. Through price regulations the state has tried to ensure a transfer of value from agriculture to industry. The prices of wage goods particularly have been kept low to ensure low wages in industry. However, short-term political considerations prior to elections have resulted in high floor prices for certain crops but, on the whole, real prices received by farmers have been in decline. This trend has increased even since the crisis of the import substitution industrialisation which led to the crashing of wages. Domestic market-oriented industrialisation was compatible with high support prices for agricultural goods which create a large internal market. But export-oriented industrialisation could not bear high prices for agricultural products, since this would increase production prices through wages. Therefore, to maintain the competitiveness of industry, support prices for agricultural products had to be kept low. This is a direct result of Turkey's new role in the world division of labour.

It is now evident that the incorporation of Turkey into the capitalist world economy had resulted in the development of a dependent capitalism with its historically specific class relations. Dependent capitalist development has created another dependency relationship within Turkey: regional underdevelopment. The regional underdevelopment in Turkey is not a result of racist state policy, but is an outcome of the uneven development of Turkish capitalism.

In the third chapter we shall try to illuminate the features of underdevelopment in the Southeast region of Turkey by giving some indices.

Notes to Chapter Two

1. Keleş, 1964
2. Keleş, 1964, 106
3. Keleş, 1964, 101-108
4. Myrdal, 1957
5. We have no reliable statistics regarding the number of

Kurdish-speaking people in these areas. The general reliabil of official Turkish data sources is questionable, particularl on such a sensitive topic as the Kurdish question. However, according to the State Institute of Statistics, in 1965 the number of Kurdish-speaking people was 1,389,421, compared with 1,286,611 Turkish-speakers in the nine provinces of Southeastern Anatolia. For unspecified reasons, the State Institute of Statistics abandoned the practice of publishing statistics giving the number of Kurdish-speaking people after 1965.

6. Boran, 1970
7. Boran, 1970, 183-194
8. Beşikçi, 1977, 205
9. Beşikçi, 1977, 206 (my translation)
10. For a similar argument, see Ozankaya, 1969 and Beşikçi, 1969
11. Bettelheim, 1972, 301 (emphasis original)
12. Wolpe, 1975
13. Wolpe, 1975, 233
14. In fact he devoted a whole book to showing the unscientific nature of the denial of the Kurdish nation by the Turkish state. See Beşikçi, 1975
15. Wolpe, 1975, 241
16. Wolpe, 1975, 248
17. Wolpe, 1975, 249
18. See Mandel, 1974, 373 and Mandel, n.d.
19. Mandel, n.d., 2-5
20. See Luxemburg, 1951, Ch. XXX, especially 439-445
21. Ökçün, 1968
22. For this point, see Avcıoğlu, 1968 and Yerasimos, 1975, 650-660; also Cem, 1970, 261-265. Kurmuş, 1974 investigates the penetration of Western Capitalism into Western Anatolia and the gradual development of capitalist relations in the area between 1850 and 1913. The development of capitalist relations in the Çukurova region is dealt with by Novichev, 1966.
23. See Avcıoğlu, 1968; Cem, 1970; Fişek, 1969; Tayanç, 1973;

Yerasimos, 1975

24. For the phases of Turkey's integration into the world capitalist system and a comparison of Latin American development strategies with those of Turkey, see Gülalp, 1983
25. Tökin, 1934, 176-179, 193. See also Tankut, 1939
26. Keyder, 1981, 129
27. Keyder, 1981
28. Keyder, 1981, 25
29. Keyder, 1981, 28-37
30. Tökin, 1934, 147
31. Cem, 1970, 272
32. See Laws nos. 329, 535, 572 in Düstur: Üçüncü Kitap (Code of Law: Third Book) IV, 72, VI, 547, VII, 423
33. Hershlag, 1958
34. Özgür, 1975
35. Hershlag, 1958, 56
36. Tökin, 1934, 150 (my translation)
37. For a detailed treatment of capital accumulation and the impoverishment of the peasantry between 1923 and 1938, see Silier, 1981
38. Zhukovsky, 1951, 130 notes that the aşar tax could be as much as a quarter of the crop
39. Timur, 1971, 105
40. Tonguç, 1938
41. For the specific conditions and the degree of survival of traditional handicraft industry in the periphery, with specific reference to Turkey in the 1920s, see Keyder, 1981, 46-67
42. Ökçün, 1971
43. For this point of view, see Yerasimos, 1976, III, 1263-1264; also Boratav, 1974, 32; Özgür, 1975, 93; Küçük, 1971, 213
44. Hershlag, 1958, 61
45. Yerasimos, 1976, III, 1264
46. Hershlag, 1958, 63
47. Hershlag, 1958, 64
48. Karaosmanoğlu, 1968

49. See Boratav, 1974, 35-38. For a detailed account of how the State Treasury was used for the enrichment of some people, see especially Boratav, 1971, 37-38 and Ökçün, 1971, 55-60, 113. See also Avcıoğlu, 1968, 194-200
50. Timur, 1971, 116
51. Ökçün, 1971, shows that, in the 1920-1930 period, foreign capital entered Turkey to a considerable extent under the disguise of a Turkish national costume. During this period, foreign capital took part in 66 out of 201 Turkish incorporated companies. The total capital invested by these companies was TL73 million, of which TL31.5 million belonged to companies with foreign capital
52. For a similar point, see Timur, 1971, 45
53. See Gülalp, 1938, 157; Keyder, 1981, 11-67
54. See Silier, 1981, especially 40-46
55. See Birtek and Keyder, 1975; Hershlag, 1968
56. See Gülalp, 1980, 60-61
57. See, for instance, Aker, 1975; Avcıoğlu, 1968; Boratav, 1974; Hershlag, 1968; Ilkin and Tekeli, 1977
58. See Bayar, 1954, 58; Boratav, 1974, 165
59. Hershlag, 1958, 104-105
60. Timur, 1971, 179
61. Hershlag, 1968, 106; Karpat, 1959, 88
62. Boratav, 1974, 291
63. Özgür, 1976, 180
64. Özgür, 1976, 181
65. Boratav, 1974, 292
66. Boratav, 1974, 357
67. Thornburg, et al., 1949, 94-138
68. International Bank for Reconstruction and Development, 1951
69. Günce, 1967, 24-25
70. Tayanç, 1973, 118
71. Avcıoğlu, 1968, 402-403; Küçük, 1971, 220-225
72. Yerasimos, 1976, III, 1360
73. Karpat, 1967, 261
74. Avcıoğlu, 1968, 403; Küçük, 1971, 224

75. Hinderink and Kıray, 1970, show an aspect of the development of capitalism in agriculture in the Çukurova region by investigating four villages in which different levels of technological development were apparent. For a similar assessment, see Akşit, 1967

76. The argument which follows relies heavily on Gülalp, 1983, 44-67

77. Gülalp, 1983, 51

78. For Turkey's relations with international organisations, see Doğan, 1980

79. Nokta, 20-26 August 1984, 8-11

80. State Institute of Statistics: Agricultural Census of 1980

81. Varlier, 1978, 51

82. State Planning Organisation: First (1963-67), Second (1968-72), Third (1973-77) and Fourth (1979-83) Five-Year Development Plans

3. The Structure Of Southeastern Anatolia

In this chapter an attempt will be made to show that the eastern and southeastern parts of Turkey are the most underdeveloped regions. This is reflected in the backward nature of production, the low level of development of the infrastructure and the limited availability of services. The inequalities among regions are intensified by state policies which try to ensure capitalist development. An important factor in the intensification of regional underdevelopment is the continuous transfer of surplus (labour and product) from underdeveloped to developed regions. The aim of this chapter is twofold. First, an attempt will be made to exemplify the nature of regional underdevelopment in Southeastern Anatolia by highlighting particular aspects and characteristics of the region. These will then be contrasted with their national equivalents. The second objective is to acquaint the reader with the larger area within which the fieldwork was carried out in the villages of Gisgis and Kalhana.

Southeastern Anatolia

The Southeast Anatolia region comprises nine provinces: Adıyaman, Bitlis, Diyarbakır, Gaziantep, Hakkari, Mardin, Siirt, Urfa and Van, which account for 14.3 per cent (116,720Km^2) of the total area of Turkey (814,578Km^2). (See Fig.1)

Population

According to the 1980 census, the population of our region was 4,002,716, representing 8.9 per cent of the total population (44,736,957) of Turkey. The proportion of the region's population classed as rural (60 per cent) does not, at first sight, seem to be far above the national average (55.7 per cent), but it is necessary to treat these figures with caution when considering the rural or urban nature of the population. In Turkish statistics, areas with fewer than 2,000 inhabitants are considered to be rural and those with 2,000 or more urban. In fact there are many places with more than 2,000 inhabitants which display predominantly rural characteristics.

A better indicator to show whether a certain area is rural or urban is the size of the economically active population and the nature of their activities. For example, in 1980, out of the total economically active population of Southeast Anatolia, 71 per cent were engaged in agricultural activities, compared with 58.9 per cent in the other regions as a group and 60.0 per cent in Turkey as a whole (see Appendix Table A7). Despite the dominance of agriculture as the main economic activity in the region, there are a number of large cities, such as Gaziantep and Diyarbakır. These exist not as a result of industrialisation and the consequent increase in the number of industrial workers and workers in the service sector, but largely due to the rural exodus caused by mechanisation and the destruction of the natural economy in agriculture. The shanty towns of the big cities in the region accommodate almost 50 per cent of the population of the cities. (1)

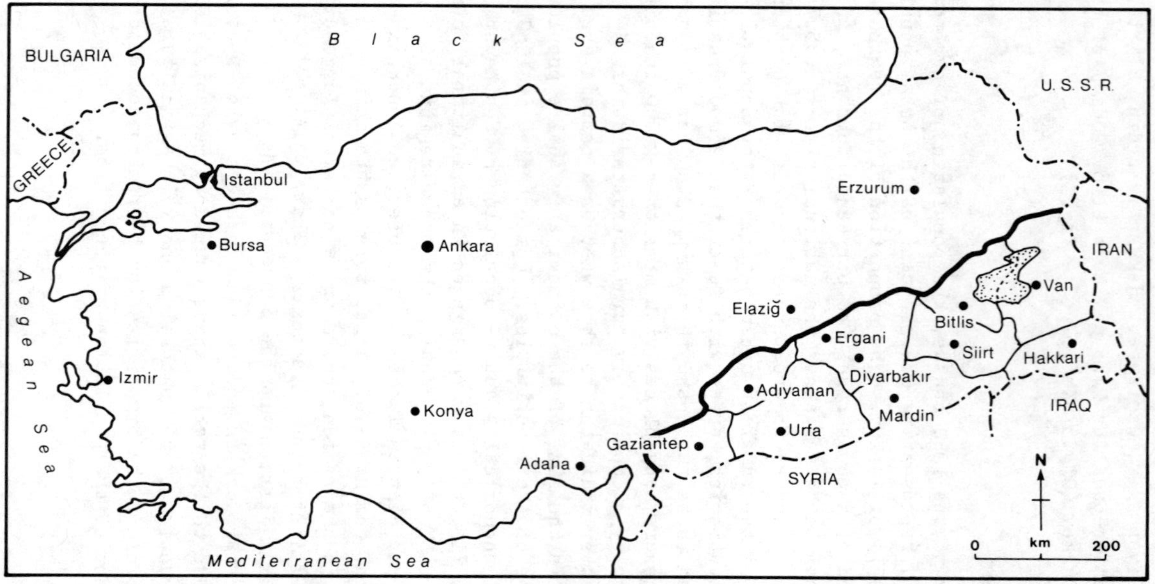

Fig. 1. Map of Turkey showing Southeastern Anatolia

Industry

The level of industrialisation is too low to absorb the labour force that has been freed from agriculture and their dependence on landlords. Furthermore, as in many other aspects, the disparity between the region and the rest of Turkey is also evident in the degree of industrial development. Of Turkey's 6,317 public and private industrial establishments in manufacturing industry, only 150 are to be found in this area. This 2.4 per cent of Turkey's total manufacturing industry employs some 10,108 people, only 1.5 per cent of the total work force in manufacturing industry in Turkey in 1975.

Nevertheless, although the term 'manufacturing industry' is used in the 1975 Annual Survey of Manufacturing Industry by the Turkish State Institute of Statistics, most of the private establishments in the region hardly deserve to be given the name 'industrial'. They may, at best, be called 'workshops', given the fact that the 130 private establishments which constitute 86.7 per cent of the total public and private establishments, only employ 4,224 workers. This figure represents only 41.8 per cent of the total work force employed in 'manufacturing industry' in the region, and the average number of workers per establishment in the private sector in the region is 32.5; a figure which hardly justifies the label 'industrial'. On the other hand, the 20 state-owned establishments (13.3 per cent of the total) employ 5,884 workers (58.2 per cent of the total), thus giving an average of 294 workers per establishment. (2)

According to the findings of the State Institute of Statistics, relative to the size of its population Southeastern Anatolia lags behind the national averages for number of industrial establishments and average number of employees employed in manufacturing industry. For example, in Southeastern Anatolia there is one industrial establishment per 26,288 people, while nationally it is one establishment per 6,387 people. Similarly, the percentage of employees in manufacturing industry with regard to total number of employees is very low. (3)

Transportation and communication

Communication and transportation are limited in this area compared with the rest of Turkey. In 1981 there were 60,712km of state and provincial roads in Turkey. Out of this total, Eastern Anatolia has 25 per cent of the state highways and 25 per cent of provincial roads. The figures give the impression that the region is quite well-off in terms of roads, but it is important to note that the roads in Eastern Anatolia are susceptible to weather conditions far more severe than those of other regions. In particular, most of the provincial roads, which permit intra-regional transportation and communication, and link villages and towns with each other, are not all-weather roads. In fact, 15 per cent of the state highways and 65.2 per cent of provincial roads in Eastern Anatolia are not all-weather roads.

Furthermore, rural areas and villages in Eastern Anatolia are less integrated than their counterparts in the other regions, in terms of communication facilities. For instance, only 4.6 per cent of the villages in the region had telephones, while the percentage in the other regions is 22 per cent. (4)

Education

The unequal development among the regions is also reflected both in the level of education and in the number of schools in the region. According to the State Institute of Statistics, 69.3 per cent of villages in Eastern Anatolia did not even have a primary school, while in other regions 37.7 per cent of the villages did not have primary schools. (5) This is reflected in the fact that the rate of illiteracy in the Southeast is much higher than in the rest of Turkey; 57 per cent in Southeast Anatolia in 1980; 30 per cent in the other regions. (6) The socio-economic structure of Eastern Anatolia acts as a hindrance to equal opportunities in education: first, there are not enough schools; second, the existing schools are severely understaffed, especially at secondary level. It is not unusual to see a statement in the graduation certificate of a secondary school student from this region to the effect that 'the graduate has not had physics, chemistry etc. lessons'. This is crucial for the student's future career, because the university candidates from this region have to compete with the better prepared candidates of other regions in the university entrance examinations. Given that only 10 to 20 per cent of all candidates applying are accepted by the universities, the graduates of Eastern Anatolian schools have a very poor chance. According to the State Institute of Statistics, only 3.6 per cent of university graduates came from Southeastern Anatolia (9 provinces) in 1980 (7) compared with 96.4 per cent from the other 58 provinces of the country, whereas Eastern Anatolia constituted 9 per cent of Turkey's total population in the same year. Within this unequal structure women occupy an even more underprivileged position: they constitute only 12 per cent of Southeastern Anatolia's 30,979 university graduates.

Health

The Southeast region, like the Eastern region, lags behind other regions in terms of available health services. Of the total for the whole country, 8.1 per cent of the hospitals, 5.1 per cent of the beds in hospitals, 2.5 per cent of the doctors and 6 per cent of the nurses were to be found in Southeast Anatolia in 1980. Furthermore, there is one bed for every 793.2 persons in the region, while there is one bed for every 433 persons in the other regions. (8)

The disadvantaged situation of the population of the Southeast, as well as Eastern Anatolia, with regard to health services has attracted the attention of politicians and successive governments. In 1963, for example, it was decided that the socialisation of health services would start first in Eastern Anatolia. Since that time quite a number of health centres have been initiated in the region but, owing to the shortage of qualified staff (doctors, nurses, etc.), most of them do not function properly.

Agricultural inputs

It is of interest to examine the usage of modern inputs which are crucial in terms of the level of productivity in agriculture. The Southeastern Anatolia region stays well behind the national average in terms of the use of modern inputs in agriculture. (9) For instance, 70.4 per cent of the total 3,558,815 holdings in Turkey use artificial fertilisers, while only 45.4 per cent of the total 331,953 holdings in Southeastern Anatolia use artificial fertilisers. The figures for the use of tractors are 44.69 per cent in Turkey as a whole, and 39.30 per cent in Eastern Anatolia. Similarly, while 57.82 per cent of holdings use insecticide/pesticide and other chemicals on a national scale, the figure in Eastern Anatolia is 30.99 per cent. The same trend can be detected in the use of irrigation. Compared with a 48.1 per cent national average, only 33.6 per cent of holdings in Southeastern Anatolia make use of irrigation.

In addition to the lower average use of modern inputs within the region, compared with the national average, it is also evident that the use of modern inputs in the region manifests further inequality between holdings of different size. For example, for large holdings with 500 decares (10) or more land, 71.02 per cent make use of artificial fertilisers, 64.06 per cent use tractors in farming and 57.94 per cent use agricultural chemicals, while these percentages for small holdings with 100 decares of land or less are 19.36 per cent, 34.84 per cent and 30.24 per cent respectively.

The technology and farming methods of the region are predominantly primitive. The extent of use of modern equipment and machinery in the region remains very limited compared with traditional equipment. While tractors numbered only 12,757, there were 145,397 wooden ploughs, and 19,410 walking ploughs; while combine harvesters numbered 781, there were a total of 47,856 threshing sleds. (11)

State policies

The emergence of the multi-party system in 1946 led politicians to pay special attention to eastern Anatolia, with regard to public investment, in order to secure more votes. Although they emphasised from time to time in their political rhetoric, that the state should invest in the east, there was no substantial state policy to overcome regional inequalities until 1960. However, some attempts were made to invest in the east, but they were far from overcoming the underdeveloped state of the region, or from closing the gap between the east and the other regions. For instance, a specific budget for the development of the east was included in the 1949-50 state budget. (12) Although this procedure was abandoned in subsequent years, a few import-substitution industrial establishments were opened in the region. (13) Nevertheless, on the whole, the free market mechanism was believed in for economic development, and productivity and profitability were the main concern in decisions relating to the locations where state investments were to be established.

Inter-regional inequalities have been recognised as a problem since the first Five Year Development Plan (1963-1967), and various policies have been adopted in the hope of getting rid of these inter-regional inequalities. Nevertheless, according to the Fourth Five Year Development Plan (1979-1983), 'despite all envisaged policies and efforts inter-regional imbalance has gradually increased'. (14)

In the period of the three five-year development plans, one of the important reasons for the increase of regional imbalance is that the share of the underdeveloped regions in public investment gradually declined. Furthermore, the private sector was not directed to those regions, according to the Fourth Five-Year Development Plan.

In the first five-year planned period, per capita investment in the East and Southeast regions was higher than that in other regions, but most of the investments were in the service sector, while in the other regions the share of industry is higher than that in the East and Southeast regions. In the second five-year planned period, the share of industrial investment exceeds that of services and agriculture in the East and Southeast regions but, when these figures are compared with those of other regions, it becomes evident that per capita investment in industry and services in the East and Southeast regions lags behind that in other regions. These differences increase further in the third five-year planned period. In particular, per capita investment in industry for the other regions is almost twice that of the East and Southeast regions. Also, the average per capita investment in the East and Southeast regions lags well behind that of the other regions in the third planned period (1973-1977). (15)

Despite all statements and intentions to the effect that priority would be given to the development of the East and Southeast regions, in the application of the plans priority has in fact been given to the developed regions and the gap between the developed parts of Turkey and the underdeveloped East and Southeast has widened rather than narrowed. In most of the investments made, questions of productivity, proximity to big markets and transport facilities have been kept in mind, and so the underdeveloped East and Southeast regions have been neglected in the allocation of investments.

In contrast to the above indicated inequalities between the Southeast and the rest of Turkey, the East and Southeast regions have been a major cheap labour source for the development of Turkish capitalism. Especially after the 1950s, with the mechanisation of agriculture, quite a large part of the labour force became available. A study of internal migration in Turkey by Tümertekin (16) has shown that the East and Southeast regions have been losing population through out-migration. Although some centres, such as Diyarbakır, Muş and Bitlis, have taken in population between 1955 and 1960, this is negligible when we consider the region as a whole. The trend has still continued in recent years. The developed centres still attract a labour force from the East. The out-migration of population is of considerable importance for the region. This is especially so as mainly young people endeavour to migrate and the resulting age structure of the economically active population in the region changes and therefore the productivity of labour is also affected indirectly. Furthermore, in the case of seasonal labour migration the region supports the labourers in the off-season and thereby reduces the production costs of the labourers' employers. It may, therefore, be concluded from the previous discussion that, whereas the Southeast region receives less than its fair proportion of services, capital inputs, etc., it is a major contributor of labour for the rest of the national economy. Given the importance of this factor, it will be discussed at some length in Chapter Ten.

Economic structure of Southeast Anatolia

In order to assess the role and function of the region within the Turkish economy as a whole, we shall examine the structure of the economy of the region. Since agricultural production is the major part of the region's economy, we shall first deal with land tenure, and the main relations of production in agriculture. This will be followed by a brief discussion of agricultural production in the region.

Land Tenure

The distribution of land in Southeastern Anatolia is highly differentiated. In 1980, while 11.6 per cent of the total households owned 59.9 per cent of the total lands owned, small landowners, which constitute 56 per cent of the landowning households, owned only 8.7 per cent of the total (17) (See Appendix Table A.9). It should be pointed out that the above figures do not take into consideration the number of landless families, which account for quite a large part of the rural population in the area. In 1973, for example, 189,403 households, 30.1 per cent of the total of 628,578 rural households were landless. Of these 125,751 (66.4 per cent) were engaged in farming, mostly through sharecropping arrangements, and the remaining 63,652 (33.6 per cent) households earned their main income as labourers. (18) The explanation given in the sources used about the nature of these labourers is far from clear. In the Turkish text the term 'straight labourers' is used, without any clarification. Given the fact that the level of industrial development is almost negligible in the area and that these households are located in population centres of less than 2,000, where there are no industrial establishments, we can assume that they are not engaged in a wage economy related to industry. Then who are these 'straight labourers'? Are they seasonal labourers? Or artisans? Or what? However, one thing is clear, the ratio of landless households in the area is quite high and much higher than that in Turkey as a whole: 22.26 per cent and 13.27 per cent respectively. (19)

Owing to factors such as absenteeism, renting and share-cropping arrangements and the illegal use of public lands, etc., the distribution of holdings in the region differs from the distribution of landownership. The important point is that the distribution of holdings has shown little change over a 30 year period, as shown in Appendix Table A.9. The numbers of small and big holdings have increased at the expense of medium-sized holdings but, in spite of an increase in the number of small holdings, the amount of land cultivated by these holdings has actually decreased. The existence of very large holdings has been one of the most important features of the region since the sixteenth century, simply because large amounts of land were granted to local notables, tribal leaders, etc. of the area, by the Ottoman administration for political reasons. (20) In fact, remnants of the yurtluk/ocaklık system can still be seen in the area. This is revealed by the fact that some families own one or more villages in the region. According to the Village Inventory surveys carried out by the Ministry of Village Affairs between 1963 and 1971, out of a total of 4,194 villages in Southeast Anatolia 3,767 belonged to the inhabitants of the villages, 170 belonged to individuals, 161 belonged to families and 96 belonged to dynasties. This gives a total of 427 villages owned by individuals, families or dynasties, which is 11.4 per cent of all villages. (21)

A number of landowners give some of their lands to share-croppers for various reasons. Some landowners, such as civil servants, teachers, merchants, who have no time for farming, give their lands to sharecroppers for a supplementary income.

Big landlords and capitalist farmers also give some of their lands to sharecroppers, though for different reasons. For instance, they may give some of their marginally less productive lands to sharecroppers in order to secure a readily available labour force for peak seasons.

Sharecropping plays an important role in reproducing the political and economic power of landlords, some of whom are also tribal leaders. It is through sharecropping arrangements that landlords strengthen their political dominance, which in turn enables them to have access to credits, fertilisers, etc., and therefore to intensify their economic dominance over the sharecroppers. The extent to which sharecropping is used, therefore, is an important feature of the political economy of this region. The widespread application of various types of sharecropping in Eastern Anatolia has been very well documented by Varlier, who shows that in Eastern Anatolia 99,783 (79.3 per cent) of a total of 125,751 landless households engage in sharecropping or renting arrangements. (22) This supports the view that landlords try to tie the landless poor to the land in order to secure a labour force for peak seasons. (23)

Absentee landlords who give their lands to sharecroppers or renters play a very important role in the transfer of the surplus product from the rural areas to urban areas. Although absentee families account for only a small proportion of the landowning families (6.2 per cent of the total) they control 57.3 per cent of the total land in Southeast Anatolia. The figures for Diyarbakır province are well above average. The absentee landowning families, while constituting only 3 per cent of the landowning families in the province, control 88 per cent of the total land. (24) As Beşikçi points out, the absentee landlords dwell in towns and cities, running their farms through their kahya (bailiff) or, as in the case of big landlords, they sometimes run their farms personally and invest in more profitable areas such as commercial activities, running an hotel, cinema or shop, or buying apartments, etc.

According to Beşikçi, ex-feudal landlords and the newly emerging town bourgeoisie are the same people. (25) Without subscribing to the last statement, we can conclude that the rural surplus extracted from the direct producers in various forms by the absentee landlords who are also a part of the town bourgeoisie are transferred to other regions through the luxury consumption habits of the big landlords. In some cases the surplus is transferred directly to the developed western part of the country, because the big landlords have moved to the big cities in the West, such as Istanbul, Izmir and Ankara, living luxuriously, educating their children in expensive private foreign schools, engaging in commerce, transportation, real estate speculation and so on.

Unequal land distribution is further reflected in the unequal income distribution in the rural sector of the region. While income in the majority of households (67 per cent of the total) does not exceed TL15,000 per annum, 3 per cent of the total households enjoy annual incomes of TL100,000 or more. This should be compared with a 1973 national per capita income of TL6,898.

It has been argued that the existing 'system of landownership hinders increased production and is contrary to the goals of social justice; it must therefore be reformed'. (26) Although the State Planning Organisation 'experts' recommend land reform and many governments have included land reform in their programmes, land reform has been a protracted story of the Turkish Republic from its inception. The existence of a strong landlord class in Turkey and their effective role in Turkish politics has not allowed the implementation of any extensive land reform programme. (27)

Apart from the lack of 'social justice' caused by the unequal distribution of land, and therefore of income, the existing landownership pattern hinders any rise in productivity in the region. The producers with low income cannot afford to buy highly expensive agricultural machinery, chemicals, improved seeds, etc. Also, some absentee landowners tend to neglect their lands.

Rural Production

Cereals constitute the most important items of agricultural

production in terms of both the volume of production and the area under cultivation in Southeast Anatolia. In 1981, 1,728,606 hectares (90 per cent) of the total 1,920,054 hectares of cultivated lands were assigned to cereal production. Of the cereals, wheat is the most common: out of the total 1,728,606 hectares under cereals, 1,347,079 hectares (77.9 per cent) were under wheat, 361,690 hectares under barley, 5,854 hectares under millet, 3,600 hectares under rye, 7,494 hectares under rice, 2,539 hectares under maize and 350 hectares under mixed grain. Wheat, being the staple, was not only at the top of the table in terms of area cultivated, but also in first place in terms of the volume of production, accounting for 76 per cent (1,840,977 tons) of the total cereal production and 60.3 per cent of the total agricultural production, which was 3,053,004 tons in 1981. (28)

Compared with cereal production the production of other agricultural crops remains limited. However, with the government's anxious efforts to increase the production of commercial crops, crops such as sugarbeet and cotton seem to be gaining importance. Apart from commercial crops, lentils are one of the most extensively marketed products in the region. Lentils were the third largest crop in terms of area under cultivation in the region in 1981. This is because lentils are an important constituent of the peasant diet in the region, as well as being a marketable crop. However, the importance of lentils as a main item in the peasant family's diet has been eroded by the rise in the price of lentils in the market. Instead of having lentil soup with bread for breakfast, peasant families now tend to have tea, which is much cheaper. This was observed in the villages of Ergani during our fieldwork.

Many varieties of vegetables and fruits are also grown in the region, but the production of vegetables and fruits is not so great that it can be considered a major determinant of rural production in the region. The marketed part of the vegetables and fruit brings supplementary cash to the producer households. In 1981, 56,543 hectares were used for 'market garden' produce, which amounted to 874,767 tons according to the State Institute of Statistics. (29) Of the 'market garden' crops, melons, watermelons, tomatoes, aubergines, cucumbers and peppers were the most extensively grown items in order of production output. In 1981, 476,742 tons of fruit were produced from 15,626,153 fruit trees. At the top of the table, with 383,402 tons of production, were grapes. Among other 'orchard' crops, walnuts, pomegranates, almonds, apples, pears, plums and apricots were the most produced items in the Southeast region. (30)

Livestock production is the second major economic activity in the region. In some areas within the region, livestock breeding is even considered the main source of livelihood. For instance, Beşikçi (31) claims this to be the case in Adıyaman, Bitlis, Siirt and Van provinces. Despite the fact that seven provinces of the region (Bitlis, Diyarbakır, Hakkari, Mardin, Siirt, Urfa and Van, which constitute the sixth agricultural region according to the State Institute of Statistics) have 21.1 per cent of the livestock of the whole country, they only account for 19,475 tons of the country's 225,000 tons of meat production. (32) This is partly due to low productivity, and partly due to cattle-smuggling into the neighbouring countries, Syria, Iraq and Iran.

Low productivity is also a main feature in the production of other animal products, such as dairy goods, wool, mohair, honey, etc. The technology and methods of production are old-fashioned. For instance, most of the milk produced in the region is processed into yoghurt, cheese and butter by individual households. Prior to 1963 there was no modern creamery in the region. However, in order to meet the increasing demand for milk and dairy products in the industrialised parts of the country, governments have planned to open creameries in Eastern Anatolia. Thus the second Five Year Plan envisaged seven creameries being opened in Eastern Anatolia during 1972 and 1973.

So far we have seen the structure of agricultural production in the Southeastern region of Turkey. The agricultural products produced in the region are transferred to the industrialised parts of Turkey or to overseas markets by government agencies such as Toprak Mahsulleri Ofisi and Tekel, or by government-supported sales co-operatives such as Çukobirlik and by merchants. Also, rural resources flow out of the region via absentee landlords. In addition to being a source of cheap labour for developing capitalism, the region is also a food-stuffs depot for the industrial regions: a factor which will also be discussed at some length in Chapter Eight.

We have shown that the Southeast region is the most under-developed region of Turkey. The region is mainly of a rural nature. Although Turkey as a whole shows rural characteristics, these are more distinguishable in the Southeast region, where there is almost no industry, the transportation and communication facilities are less developed, the level of education is very low, and health facilities are very inefficient. Although the region is more agricultural than the rest of Turkey, the level of technology and agricultural inputs are more backward. The State has not been able to reduce the discrepancies between the Southeast region and the rest of Turkey. Moreover, it is possible to argue that state policies have intensified the discrepancies between this region and the rest of Turkey. The surplus (labour and products) created in the region has been transferred to the developed part of the country. In the following chapters we shall attempt to show how this surplus is created and transferred from the region. The analysis in the following chapters will be based on the fieldwork carried out in Gisgis and Kalhana villages in 1977. We shall argue that it is the peasant household which creates this surplus labour and product. The organisation of the household economy vis à vis larger structures renders possible the creation and transfer of this surplus, which is used in the development of urban capitalism. We shall argue that the peasant household as an economic unit carries the burden of this development. Before going into the details of ownership of means of production, relations of production, division of labour, etc. it seems appropriate to acquaint the reader with Gisgis and Kalhana, where the fieldwork was carried out.

Notes to Chapter Three

1. Ozankaya, 1969
2. State Institute of Statistics, 1977a
3. Ibid.
4. State Institute of Statistics, 1963, cited in State Planning Organisation, Co-ordination Department, 1972; Statistical Yearbook of Turkey, 1983
5. State Planning Organisation, Co-ordination Department, 1972, 60
6. Calculated from the 1980 census: State Institute of Statistics, 1984a
7. Ibid.
8. Calculated from ibid.
9. Varlier, 1978. Varlier's work is based on data gathered in 1973 by the Institute of Population Studies, Hacettepe University
10. One *decare* equals one-tenth of a hectare. Official statistics use *decare* and *dönüm* interchangeably.
11. State Institute of Statistics, 1984b
12. State Planning Organisation, Co-ordination Department, 1972, 39-41; Ozankaya, 1969, 99-100
13. Ozankaya, 1969, 99
14. Fourth Five-Year Development Plan published in *Resmi Gazete*, 12 December 1978, 51
15. Per capita investment (TL) during the planned period (1963-77) was as follows:

	1st Plan	2nd Plan	3rd Plan
(i) in agriculture			
East and Southeast regions	95	173	291
Rest of Turkey	118	129	305
(ii) in industry			
East and Southeast regions	298	637	1,515
Rest of Turkey	305	768	3,002

	1st Plan	2nd Plan	3rd Plan
(iii) in service activities			
East and Southeast regions	324	441	1,511
Rest of Turkey	261	525	1,767

16. Tümertekin, 1968
17. Calculated from State Institute of Statistics, 1980
18. A brief comment on some of the statistics we are using in this part seems to be necessary. Although we have tried to use statistics concerning only the Southeast region whenever they were available, owing to the tendency of some sources to combine the Eastern and Southeastern Anatolian regions of Turkey, we have had to make use of figures pertaining to both regions. Therefore, in this section figures concerning Eastern Anatolia include those of Southeastern Anatolia, unless otherwise stated. Another point is that the figures given in these statistics are based on the declarations of the owners and should be regarded with caution. In most parts of Eastern and Southeastern Anatolia, as in other parts of Turkey, cadastral surveys are in their infancy. Nonetheless, the figures we use can give us a basic idea as to what the situation is like in the region.
19. Varlier, 1978
20. See Chapter Five
21. Calculated from Köy Işleri Bakanlığı Village Inventory Surveys of the provinces of Southeastern Anatolia
22. See Varlier, 1978
23. See Chapter Six
24. Calculated from Village Inventory Surveys
25. Beşikçi, 1969, 122-123
26. State Planning Organisation, 1963, 47-48
27. See Chapter Two; also Aktan, 1971
28. State Institute of Statistics, 1984b
29. *Ibid.*, 20
30. *Ibid.*, 19

31. Beşikçi, 1969, 23
32. State Institute of Statistics, 1984b

4. Physical Environment , Population And Agriculture

Before discussing, in later chapters, the nature of the social relations of production, social structure, landownership, access to land, role of the household, etc., it is necessary to highlight some general characteristics pertaining to the two villages under consideration. It is for this reason that this chapter has been divided into two sections. The first section will examine the physical environment and population in Gisgis and Kalhana, while the second section will focus on some general features related to agrarian activities.

Physical Environment & Population in Gisgis and Kalhana

Gisgis and Kalhana villages are in the Ergani district of the province of Diyarbakır, which is about 958km southeast of the capital city, Ankara. Both villages are on the stabilised road that runs between Ergani and Çermik district centres, the distances between Kalhana and Gisgis and Ergani being six and eighteen kilometres respectively.

Gisgis : Physical environment

Gisgis village is one of the villages which borders on the Çermik district. It is situated on the main road between Ergani and Çermik which cuts through the village from east to west. The area in which the village is situated is a long flat strip lying between two parallel mountain ridges which form part of the Taurus chain. The mountain to the south of the village is locally named Kemertepe and at its foot is the Milik Çayı, a stream which runs about three hundred metres away from the village settlement. In the area between the Milik Çayı and the village there lie vegetable gardens of various sizes. The mountain about one and a half kilometres to the north of the village is much higher than Kemertepe. The fields within the village boundaries are not of an even nature. A number of hills act as reference points for the locational description of fields, vegetable gardens, or vineyards; for example: 'the field behind Kemertepe' or 'the vineyard on Demirtepe' are typical directions used by peasants.

Gisgis village has boundaries with Sincik (Çayirdere) village in the northwest, Zirkiilyan (Dağarası) village in the northeast and east, Ziyarek (Tevekli) village in the southeast and Zimoyik (Dibektaşı) village in the south, as well as Çermik district in the west. The mountains and hills around all these villages carry some form of vegetation, albeit sparse, such as oak trees, hornbeams, and dwarf bushes, which are rapidly disappearing since the people from the surrounding villages cut them for fuel and in order to open new fields. Most of the fields cleared in this way are planted with vines. We came across areas of fruit trees and vegetable gardens on the lower slopes of the locally named Sincik Dağı to the north of the village. About thirty or more springs around the village serve as water resources for small-scale vegetable production.

The village stretches along the Ergani-Çermik road from east to west and the houses line up side by side on both sides of the road. However, there is one line of buildings on the south of the road, while the rest are on the north side. All the windows and doors face towards the south in order both to get as much sun as possible in the cold season, and to be less affected by the westerly and easterly winds, since the village is well protected from northerly and southerly winds by the parallel ridges of mountains lying to the north and the south.

Most of the houses (Fig. 2) have two storeys with flat roofs. The ground floor, which is generally bigger than the upper floor, is used as an animal barn and storage space for straw and hay. A ladder is used in order to climb up to the roof of the ground floor through a hole in the ceiling. Half of the flat roof of the ground floor serves as a large balcony in front of the upper rooms. The whole family sleeps on this roof/balcony in the summer because it is too hot inside. The upper floor generally consists of two rooms and a kitchen/pantry. Generally there is no toilet in the house. The materials used in the buildings are mostly <u>kerpiç</u> (sun-dried bricks of mud and straw) and stones. Cement has been used in a few buildings, such as the school, the gendarmerie and the health centre. Although there is an abundance of drinking water, none of the houses had water inside. Water is obtained from the six fountains in the village. (See village plan, Fig. 4)

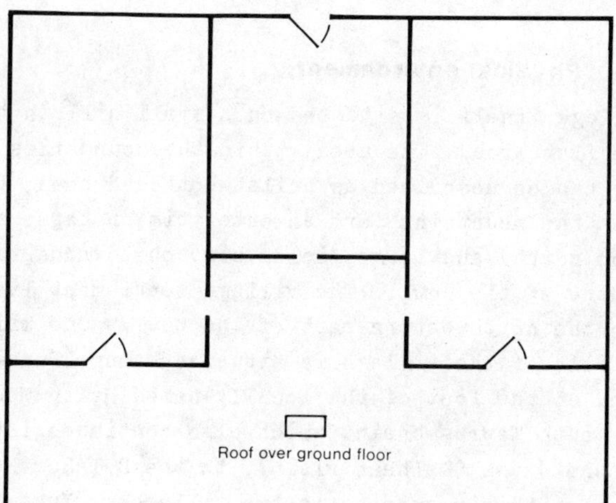

Fig. 2. Plan of typical village house

There are two shops and two coffee houses in the village, but one of the shops was closed during our fieldwork and the owner did not intend to reopen it. The coffee houses are the places where most men spend their spare time. Educated youths preferred to patronise one of the coffee houses rather than the one frequented by elderly people. (1) The only shop that was in operation was also supposed to be the Post Office. However, during our stay in the village we never saw anybody taking a letter to the Post Office. Since there are always people going to the town, letters are sent with them to be posted from there.

The village school had 119 students and two teachers in 1977. The two classrooms were too few for the five classes of children aged between seven and twelve, so the first, second and third year students were taught in one classroom while the fourth and fifth year students were taught in the other. The gendarmerie station, situated about 200 metres west of the village, had six soldiers and a sergeant who were responsible for maintaining law and order in Gisgis and the surrounding villages. The health centre and its three-storey residential building constitute the westernmost section of the village.

Kalhana : Physical environment

The village itself is situated on a small hill in the middle of a large flat area. The area within the boundaries of the village can be described as a flat-bottomed bowl, broken on one side, as the mountains form an outer rim on three sides (south, west and north) and large fields stretch towards the east from the centre of the bowl. The village settlement lies on a small hump in the northwestern part of the bowl. One kilometre or so to the west of the village is situated Malan (Pinarkaya) village, at the foot of the locally-named Malan Mountain, part of the South Taurus chain, which also continues into the south of Kalhana Ovası (Kalhana Plain), to the Balahur Mountain. At the foot of this mountain are two villages: Yukarı Balahur (High Balahur) and Aşağı Balahur (Lower Balahur). Keydanevleri

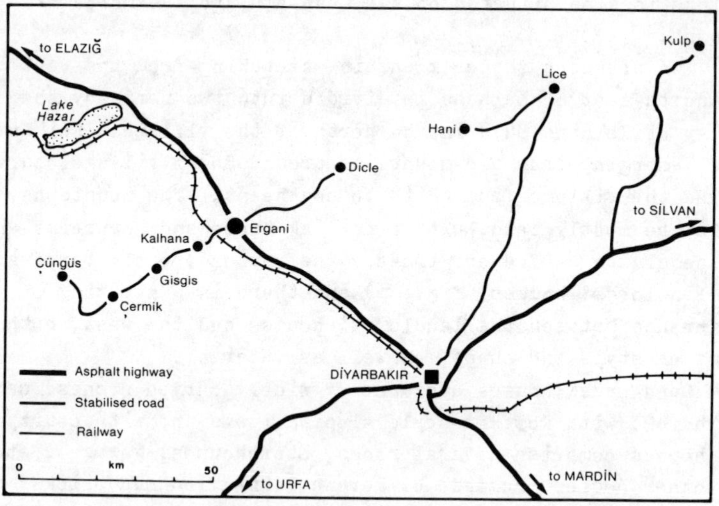

Fig. 3. Map showing location of Gisgis and Kalhana

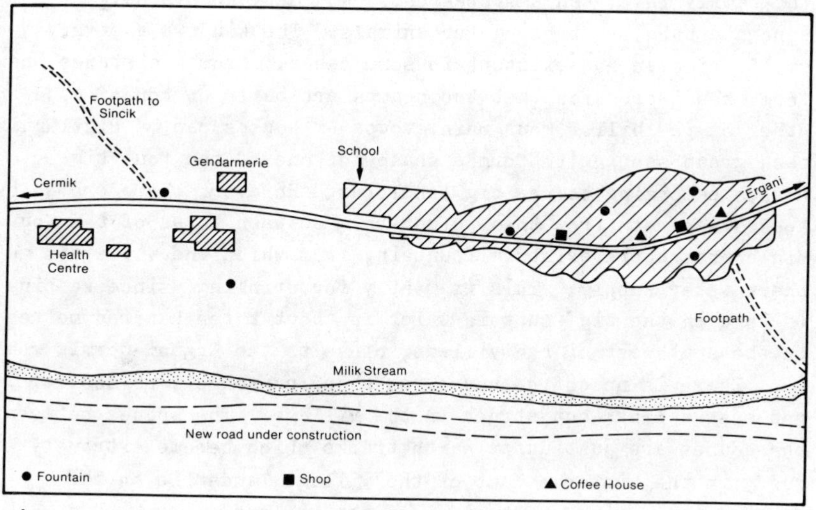

Fig. 4. Sketch of Gisgis village

village is also situated on the mountain, to the north of Kalhana.

The crescent-shaped mountain stretching from the west to the north-east of Kalhana is divided into two parts by the valley of Kalhana Suyu in the north of the village. Kalhana Suyu, emerging from the mountains around Boğaz village, curves around the village from north to southeast. The mountains and hills are mostly bald, with a few oak trees and hornbeams and sparse clusters of dwarf trees. The houses are clustered around the landlords' houses (Fig. 5) and there is a striking difference between the landlords' houses and the rest, both in terms of style and shape, as well as material.

Landlords' houses are made of nicely carved stones, cement and brick, with western-style sloping roofs and with courtyards. The houses comprise several rooms, storehouses, garages, etc. The other houses are made of kerpiç (sun-dried mud bricks) with ceilings so low that one has to stoop on entering through the door. The roofs, covered with timber, rushes and soil, are flat. These houses usually have just one or two rooms, where the family live, and a store-room. Not many houses have a separate barn or stabling for animals. The windows are very small, or even non-existent in some cases. From a distance one forms the impression that the houses are built on top of each other on the hill. Four main groups of houses can be distinguished, each group seeming to form a shadow of one of the four big houses belonging to the big landlords. However, there are a few houses separate from these clusters. Between three of the four big houses there exists a fountain, from which the villagers get their water supply. This is mostly for drinking, since washing is done in the big fountain which is about three hundred metres to the southwest of the village, close to the Ergani-Çermik road.

There is no coffee house, no shop, no school, no mosque, not even a clear-cut street in the village. The spaces between the houses are just dusty earth tracks which become extremely muddy in the winter. Most of the village lands lie on the eastern and southeastern sides of the village.

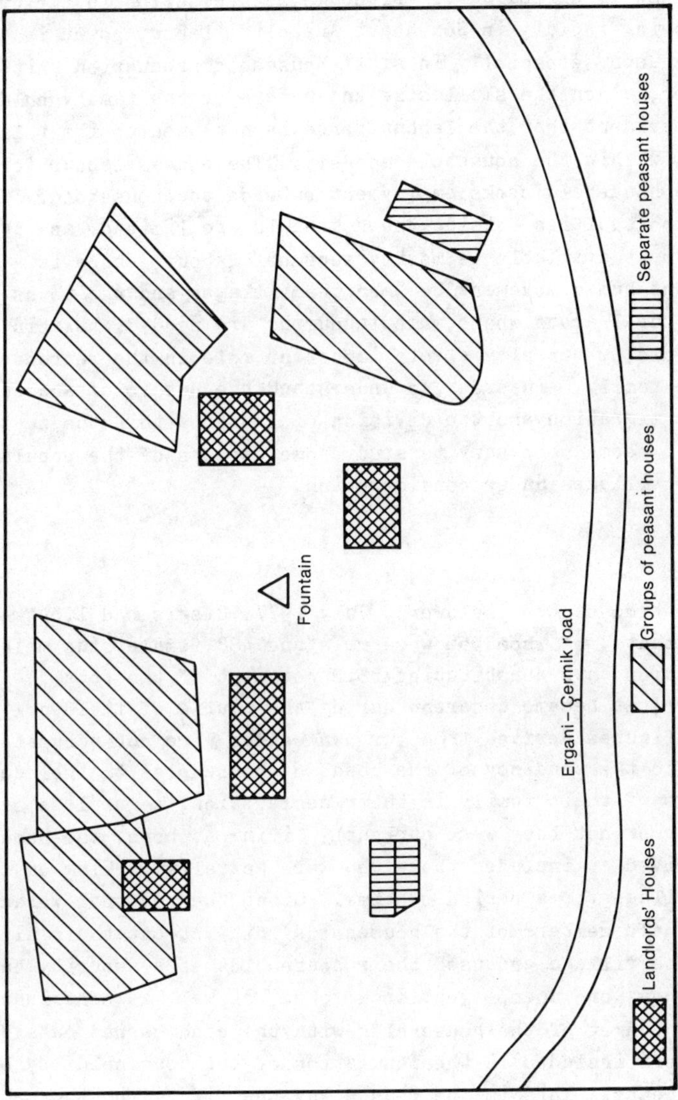

Fig. 5. Sketch of Kalhana village

Population in Gisgis and Kalhana

Labour power is very important in villages where the main source of income is agriculture. Although mechanisation in agriculture is growing rapidly in Southeast Anatolia, labour power is still widely used, especially in small household production units. However, given the small size and nature of the family holdings, it is evident that the labour force is not used to its full extent within the household economy. The excess labour force of the household seeks employment outside the household. Since job opportunities outside the household are limited, and the employment available is mostly seasonal labour, there is constant human movement between the villages and the towns and other rural areas where wage labourers are needed. Within the household, women play a very important role in the reproduction of the family. In order to understand the nature of seasonal labour migration and the division of labour within the household it seems necessary to study some aspects of the population in the villages under consideration.

Gisgis

At the time of the fieldwork, July 1977, Gisgis had 1,044 inhabitants, of whom 556 were male and 488 female, the male population thus constituting 53.2 per cent of the total. However, it became apparent during the course of fieldwork that these figures derived from our own census were not accurate. Owing to the tendency of the heads of households to include all members of their family in their declaration, regardless of whether or not they were currently living at home, the numbers we arrived at included those who were actually working outside the village for a period of time. Since the seasonal workers (some male members of the households) did not cut their ties with the village and used their households as a security base when they were unemployed, sick, etc., as well as contributing to the budget of the households with the cash earned outside, they were included in the population of the households by our respondents. This is one reason why the figure for the male population is higher than that for females.

Although, in rural areas of Southeast Anatolia, children start to work when they are about 7 to 8 years old, helping their parents in simple jobs, we considered those under 14 as relatively unproductive, since they spend most of the year going to school. Table 1 shows the age and sex structure of the village population. In order to differentiate the physically active population, in terms of production, from those who are inactive, we have arbitrarily divided the population into three groups: those aged 0-14, 15-65 and over 65 respectively. We are aware of the dangers of arbitrary categorisations like this; however, the first and third groups include those who are basically dependent on the production of the economically active, and the table presents a general picture of the work force in the village.

It is clear from Table 1 that the population of the village consists of a large proportion of young people. Only 2 per cent are above the age of 65, whereas the active group (aged 15 to 65) comprises 53.1 per cent of the total and children comprise no less than 44.9 per cent. Among those aged 15 to 65, males constitute 55.4 per cent.

The marital status of those over 14 years of age is shown in Table 2. In Gisgis, 62.8 per cent of the male population above the age of 14 are maried, as against 84 per cent of the females in the same age group. This is largely a result of females being treated as objects of monetary transactions. Women constitute a very decisive part of the household economy. Not only do they do all the housework, but they also work in the production of the goods produced by the household, and are valuable assets of the household economy, especially since they work without any remuneration. Being a source of free labour, they are bought and sold in the context of an ideological structure called *başlık* (2), which legitimises the commercial transaction. Marriages in the village are arranged, and neither the boys nor the girls have any say in the choice of marriage partners. Fathers would marry off their daughters to whomsoever offers more money as a *başlık*, the age

TABLE 1 POPULATION BY AGE GROUP AND SEX IN GISGIS

AGE GROUP	MALES NUMBER	MALES PER CENT	MALES PER CENT OF TOTAL	FEMALES NUMBER	FEMALES PER CENT	FEMALES PER CENT OF TOTAL	TOTAL NUMBER	TOTAL PER CENT OF TOTAL
0-14	240	43.2	23.0	229	46.9	21.9	469	44.9
15-65	307	55.2	29.4	247	50.6	23.7	554	53.1
66+	9	1.6	0.8	12	2.5	1.2	21	2.0
Total	556	100.0	53.2	488	100.0	46.8	1,044	100.0

TABLE 2 MARITAL STATUS OF THOSE OVER 14 IN GISGIS

STATUS	MALES	PER CENT	FEMALES	PER CENT	TOTAL	PER CENT
Married	196	62.8	215	84.0	411	72.4
Unmarried	116	37.2	33	13.0	149	26.2
Widowed	-	-	8	3.0	8	1.4
Total	312	100.0	256	100.0	568	100.0

TABLE 3 POPULATION INCREASE IN GISGIS

YEAR	MALES	FEMALES	TOTAL	INDEX
1955	318	397	715	100.0
1960+	319	398	717	100.2
1965	383	387	770	107.6
1970	433	431	864	120.8
1975	514	484	1,003	140.2
1977++	556	488	1,044	146.0

\+ Figures for 1960 are taken from Beysanoğlu, 1962

++ Population census carried out during our fieldwork

Source: State Institute of Statistics, Population censuses for the relevant years

of the future bridegroom being unimportant so long as he can pay the <u>başlık</u>. Such lack of consideration sometimes results in dramatic events, such as the girl committing suicide. Fathers with daughters generally want to get rid of them as soon as possible in order to obtain the <u>başlık</u> money. On the other hand, fathers with sons may be reluctant to marry off their sons, because of the <u>başlık</u> money they will have to pay. When they do decide to marry their sons, they start to look for young, healthy and strong girls as brides for their sons, so that they can use their labour for a long time. For these reasons, the girls in the village get married at a very early age, sometimes when they are just 12 years old. Another reason for the predominance of married women over married men is the persistence of polygamy, in spite of its being illegal. In particular, some of the relatively rich farmers have more than one wife.

Regarding the role of <u>başlık</u> in determining marriages, it might also be pointed out that, in Gisgis, 26.2 per cent of the people above 14 years of age are not married (149 out of 568) and, of these, 77.8 per cent (116) are male and 22.1 (33) are female. This disparity is due partly to the inability of young men to collect money for the <u>başlık</u> and partly to the ability of some of the relatively rich villagers to buy more than one wife.

We did not come across any widowers in the village during our fieldwork, but there were eight widows. This is due to the fact that those men who are divorced or widowed remarry. Some of the widows also remarry, but the prospects of remarriage for widows are very slim if they are over thirty, simply because men want to marry a young, healthy woman who will be more industrious in the reproduction of the household. It is not unusual, for example, to see a man in his fifties marrying a teenage girl.

The population of Gisgis increased by 46 between 1955 and 1977 (Table 3), but the rate of increase has fluctuated considerably. Whereas between 1955 and 1965 it amounted to only 7.6 per cent, between 1965 and 1975 it was about 30 per cent.

The relatively slow rate of population growth between 1955 and 1965 can be explained by out-migration from the village.

With the promotion of agricultural development by the Democrat Party government from 1950 onwards, the production of cash crops, especially in areas like the Çukurova, where capitalist farming had long been established, increased rapidly. Around Adana and Tarsus, not only did cotton production increase but, in addition, cotton textile industries developed at a fast rate. Cotton production, which is very labour-intensive, and the newly-established or enlarged industries in the Çukurova region (particularly in Adana and Tarsus) were the main factors attracting the landless or poor peasants from other regions, especially those of Southeastern Anatolia, where control of the land is in the hands of a few landlords, and quite a number of peasant families work as sharecroppers, agricultural workers and the like.

The demand for workers in the Çukurova region was satisfied within a decade, and migration from other areas for permanent settlement in that region has slowed down. Capitalist cotton production still requires seasonal labour, however, thus causing seasonal population movements between regions. This point will be dealt with at greater length when we consider the migration problem in Chapter Ten.

It may be argued that the increase or decrease in population is also related to factors such as health services, nutrition, etc. There is no doubt that improvements in medical treatment and health services increase the life expectancy of the people; we cannot be certain, however, about the extent of the effect on the medical care of the people in the village of the opening of the Sağlık Ocağı (health centre) in 1965. The Sağlık Ocağı was opened in Gisgis for political reasons and does not function as it should. There is no doctor in the Sağlık Ocağı, only one health officer, one nurse and a caretaker. Apart from basic things such as alcohol, aspirin and tincture of iodine, essential medicines are not stored in the centre. In fact the only services the Sağlık Ocağı can provide are the assistance of a nurse in the case of a birth, and bandaging of wounds or cuts. Given the nature and limitations of the health services in the village, it is too difficult to determine the effects of these services on the population increase in Gisgis.

Social and economic values attached to the number of children are also effective factors in the population increase in the village. To have sons is very desirable. This is due to the fact that there is no social security for old age and it is the sons' duty to look after their elderly parents. Furthermore, the high rate of infant mortality in the village encourages people to have as many children as they can, in case some of them die before reaching maturity. In Table 4 we see the number of children per family and the incidence of infant mortality are recorded by our fieldwork.

TABLE 4 LIVE BIRTHS AND INFANT MORTALITY IN GISGIS

LIVE BIRTHS PER FAMILY		LIVING CHILDREN		INFANT MORTALITY CASES	
NO. OF BIRTHS	NO. OF FAMILIES	NO. OF CHILDREN	NO. OF FAMILIES	NO. OF DEATHS	NO. OF FAMILIES
0-2	20	0-3	33	0	44
4-6	49	4-6	87	1	40
7-9	75	7-9	44	2	32
10-12	13	10+	-	3	13
13+	7		164	4	19
	164			5	12
				6+	4
					164

It is clear from Table 4 that there is a high birth rate in the village, as well as a high rate of infant mortality. The high death rate is caused in part by malnutrition and lack of medical care, as well as other factors such as the frequency of pregnancy and the young age of the mothers at the time of their first pregnancies. (3)

The desire to produce sons stems not only from economic but also from social necessities, such as being strong in kabile (large family group) disputes which generally end up in fights. The strongest _kabile_ always controls political power in the village, reflected in the election of the village headman. However, despite the general tendency to desire many children, it emerged that families with a low income and relatively well-educated families were not very keen on having large numbers of children. Ignorance, economic inability to buy contraceptives, social stigma attached to birth control and the distance from the towns where doctors live are the main factors inhibiting the practice of birth control. However, this does not mean that some of the women do not try to take preventive measures against childbirth. The practice of traditional abortion methods in some cases has tragic results, such as the mother losing her life. Also, in some cases women may try to use each other's medicine to prevent conception or to abort the foetus. For instance, one of my respondents told me that his wife had used her neighbour's injection, which had been obtained from a chemist without any prescription. It should be noted that those people who use medical contraceptives (albeit in some cases belonging to others) are very much in a minority.

Despite the high rate of infant mortality and out-migration, the data collected show that population growth in Gisgis remains rapid and the population has risen from 715 in 1955 to 1044 in 1977.

Kalhana

The population of Kalhana village was 258 in 1977. Females outnumbered males in the village, comprising 53.5 per cent of the population. This was due partly to the fact that some of the male population of the village had left in order to find work, and partly to the natural population increase. The total number of males in the village is 120, and females number 138. As in the case of Gisgis, we have broken down the population into three age groups, so as to be able to see the extent of the working and dependent population in the village. (Table 5)

The village population has a very youthful age structure, those under 14 comprising almost half the total. This is

TABLE 5 POPULATION BY AGE GROUP AND SEX IN KALHANA

AGE GROUP	MALES NUMBER	MALES PER CENT	MALES PER CENT OF TOTAL	FEMALES NUMBER	FEMALES PER CENT	FEMALES PER CENT OF TOTAL	TOTAL NUMBER	TOTAL PER CENT OF TOTAL
0-14	66	55.0	25.6	56	40.6	21.7	122	47.3
15-65	49	40.8	19.0	80	58.0	31.0	129	50.0
66+	5	4.2	1.9	2	1.4	0.8	7	2.7
Total	120	100.0	46.5	138	100.0	53.5	258	100.0

TABLE 6 MARITAL STATUS OF THOSE OVER 14 IN KALHANA

STATUS	MALES	PER CENT	FEMALES	PER CENT	TOTAL	PER CENT
Married	32	59.2	48	58.5	80	58.8
Single	21	38.9	31	37.8	52	38.2
Widowed	1	1.9	3	3.7	4	3.0
Total	54	100.0	82	100.0	136	100.0

TABLE 7 POPULATION INCREASE IN KALHANA

YEAR	MALES	FEMALES	TOTAL	INDEX
1955	65	91	156	100.0
1960+	101	100	201	128.9
1965	103	111	214	137.1
1970	111	112	223	142.9
1975	126	140	266	170.5
1977++	120	138	258	165.3

\+ Figures for 1960 are taken from Beysanoğlu, 1962

++ Figures for 1977 are derived from the questionnaire applied in the village in the summer of 1977

Source: State Institute of Statistics, Population censuses for the relevant years

hardly surprising, given the economic structure of the village. The majority of households in the village do not have any land at all, and the work possibilities created by commercial farming are not sufficient to keep pace with the population growth in the village as well as immigration into the village. Therefore some of the work force, particularly adult sons, leave the village to work outside. This also partially explains why females outnumber males in the middle age group. The same tendency is also evident from the fact that, whereas male children outnumber female children, when we move to the second group the reverse is the case, namely females are more numerous than males. The very low number of old people, those over 65, can be attributed to the fact that people do not have enough food, especially those foods containing high protein, the difficult working conditions causing people to age rapidly, sanitary conditions and medical help being at a very low level.

As in Gisgis, marriage is a contractual transaction between the couple's families. The bride is generally chosen for the boy by his family. Neither boys nor girls have any strong say in the choice of marriage partner. The only thing they can do is comply with the wishes and decisions of their seniors, namely their parents, grand-parents, uncles, elder brothers etc. Very large sums of money are demanded by the girl's father as <u>başlık</u>, which has to be paid by the bridegroom's family. The <u>başlık</u> mechanism, while leading to the early marriage of girls, affects young males in a different way, creating an obstacle to marriage when young. Table 6 shows the marriage situation in the village.

In Kalhana, 59.5 per cent of males and 58.5 per cent of females over 14 were married. In absolute terms married females outnumbered married males owing to the fact that, although polygamy is officially illegal in Turkey, some men, particularly those who are relatively rich, have more than one wife, and our population census included only those who were present in the village, and therefore did not take into account those husbands working outside. Single men constituted 28.9 per cent of the males, whereas 37.8 per cent of the females were single.

There were one widower and four widows in the village. Two of the widows had recently lost their husbands in an accident and were living with their brothers-in-law's families.

At this point it might be of interest to point out that, until the last decade, men felt obliged to marry their brothers' widows, because it was believed in the village that it was immoral for a widow to live alone. The honour of the whole family would be at risk if she lived alone. Of course this was a kind of rationalisation mechanism, which had developed over the years so as to justify marriage with the brother's widow. I assume the real reason behind this was economic, and to a certain extent social. In order to keep the dead brother's property within the family and to have absolute control over it, and also to protect his children as well as make use of their labour when they are able to work, the elder brother would marry his brother's widow. However, this tradition of marrying one's brother's widow is dying out in that brothers easily avoid marrying their brother's widow if there is no land or property involved. If the property left by the dead brother is valuable, then marriage may be considered. Of course, this was a custom that applied equally to both villages. The fact therefore that there are widows left unmarried in both cases is an indication of the increasing poverty of the peasants.

Population increase in the village seems to be very rapid, but it would have been much higher were it not for migration from the village. In order to understand the speed of population increase in the village we noted the number of deaths and births in the village and calculated the rate of population increase in the village for the year 1976 as being 5.7. (4) It is wrong to assume that the rate of population growth in the village will be 5.7 per cent every year; however, for the sake of convenience let us assume a 5 per cent rate of population increase; then the population of the village would have been much higher than the existing level. Surprisingly enough, the population of the village seems to have decreased in the last few years preceding 1977. This can be explained by two factors: first, out-migration might have reached such a rate that the natural population increase could not keep pace with it; second, it begs the question of the validity of the statistics we are using. Our suspicion regarding the validity of our figures concerning the whole province was confirmed by the fact that the interviewers in Ergani in the 1975 population census were told by their superiors to inflate the figures for the population of the whole district, simply because it was believed that the district would then be given priority over other districts in the allocation of financial aid and investments within Diyarbakır province if it was shown to have the highest population among the districts of that province. In short, the figures for Kalhana for the year 1975 might have been inflated in accordance with this general application. The jump in the index from 142.9 in 1970 to 170.5 in 1975 seems to be rather unrealistic compared to the increase from 128.9 in 1960 to 137.1 in 1965 and 142.9 in 1970. Furthermore, the index for 1977 calculated from our own population census is much lower than the one based on the 1975 population census.

However, one conclusion we can draw from the above discussion is that the population is growing at a high rate in Kalhana, just as in Gisgis. Although the level of health services and medical care is very low in the whole of South-eastern and Eastern Anatolia compared to other parts of Turkey, there has, nevertheless, been an improvement in services and medical care over the past thirty to forty years. Of course this does not mean they are efficient or efficiently organised. For instance, there were only two doctors in Ergani district hospital and they were also working in the Ergani Sağlık Ocağı, which would only deal with people of a certain area. The 71 villages of Ergani were divided into health zones for the purpose of receiving help from the Sağlık Ocağıs. In some cases the allocation of the villages to one health zone or another seems to have been made regardless of the locality of the village.

For instance, Kalhana is about six kilometres from the town of Ergani and has all its economic and social relations with Ergani, yet the village was included in the Kesentaş health centre zone, despite the fact that Kesentaş is about fifteen kilometres from Kalhana in the opposite direction from Ergani. Ergani health centre would not look after patients from Kalhana but would refer them to Kesentaş health centre, where there was no doctor. Furthermore, it is economically disadvantageous for the people of Kalhana to go to Kesentaş. The only means of transport available are minibuses and dolmuş taxis (shared taxis) running between Ergani and Çermik, which pass through several villages, including Kalhana and Gisgis. It is more or less impossible to get a space in one of these vehicles from Kalhana because, first, they are not very frequent and therefore become full even before they leave Ergani and, second, it is so expensive that poor people cannot afford the fare; drivers charge full fare to passengers boarding the minibus or taxi anywhere on route. Instead of facing all these difficulties, people tend not to bother about their illnesses unless they are very severe. However, we may say that the relative improvement in medical care and health services over the years might have contributed to a very limited extent to the population increase.

Social factors, on the other hand, are more important than the medical factors in the increase of population. Children are considered to be the source of social security for the parents in their old age, and male children especially are highly valued for this reason. All the families interviewed wanted to have boys rather than girls, who are commonly considered to be <u>el malı</u> (the property of strangers). Those who do not have male children try various sorts of remedies. A very common strategy based on superstition is to move house in order to change the family's luck; this is locally called <u>kapı değiştirmek</u> (literally: to change doors). Alternatively, people may go to sheikhs or they may entreat divine intervention by vowing to make a sacrifice in the event of success. Men may eventually remarry, with or without divorcing their current wife.

As to the number of children, poorer families did not seem to be very keen on having many children. Those without any land, animals or permanent job especially did not want to have more than two or three children, but neither did they do anything about not having many children. None of the poor families used any contraceptives, and most of them did not even know anything about such matters. Although a very small minority of the poor had heard about contraceptives, they never tried to obtain any because of several factors, such as ignorance of where or how to obtain them, religious belief that it is a sin to interfere in God's work, fear of other people hearing of their use of such sinful medicines or methods, etc. Nevertheless, poor and uneducated people in the village do use traditional methods to induce miscarriage before the pregnancy reaches its full term, but such methods tend to be extremely primitive and may result in death for the pregnant woman.

In addition to the above, the high rate of infant mortality in the village acts as a catalyst for people not to take measures against pregnancy. For instance, 12 families out of 44 had not lost any children before the time of our fieldwork; 7 families had lost one child, 10 families had lost 2 children each, 5 families had lost 3 children and the rest had lost 4 or more children since their marriage. As we stated for Gisgis, the high rate of infant mortality is aggravated by malnutrition and the lack of proper medical care and sanitation.

In distinct contrast, the big landlords who are well educated were very conscious of the fact that more children mean more problems to face and more money to have to spend. The highest number of children among the big landlords was four. These families were aware of all sorts of contraceptives and were using them successfully.

Agriculture in Gisgis and Kalhana

In this section, we shall examine in some detail some of the general characteristics pertaining to agrarian activities in the two villages. This should constitute, along with the previous section, the necessary background within which we shall examine social relations of production in Gisgis and Kalhana in later chapters.

Gisgis

To take agriculture as the primary source of income and proceed from it may lead us somehow to false conclusions. The fact that 95 out of 164 families (57.8 per cent) obtain their livelihood primarily from agriculture (Table 8), is not enough to give the whole picture. Although 69 families seem to derive their livelihood from work other than agriculture, most of them are related to agriculture in some way. In some families agriculture is a secondary source of income; direct involvement with agriculture on the part of some members of the family or indirect involvement of some families with agriculture, constitute a secondary source of income. In the first case, the head of the household may work outside agriculture as a civil servant, worker, grocer, teacher, etc., and his wife and children would cultivate the land. In the second case, the lands of the household may be given to sharecroppers. In short, we may derive the conclusion that, in spite of the tendency of more and more people in Gisgis to seek work outside agriculture, the economic structure of the village is still based on agriculture.

Agricultural Resources

Land is the main resource in agriculture. Factors such as the amount, distribution, nature, topography and chemical composition of the land are some of the determinant conditions of agricultural production. Water resources are equally important in agriculture. The agricultural resources of Gisgis are examined in some detail below.

Land. Leaving aside the landless families, 124 families included in our questionnaire owned 5,306 *dönüms* of land. The average land per household, including the landless households, is 32.4 *dönüms*. This figure becomes 42.8 *dönüms* if the landless households are excluded from the calculation and, if the farming households only are considered, the average land owned

TABLE 8 LANDOWNERSHIP BY PRIMARY JOB IN GISGIS

OCCUPATIONS	LAND OWNED (donums)						
	LANDLESS	1-10	11-20	21-50	50+	TOTAL	PERCENTAGE
Farmer	8	16	6	39	26	95	57.9
Artisan	-	1	-	-	-	1	0.7
Stoner/Mason	6	2	1	-	-	9	5.5
Permanent labourer (including drivers)	3	2	1	4	1	11	6.7
Civil Servant/Teacher	6	-	-	1	-	7	4.3
Casual labourer	12	7	3	2	-	24	14.6
Grocer/Coffee House owner	-	1	-	1	2	4	2.4
Merchant	-	-	-	-	2	2	1.2
Unemployed	5	4	1	1		11	6.7
Total	40	33	12	48	31	164	100.0

is 55.9 dönüms per household. It is evident that to rely on average numbers obscures the inequality that exists in the distribution of land. However, our main concern here is not to deal with the inequalities in the distribution of land in Gisgis, but rather to indicate the fact that holdings in Gisgis are, for the most part, too small to maintain the owning household. It is not surprising, therefore, that many households or some members of the households seek to obtain supplementary income for the sustenance of the household.

Regarding irrigation, 39.4 per cent of the total land (1,499 out of 5,306 dönüms) is irrigated. Although Gisgis is very rich in terms of water resources in comparison with other villages in the Ergani plain, these resources are not used to their full extent. Numerous pinars (natural springs) are used to water mainly vegetable gardens. There is no water pump in the village because, in the first place, it is very expensive to buy and, in the second place, nobody has a large enough area of land to be able to use a pump to its full capacity. The Milik Çayı (Milik Stream) which passes south of the village and is fed by the waters originating from the neighbouring mountains and high hills, as a result of the melting snow which lies for a long time on the high mountains, is not used to its full extent for irrigation simply because the topography of the surrounding fields does not allow for its use in this way. The fields around Milik Çayı are much higher than the level of the river and the use of Milik Çayı for irrigation would necessitate irrigation canals or water pumps which do not exist in the village, for the reasons stated above. Secondly, by mid-July Milik Çayı dries up, due to the excessively hot weather conditions.

Tables 9 and 10 show the distribution of both the irrigated and unirrigated lands in the village. Since the land-ownership pattern will be dealt with later, we will not deal with these tables in detail at this stage.

According to Table 11, which indicates the distribution of land among different sections of agriculture, field agriculture (5) covers the largest amount of land. Production of grain is carried out on unirrigated land, whereas the majority of the irrigated lands have been assigned to vegetable gardening, which

TABLE 9 IRRIGATED LANDOWNERSHIP IN GISGIS

IRRIGATED LAND OWNED (*dönüms*)	NUMBER OF HOUSEHOLDS	PERCENTAGE OF HOUSEHOLDS	TOTAL LAND OWNED (*dönüms*)	PERCENTAGE OF LAND
Landless	56	34.2	-	-
1-10	64	39.0	303	20.2
11-20	24	14.6	450	30.0
21-50	16	9.8	530	35.4
51+	4	2.4	216	14.4
Total	164	100.0	1,499	100.0

TABLE 10 UNIRRIGATED LANDOWNERSHIP IN GISGIS

UNIRRIGATED LAND OWNED (*dönüms*)	NUMBER OF HOUSEHOLDS	PERCENTAGE OF HOUSEHOLDS	TOTAL LAND OWNED (*dönüms*)	PERCENTAGE OF LAND
Landless	48	29.3	-	-
1-10	39	23.8	191	5.0
11-20	17	10.3	228	6.0
21-50	31	18.9	834	21.9
51+	29	17.7	2,554	67.1
Total	164	100.0	3,807	100.0

TABLE 11 LAND UTILISATION IN GISGIS

TYPE OF AGRICULTURE	AMOUNT OF LAND (*dönüms*)	PERCENTAGE OF LAND
Field agriculture	3,765	70.9
Garden agriculture	869	16.4
Vineyards and Orchards	672	12.7
Total	5,306	100.0

serves, with vineyards, to cover some of the cash needs of the families. Among the field crops, wheat is the most produced, followed by lentils and then barley. All three are produced mainly for home consumption. Since bread and cracked wheat (bulgur) are the staple foods of the families in Gisgis, some households have to buy supplementary wheat when they cannot produce enough for their own consumption. On the other hand, the production of vegetables such as tomatoes, green peppers, aubergines, marrows, cucumbers and onions and of fruits such as grapes, sweet melons and water melons, is the main source of cash income for the farming households.

Fruit production is not carried out with the aim of deriving any income from it. A few trees of almonds, cherry, black cherry and apricots can be seen scattered around in vineyards; however, the produce of these trees is mainly consumed by members of the families in the village, especially by children, who sometimes declare ownership of a particular tree in a field and do not let anybody approach their tree without their permission. The fertility of a particular child's tree brings him prestige among his friends, and it is not unusual to hear children boasting about their trees, saying 'my apricot tree is bigger than yours' or persuading younger siblings to do something by saying 'I will let you have so many apricots from my tree' and the like. Before digressing too much, let us reiterate that the negligible production of fruit (apart from grapes and melons) is mainly for the consumption of the local households, not for the market. Although the production of vegetables, grapes and melons is mainly for the market, this does not mean that these things are not consumed by the village households at all.

Unlike vegetables, sweet melons and water melons are cultivated in unirrigated lands. Therefore the melons and water melons do not grow very large; however they are very sweet. In Diyarbakır and around the River Tigris, melons and water melons are cultivated in the alluvial lands which allow the fruit to grow bigger. Incidentally, the Diyarbakır region is very famous for its watermelons, the weight of which sometimes exceed 40 kilogrammes (about 100 pounds), and it is not unusual to see watermelon sellers selling their melons in huge slices, weighing about three to five kilos each, in the streets.

The *mera* (common pasture land) constitutes a significant part of the rural resources, given the place of animal husbandry in the economy of the village. The *meras* are communally used lands whose ownership lies with the state and over which the village community has usufructory rights. According to the village headman's estimate, there exist about 10,000 *dönüms* of pasture land in Gisgis. Although everybody has the right of grazing their animals on the *meras*, the uneven distribution of animals among the households renders it possible for households with large numbers of animals to make more extensive use of the *meras* than those with few or no animals. There are households that do not take advantage of the *meras* at all. Furthermore, the nature of ownership of the *meras* paves the way for negligence regarding the improvement and upkeep of these lands. And so the *meras*, exposed to water and wind erosion, fertilised only by natural manure and subject to over-grazing, are being exhausted year by year.

Animals. Sheep outnumber other animals in Gisgis, followed by goats and cows. *Karaman koyunu* (a fat-tailed sheep, named after the Karaman district of Konya province) is the most numerous breed of sheep, but there are also a few merino sheep. The distribution of sheep and goats in the village is highly unequal. (6) Although the number of cows is not as high as that of sheep and goats, their distribution among the households is more or less equal. Oxen are used as draught animals, whereas donkeys and to a limited extent horses are used as transport animals. Poultry are also more or less equally distributed among the households. None of the households has poultry as its main source of income, although once in a while some eggs or a few chickens may be sold in the market. In Gisgis there were 263 cows, 716 sheep, 304 goats, 133 donkeys, 13 horses and 281 poultry at the time of the fieldwork.

Kalhana

Agricultural Resources

As Table 12 shows, farming is the main source of livelihood for sixteen households in Kalhana. When the three tractor-drivers and one animal-breeder are added to this figure, the number becomes 20 out of 46 households. Furthermore, if we add people like casual labourers, who earn part of their income from agriculture, and permanent labourers, such as factory workers, who leave their families in the village and go to other places to work while the families stay in the village to work as seasonal labourers, we may say that agriculture plays a very important role in the economy of Kalhana.

Land. As we stated in the case of Gisgis, land is one of the most important factors in agriculture, and the quality and quantity of the land, amongst other things, are important determinants of agricultural production. Only ten households in the village own land. Given the formidable discrepancy in the distribution of land among the inhabitant households of the village, it would be very misleading to talk about an average holding per household. Only 526 dönüms out of a total of 11,516 dönüms of land owned (4.6 per cent) are not irrigated. Each piece of land has a period of time allocated to it for irrigation. Despite all our efforts to find out the criteria by which the distribution of the water to the fields was determined, we could not obtain any information at all. We were simply told that land was inherited or bought with certain hours per week of irrigation rights. The time of irrigation alternates periodically between nights and days in order to eliminate any sort of injustice. Fields in the northern and some in the eastern part of the village are irrigated with the water of Kalhana Suyu (Kalhana Stream) and those in the southern part of the village with the water of Hilar Çayı (Hilar Stream).

Owing to the flatness of the land, old-fashioned irrigation canals without any sophisticated machinery are good enough to

TABLE 12 LANDOWNERSHIP BY PRIMARY JOB IN KALHANA

OCCUPATION	LAND OWNED (dönüms)					
	LANDLESS	1-50	51-100	101+	TOTAL	PERCENTAGE
Farmer	7	4	1	4	16	34.8
Stoner/Mason	2	-	-	-	2	4.3
Permanent labourers (including drivers)	11	-	1	-	12	26.1
Civil Servants/Teachers	1	-	-	-	1	2.2
Casual labourers	12	-	-	-	12	26.1
Unemployed	1	-	-	-	1	2.2
Pedlar	2	-	-	-	2	4.3
Total	36	4	2	4	46	100.0
Percentages	78.3	8.7	4.3	8.7	100.0	

TABLE 13 LAND UTILISATION IN KALHANA

TYPE OF AGRICULTURE	AMOUNT OF LAND (dönüms)	PERCENTAGE OF LAND
Field agriculture	11,305	98.2
Garden agriculture	45	0.4
Vineyards and Orchards	166	1.4
Total	11,516	100.0

irrigate the fields, but the system necessitates a vast labour force. To build a modern irrigation system would necessitate a huge investment, which none of the farmers could afford. The state is the only body which could afford to invest in infrastructural establishments such as irrigation canals and the like in Eastern Anatolia. When the Karakaya Barajı (Karakaya Dam), which has been under construction for several years on the River Euphrates in Çüngüş district, some 50 kilometres away to the northeast of Ergani, is finally completed a network of irrigation canals in the region will, we believe, change the structure of its agriculture. Some relatively high fields, or the fields very far from the two streams, are not irrigated at present.

Since we have dealt with the landownership pattern in the village elsewhere, (7) and the amount of unirrigated land is very small, we shall not deal here with the distribution of irrigated and unirrigated lands separately. We must, however, draw attention to the allocation of the farmland among the three main types of agriculture - field agriculture, garden agriculture and vineyards and orchards. (Such a classification is, of course, in no way exhaustive. For instance, it excludes animal husbandry as a part of agriculture; however, the purpose of our classification is only to show the ways in which the land is utilised.)

As is evident from Table 13 , the category field agriculture is dominant in Kalhana, occupying 98.2 per cent of the total lands, while vegetable gardens, vineyards and orchards occupy only 1.8 per cent of the total. Field agriculture includes mainly cotton production and the production of lentils, wheat, sesame seeds, sugar beet, etc. Cotton, sesame seeds and sugar beet are produced exclusively for the market, whereas wheat, lentils and barley may be produced both for the market and for home consumption, depending on the nature of the farm: whether it is a peasant farm or a capitalist farm.

As Table 13 shows, the amount of land assigned to vegetable gardens is very limited, being confined to a few small household plots, the produce of which is consumed at home. Vegetable gardening necessitates constant attention as well as a large labour force if it is taken up on a large scale. Given the fact that wage labour is very expensive and that the marketing of vegetables is not organised to any great extent, the big landlords prefer to engage in the production of other cash crops, such as cotton and sugar beet, the main buyers of which are the state or state-backed co-operatives like the Çukobirlik.

The big landlords allow one or two of their sharecroppers to plant vegetables on a sharecropping basis, so that they will be supplied with vegetables all through the summer. If there is an excess of vegetables it is the sharecropper who markets them, giving the landlord his share of the returns.

Unlike the categorisation pertaining to Gisgis, the third category 'vineyards and orchards' includes kavaklık (poplar trees). All the landlords in the village have five to ten dönüms of kavaklık, which brings a very good income, as poplar wood is very popular in building construction in the area. Fruit production is very limited, and is for home consumption. In the vineyards, a very special type of grape is produced: şıra üsümü. This is a very sweet grape, the juice of which is used in making pekmez (boiled grape juice), pestil (grape juice boiled with flour and starch and dried in the sun into very thin layers) and sucuk (a sausage-shaped sweet consisting of a thick outer layer of dried grape juice boiled with flour and starch, covering a string of walnuts inside). Pestil and sucuk are very expensive and only rich people can afford them, so they can be considered exotic foods. All the vineyards in the village are owned by the big landlords. Small farmers do not have any vineyards or orchards.

As to the meras, they constitute a relatively small part of the village lands, compared to the proportion of meras in the total lands of Gisgis. This is mainly due to the fact that big landlords have annexed a considerable part of the village communal lands to their own holdings, one way or another. There exist about 4,000 dönüms of meras in Kalhana. The right of all village households to graze their animals on communal lands is largely theoretical, since the existing pattern of animal ownership in the village does not allow those who have no animals to make use of the meras. What was said about soil exhaustion over a number of years in the case of Gisgis is also valid for Kalhana.

Animals. Sheep are bred for both milk and meat and are the largest animal group in Kalhana. As in Gisgis, there are two breeds in Kalhana: karaman and merino, the former outnumbering the latter. Like the distribution of land, the distribution of animals is very unequal in Kalhana. This topic is dealt with in Chapter Five and it is sufficient here to state the number of animals present in the village during the fieldwork. However, a few words seem to be essential concerning poultry. Despite the existence of a poultry farm, there are only 141 poultry in the village. This is due to the fact that one of the big landlords in the village, built a building that was supposedly a poultry farm in order to secure a large amount of credit from the Agricultural Bank. Since the money was used somewhere else, the poultry farm has never operated. In Kalhana there were 237 sheep, 142 goats, 38 cows, 11 oxen, 20 donkeys, and 141 poultry at the time of the fieldwork.

Crop Production in Gisgis and Kalhana

Owing to differences in the nature of the land and water endowments, some different and some common crops are grown, and therefore different crop rotations are followed in Kalhana and Gisgis villages. The land in Kalhana is flat and mostly irrigated, while most of the land in Gisgis is sloping, rocky and unirrigated. Cotton in Kalhana, and wheat in Gisgis are the major crops. While cotton is produced entirely for the market, wheat in Gisgis is produced mainly for home consumption.

In Kalhana, of the 11,305 dönüms of land devoted to field agriculture almost one fifth (2,250 dönüms) was fallow in 1977, while the remaining 9,055 dönüms were divided among a variety of crops as shown in Table 14. In Gisgis, on the other hand, wheat constitutes the largest crop in terms of area cultivated.

TABLE 14 LAND UNDER CULTIVATION IN KALHANA

Cotton	4,168	dönüms
Wheat	2,440	"
Lentils	1,417	"
Sugar beet	300	"
Barley	240	"
Vetch	150	"
Millet	100	"
Chick peas	100	"
Sweetcorn	75	"
Sesame seed	65	"
Total	9,055	dönüms

Table 15 LAND UNDER CULTIVATION IN GISGIS

Wheat	1,623	dönüms
Lentils	577	"
Melon/ watermelon	235	"
Vetch	179	"
Millet	148	"
Barley	143	"
Chick peas	60	"
Total	2,965	dönüms

Of the 3,765 *dönüms* of land, 800 *dönüms* were fallow in 1977 and the rest was devoted to the cultivation of the limited range of crops indicated in Table 15.

In Kalhana, irrigation permits the production of cotton. Until the 1960s a type of cotton called *yerli* cotton was grown in Kalhana. The *yerli* cotton, which originates from Asia and has been known in Turkey for many years, is a short-staple, low-yield type. It was replaced in the 1960s by a higher-yield, long-staple type, *deltapine*, of American origin. Despite the introduction of technology and better yielding varieties like *koker* and *deltapine*, cotton productivity in the village is well below that of the Çukurova region. For instance, Hinderink and Kiray (8) state that, in Sakizli and Yunusoğlu villages of the Çukurova region, the cotton yield of irrigated lands is about 200 kilogrammes per *dönüm*. The average productivity in irrigated cotton in Kalhana rarely exceeds 150 kilogrammes per *dönüm*. In most cases this is partly due to the monoculture of cotton for five or six successive years.

In Kalhana, wheat is grown mainly in rotation with cotton, and with other crops like lentils, chick peas, barley, melon, etc. Two types of wheat are grown in Kalhana: *akbaşak* and *boz*, while only *akbaşak* is grown in Gisgis. *Akbaşak*, also called *sorgül*, is a pale golden-coloured wheat, soft to grind and highly favoured for the locally preferred home-made bread, which is the staple food in the area. *Boz* wheat is hard and brownish in colour and not suitable for local bread making. The *boz* wheat is grown entirely for the market and is suitable for macaroni production. This type of wheat was introduced to the area in recent years by the official agricultural office and the big farmers of Kalhana immediately switched to *boz* wheat production, for it brings in more money than the traditional *akbaşak* type. In 1977, the price of *boz* wheat was 290 *kuruş* (9) per kilo, while that of *akbaşak* was 250 *kuruş* in the market.

Small producers who produce wheat mainly for home consumption did not make this switch from *akbaşak* to *boz* wheat, firstly because *boz* wheat is not suitable for traditional bread making and therefore had no use value for them. On the other hand producing _boz_ wheat as a commodity was not beneficial for them because it meant that they would have had to sell _boz_ wheat in the market in order to buy _akbaşak_ for their own consumption. By the time they paid for the transport of the wheat, plus a profit of the merchant for the _akbaşak_ wheat, either they would have been worse off or the difference they would have received from the selling and buying transactions would have been so meagre that it would not have been worth bothering with. Furthermore, they did not want to take the risk of venturing to grow a new variety which was totally unknown to them. However, the big landlords, who had access to information via their close relations with the agricultural office, did not hesitate to try the _boz_ wheat.

The productivity of wheat per _dönüm_ varies between 35 and 105 kilos, that is between 1 and 6 _ölceks_ (10), on poor land, and 105 to 192 kilos on medium quality cropland in the region. However, the lands in Gisgis village can only be subsumed into the first two categories in terms of wheat production, because the highest productivity rate for wheat in the village was 10 to 1, that is to say, given that 17.5 kilos (half an _ölcek_) of seed is planted in one _dönüm_ the highest productivity was 175 kilos per _dönüm_ in Gisgis in 1977. On the other hand, the majority of land in Kalhana was medium or good quality as far as wheat production was concerned. The highest productivity rate we came across was 16 to 1 (280 kilos per _dönüm_) in Kalhana. This difference between the productivity rates in the two villages is due to irrigation, fertilisation and the nature of the land. Lands in Kalhana are mostly irrigated and well fertilised, while in Gisgis they are dry and often neglected, owing to the owners' inability to obtain chemicals.

Lentils are of secondary importance to the producers, compared to wheat and cotton in Kalhana, and wheat in Gisgis. They are grown almost entirely for home consumption in Gisgis, while they are grown to a great extent for the market in the big farms, and to a very little extent in the small farms of Kalhana.

Tilling the Land

Farming patterns and land tillage not only differ between the two villages, but also vary from farm to farm, even within the same village. Knowing that no particular farm or unit of production can represent the diverse farming operations in the two villages we chose several units of production from both villages to be able to give a general picture of the farming operations as well as crop rotations in these villages.

Farm I

The first example is the largest farm in Kalhana, belonging to Fuat Aydoğan, who had taken over the running of the farm after his father's death a few years before our fieldwork. Fuat is a university graduate, single, and lives with his mother, younger brother and sister. At the time of our fieldwork, both his brother and his sister were students and had nothing to do with the farm. The farm consists of 5,000 dönüms divided into many plots. Only about 300 dönüms of the total farm lands are not irrigated, and the rest, which is irrigated, consists of medium and very good lands. The unirrigated lands and an additional 500 dönüms are given to sharecroppers, both from Kalhana and neighbouring villages such as Malan, Keydanevleri, and Aşağı Balahur. The rest is cropped as follows: 1,000 dönüms cotton, 1,000 dönüms wheat, 400 dönüms sugar beet and 400 dönüms lentils; 1,400 dönüms are laid fallow. Wheat and cotton are grown in rotation while sugar beet and lentils are the other crops grown in rotation with each other. Fuat's father, Zakir, towards the end of his life, decided that he would leave one third of his lands to rest and, since then, a kind of three field system has been used in the farm and Fuat continues to follow his father's path. In this way the land that is not given to sharecroppers is divided into six parts: three parts of 1,000 dönüms, and three parts of 400 dönüms each. Crop rotation is followed in the same way:

	FIELDS OF 1,000 DÖNÜMS			FIELDS OF 400 DÖNÜMS		
	FIELD 1	FIELD 2	FIELD 3	FIELD 4	FIELD 5	FIELD 6
Year 1	Fallow	Wheat	Cotton	Fallow	Lentils	Sugarbeet
Year 2	Wheat	Cotton	Fallow	Lentils	Sugarbeet	Fallow
Year 3	Cotton	Fallow	Wheat	Sugarbeet	Fallow	Lentils

The agricultural machinery belonging to the farm includes a tractor, a drill, a cultivator, a harrow, a threshing machine, a trailer, a cotton minzer, etc. Four permanent labourers are employed on the farm: one overseer, one tractor driver and one personal servant, as well as an animal caretaker.

In the cotton/wheat rotation, after the wheat is harvested in July and the beginning of August the land is left until the beginning of November, when the ploughing starts. During the winter, the land is worked by disc harrow several times to straighten the soil. In April, after the rains, the land is straightened again by disc harrow and cotton is sown with the cotton minzer. About 4kg of _deltapine_ seed is used per _dönüm_ and 15kg per _dönüm_ of _şeker gübre_ (sugar fertiliser), superphosphate (P_2O_5), is added to the soil. It takes one day to till a field of 50 _dönüms_ and plant cotton seed, and towards the end of April, or the beginning of May, the cotton planting finishes. Once the plants start to grow, the field is irrigated. After the first irrigation, the whole field is hoed and weeded by a team of hired workers from both Kalhana and surrounding villages. None of the members of Fuat's family work in the fields. About 50 workers are hired for 10 to 20 days for hoeing. (11) The workers are recruited mainly from the village and neighbouring villages, and most of the workers are members of the families of Fuat's sharecroppers, although some other people, like small farmers, landless poor, etc. are also employed.

Cotton fields are irrigated five times from the time of planting to the harvest time in October. Workers were paid TL15 per hour for irrigation work in 1977. Cotton is picked in October and the first half of November. The picking is done by hand where hundreds of workers, women and children, work in the fields on a payment-in-kind basis. The workers are paid one-twentieth of the amount of cotton they pick.

The wheat-growing season starts as soon as the cotton is picked. Wheat is sown from the second half of October until the end of November. The sowing is done while the field is ploughed by means of a tractor driven by a full-time driver. 17.5 kilos of tozgübre (powder fertiliser), ammonia sulphate, is used per dönüm in wheat production, although sometimes superphosphate is used instead. Harvesting is done at the end of June and the beginning of July by rented combine harvesters which are brought by their owners, mainly from Yozgat province in central Anatolia, to rent out. In 1977, farmers were charged TL25 per dönüm to have their wheat harvested.

The practice of rotating lentils with sugar beet is very new in the village. Mostly big farmers like Fuat use this method because sugar beet harvesting especially requires quite a large number of hired workers and small farmers do not have the necessary cash available for the wages. Lentils can be sown between the second half of October and the end of November, and are harvested in July and the beginning of August. Then the land is rested until the beginning of April, when sugar beet planting starts. The fields are ploughed to a depth of 20 to 30 centimetres and are levelled before planting. A mellow but firm seedbed is prepared by disc harrow. 700 grams of non-pelleted seeds are sown per dönüm. Once the crop is established, irrigation is carried out fortnightly. Harvesting requires a large labour force, where about twenty workers are hired for three weeks.

Farm II

Our second example is also from Kalhana village but is a relatively small farm compared to the first one. It belongs to Hüseyin Aslanoğlu, whose own land comprises just 10 dönüms of the 80 dönüms he cultivates. He had been sharecropping 70 dönüms of land for almost ten years in 1977. Of the sharecropped land, 30 dönüms belong to Hamdi and 40 dönüms belong to Fuat. Since he has a large family, Huseyin provides labour to the landlords at any time they wish. The extended family consists of fourteen people: Hüseyin himself, his wife, three sons, three daughters-in-law, one daughter and five grandchildren. All members of the family, including one child, participate in farming, working in the fields and looking after the animals. The household has a pair of oxen, two donkeys, one cow, four sheep and six goats. There is no agricultural machinery other than a _karasaban_ (wooden plough), _döven_ (threshing sledge) and a number of sickles, scythes and hoes, etc. Huseyin's own land is irrigated and the sharecropped land is partially irrigated. The lands are divided into four parcels of 10, 20, 20 and 30 _dönüms_ respectively. In the irrigated land, wheat, cotton and sesame are grown in rotation, while in the other lands wheat and lentils are grown in rotation with summer crops like chick peas, millet and vetch. Each parcel of land is laid fallow once in four years. The crop rotation followed by the Aslanoğlu household is as follows:

	IRRIGATED LAND (10 dönüms)	PARTIALLY IRRIGATED LANDS (20 dönüms)	(20 dönüms)	(30 dönüms)
Year 1	Cotton	Lentils	Summer crop+	Fallow
Year 2	Fallow	Fallow	Lentils	Wheat
Year 3	Sesame	Wheat	Fallow	Summer crop+
Year 4	Wheat	Summer crop+	Wheat	Lentils

+ Chick peas, millet and vetches

All fields except the cotton field are ploughed by means of a _karasaban_ (wooden plough) pulled by a pair of oxen. The cotton field is tilled by means of a rented tractor, driven by a driver employed by the tractor owner. For lentils and wheat the fields are tilled in the autumn, for the summer crops the land is tilled in December and January, and for cotton and sesame it is tilled in April. The harvesting of wheat, lentils and chick peas, millet and sesame is done mostly by scythes and sickles. Harvesting time for chick peas and vetch is the end of August and September, while millet and sesame are harvested in October. Only rarely is wheat threshed by machine, which has to be rented. Separation of the crops from the stalk is done by means of a flint-studded threshing sledge pulled by a pair of oxen. Once the crop has been separated this way, the winnowing has to be done by means of wooden forks.

All the work of preparing the fields, harvesting, transporting etc. is done by members of the household. On occasion the household may employ one or two people if they cannot cope with the work. Being tied to the landlord, the household has to give priority to his labour requirements rather than their own. Therefore it usually happens that while some members of the household work in their own fields the rest may be working in the landlord's fields.

Farm III

With few exceptions, none of the farmers in Gisgis use agricultural machinery because most of the lands are stony and, furthermore, holdings are too small to persuade tractor owners to come to the village in order to rent out their machinery. Cemal Okan is one of the many who do not use agricultural machinery. His household consists of nine people including himself and his two wives and children. He owns 50 *dönüms* of unirrigated and five *dönüms* of irrigated land, as well as 10 *dönüms* of vineyards. His livestock consist of a pair of oxen, two cows, and two female calves. Agricultural equipment owned by the farm includes a *karasaban* (wooden plough), threshing sledge, four sickles, two scythes, four hoes and four winnowing forks.

The irrigated land is planted with vegetables, mainly tomatoes, green peppers, cucumbers and, to a lesser extent, green beans, onions and marrows, in order to meet the needs of the family. On the unirrigated land, wheat and lentils are rotated with melons and water melons. Melons and water melons, vegetables and grapes are sold in the market.

In the last month of autumn, the land is tilled for planting wheat and vegetables. Tilling the land is done by means of a *karasaban* (wooden plough) drawn by a pair of oxen, and sowing is done by hand. Artificial fertilisers are not used because Cemal does not have access to the agricultural office which provides farmers with agricultural chemicals, nor can he afford to buy enough artificial fertiliser from the market, where the price is much higher than that of the agricultural office. However, a small amount of fertiliser obtained from the market is used in vegetable gardening. Since animal dung is used for fuel, called tezek (sun-dried flat round slabs of animal dung), the rest of the fields are not manured and therefore the productivity is very low due to soil exhaustion. Reaping of wheat and lentils takes place in July by means of sickles and scythes, by members of the family, although some close relatives may come to help. Separation of the crop from the stalks is achieved by the use of a threshing sledge pulled by draught animals. All the work involved in threshing, winnowing and transporting the crops is done by family members. After the harvest the fields are ploughed and left resting until the beginning of March, when they are ploughed again for melon and water melon planting. Growing melons coincides with vegetables growing as far as the growing season is concerned. Therefore, April to September is the busiest time of the year for Cemal's household.

Cemal does not let his fields lie fallow; instead he grows vetch as a summer crop every four years. The three parcels of his land are cultivated according to the following rotation:

	FIELD 1	FIELD 2	FIELD 3
Year 1	Wheat	Melon	Lentils
Year 2	Melon	Lentils	Vetch
Year 3	Lentils	Vetch	Wheat
Year 4	Vetch	Wheat	Melon

His method of crop rotation is based on tradition and is far from being scientific. He rotates those types of crops whose roots stay quite close to the surface of the ground instead of rotating crops with different root levels under the ground and thereby making use of the soil to its best extent.

The Productive Process in Gisgis and Kalhana

The level of development of the productive forces should not be taken as only a level of technological information but should rather be taken as 'a function of application of technology to the productive process and the development of the social and entrepreneurial division of labour'. (12) Nevertheless, this section examines only the technological aspects, while the social relations will be dealt with in later chapters.

Gisgis

In Gisgis village the level of technology in agriculture is very primitive, though agricultural machinery is used to a very limited extent. Traditional items of equipment used in agriculture are mainly the wooden hooked plough (karasaban), spade (bel), pickaxe (kazma), shovel (kürek), rake (tırmık), sickle (orak, or kaluç in Kurdish), hoe (çapa), scythe (tırpan), winnowing fork (yaba) and wooden thresher (döven). Among the items of metal equipment, such as the spade, pick-axe, shovel, sickle and scythe, the old-fashioned traditional ones produced by the local artisans have been superceded by factory-produced ones. Wooden equipment, such as the winnowing fork, wooden hooked plough and wooden thresher, are obtained mainly from the village carpenter or from local artisans in Ergani or Diyarbakır. Repairs of wooden equipment are usually carried out by the village carpenter; however, in some cases they are done by a male member of the household, provided that the household has access to the necessary equipment. The same thing can be said for the replacement of a broken handle of a pickaxe, shovel, etc. The backward nature of the technological level of agriculture in Gisgis village is reflected in the quantities of some items of agricultural equipment. At the time of the fieldwork there were 84 wooden hooked ploughs, 85 threshing sledges, 430 sickles, 64 scythes, 32 axes, 75 pickaxes and 92 hoes, but there were no tractors or metal ploughs.

There are several factors which do not allow the mechanisation of agriculture in Gisgis. First, the stony nature of some of the fields does not allow the use of agricultural machinery; second, excessive land fragmentation, stemming from the nature of the law concerning inheritance rights, which does not allow the optimum use of machinery; third, the high prices of machinery necessitate a sum of accumulated capital which is not likely to occur, given the low level of income of the farmers. Nevertheless there are people in the village with enough money to buy a tractor who prefer to invest their money in more profitable areas such as transportation and commerce.

Kalhana

Compared to Gisgis village, the level of technology used in agriculture in Kalhana village is highly advanced. The level of technology of Kalhana's agriculture should be considered from two different perspectives, namely that of small producers, whether they are independent peasants, sharecroppers or a combination of both, or agricultural wage-earners, and that of middle peasants and of big capitalist landowners.

The number of small peasant families with land is relatively small, comprising 8.68 per cent of the village households (here those households with 50 <u>dönüms</u> or less are considered as small peasant households). They use family labour in agriculture where the land is tilled mainly by a wooden plough pulled by a pair of oxen. However, this is not the only method of tillage, for it was observed that sometimes the family rents a tractor to till the land. This is the case either when the male members of the household are away working in other places as casual labourers in building and road construction, or they are ill, or they are involved in a sharecropping arrangement and the tilling of the land by tractor is a part of this arrangement. In the latter case, the condition imposed by the landowner, that the sharecropper should use the tractor in the tilling of the land, may emanate from two reasons: first, from the belief that land-tilling by tractor will increase productivity, and second, from the fact that the landowner himself may be a tractor-owner and may wish to increase his income by renting out the tractor. Such is the case with Hamdi Bey and Fuat Bey. (13)

We shall now dwell on the second perspective, that of big farmers who have continually been increasing their use of technology in agriculture since the early 1950s. Controlling large amounts of land and having close relations with the state officials, the big landowners have considerably greater access to improved seeds and artificial fertiliser provided by the state, and to agricultural machinery through credits granted by the Agricultural Bank. The big landowners who are producing for the market have almost totally abandonned old, traditional farming techniques on their farms. Agricultural machines like the tractor, drill, cultivator, disc harrow, threshing machine, combine harvester, etc. are widely used on the farms of big landlords. Not only do they use their machines on their farms but they also rent the machines to other farmers, peasants etc. For instance, Hamdi Bey has a tractor, a trailer, a cotton gin, a drill, a cultivator and a disc harrow, and he employs a tractor driver for a wage of TL10,000 per annum. The tractor driver works both on Hamdi Bey's land and on the lands of others who rent the tractor. When agricultural work finishes he is sent to transport building materials (bricks, sand, etc.). The same can also be said of Fuat Bey, who also has a tractor and a threshing machine. The number of farming implements in the village in August 1977 were 7 wooden hooked ploughs, 17 sickles, 31 scythes, 14 axes, 16 pickaxes, 25 spades, 21 winnowing forks, 316 hoes, 5 tractors, 3 drills, 4 cultivators, 5 disk harrows, 5 threshing machines, 5 trailers, 2 cotton minzers.

Apart from the tractors belonging to the three big landlords, we found two others owned by landless people. Three cousins (Ahmet, Izzet and Farız Güclü) own one of the tractors and one of the cousins, Ahmet, is working in West Germany. With his initiative, the other two cousins, Izzet and Farız, sold their lands and oxen to buy a tractor by instalments, and are now working as tractor drivers. According to their verbal agreement, the income from renting out the tractor and from farming is divided into three equal shares after the extraction of a salary of TL12,000 per annum. The two drivers share the TL12,000 salary between them, as remuneration for their shift work. The two driver cousins find people who are willing to give them land to sharecrop. For instance, in 1977 they were cultivating a total of 350 *dönüms* of land as sharecroppers. The owners of these lands were a merchant (absentee landlord) in Ergani, a teacher who inherited 40 *dönüms* and was unable to cultivate it for himself, and an old couple who were incapable of working.

The other landless tractor owner also engages in similar arrangements, renting his tractor to needy farmers and sharecropping land on his own account with his own tractor.

In concluding this chapter, we may say that agriculture in Kalhana is more market-oriented than in Gisgis, and that the production of commercial crops is more dominant in Kalhana. Furthermore, the nature of the land and of landownership have enabled the big landlords of Kalhana to make use of sophisticated agricultural technology and better agricultural inputs (seeds and fertilisers). In turn, this has allowed the development of new relations of production (wage-labour-capital relationship), that will be examined in the next chapters.

Notes to Chapter Four

1. Since smoking and playing cards in front of older relatives are considered signs of disrespect, most young people did not want to mix with older members of the village. The elderly people, for their part, in order to avoid being in an awkward position, turn a blind eye when they come across one of their young relatives smoking or playing cards.
2. *Başlık* means bride-price in Turkish. In the rural areas of Eastern and Southeastern Anatolia, fathers consider it their inalienable right to ask for money when their daughters get married. The girls are brought up in such a way that they think it normal for a girl to be given in marriage in return for money.
3. For a discussion of some of the factors affecting women's and their babies' health in Turkey, see Tezcan, 1979; also

Baysal, 1979

4. The number of births in the village was 23. The number of deaths was 9, a difference of 14 people in one year. The difference between 258 and 14 is 244, and from this we can say that 14 is 5.7 per cent of 244.

5. By field agriculture we mean production activities which cover the production of grain, cotton and some animal fodder, as opposed to the production of vegetables and fruit, which we prefer to call garden agriculture, and the production of grapes.

6. This theme, as well as sharecropping arrangements, will be dealt with in Chapter Six.

7. See Chapter Five

8. Hinderink and Kıray, 1970, 61

9. 100 kuruş equal 1 Turkish Lira.

10. 1 ölçek equals 35 kilos in wheat, 36 kilos in lentils, 33 kilos in barley and 30 kilos in millet, according to local measurement.

11. Hoeing is locally termed dukolan, or simply kolan, and weeding is locally termed asiv yapmak.

12. Dos Santos, 1970, 191

13. One may ask whether it would not be more profitable for the landlord to cultivate his land by himself, using his own tractor. If the land given to the sharecropper is considered alone the answer would be yes. The long-term income of the farm, however, should be taken into consideration. In the peak season the need for a labour force on the farm forces the landlord to give a piece of his land to sharecroppers who are thus tied to the farm by virtue of this arrangement. Landlords thereby avoid a possible labour shortage in the peak seasons. This also strengthens the landlords' position in imposing their will on the labourers in terms of payment. For instance, labourers are paid in kind when they are employed in cotton-picking. The amount of remuneration depends on the amount of cotton picked; in this way a healthy worker can only earn the equivalent of 60 to 70TL in cotton

during a ten-hour working day, whereas a wage labourer working in building construction for the same hours would earn about 150 to 200TL, and a labourer working in village irrigation works for 15TL per hour and would earn 150TL for a ten-hour day. The conclusion to be drawn here is that, by tying sharecroppers and landless peasants to the farm, landlords decrease their total costs in production, although in a single sharecropping arrangement, taken alone, they may appear to be on the losing side.

5. Land And Stock Ownership

Landownership in Gisgis

Gisgis is one of those villages characterised by the iltizam land system which existed before the Republican regime. In these villages, land was more or less equally divided among the peasants, and this is the basis behind the existing land distribution in Gisgis.

Figures pertaining to land tenure in Gisgis, obtained from the tax office in Ergani, seem to be greatly deflated due to the fact that they are based on the personal declarations of the owners. For instance, according to the records of the tax office there exist 2,696 dönüms of land in Gisgis whereas, according to the data we collected during our fieldwork, this figure should be 5,306 dönüms. Given the fact that landowners may also have understated the amount of land they owned during our own survey, it would be highly misleading to rely on the records of the tax office. Therefore, the findings of our own survey for land

TABLE 16 DISTRIBUTION OF LAND AMONG THE INHABITANTS OF GISGIS

LAND OWNED	NUMBER OF HOUSEHOLDS+	PERCENTAGE OF HOUSEHOLDS	CUMULATIVE PERCENTAGE	TOTAL LAND (dönüms)	PERCENTAGE OF TOTAL LAND
Landless	40	24.4	24.4	-	-
1-10	33	20.1	44.5	228	4.3
11-20	12	7.3	51.8	164	3.1
21-50	48	29.3	81.1	1,738	32.8
51+	31	18.9	100.0	3,176	59.8
Total	164	100.0	100.0	5,306	100.0

+ In Turkish civil law, property rights in real estate rest in individual persons. In contrast, in rural areas, regardless of the individual person who holds the title deeds for a property (especially for land) ownership of the property belongs to a group of people, usually the household. For this reason distribution of land is considered according to households in the two villages.

tenure in Gisgis will be used in the discussion which follows. It is evident from Table 16 that 40 of the 164 families (24.7 per cent) in Gisgis are landless. However, 8 of the 40 families, or at least their household heads, work as farmers engaged in sharecropping. Most of the 32 landless household heads work mainly as casual labourers, some have permanent work (as teachers, civil servants, drivers) and some work as stoners and masons. (See Table 8 in Chapter Four)

Given the fact that 10 <u>dönüms</u> (1 hectare) of land is too small to enable a family to survive, the families with 10 <u>dönüms</u> or less land can be considered in the same category as the landless. We shall see that more than half of the households with 10 <u>dönüms</u> or less land make their living from other sorts of activities and use the income from their land as a supplementary income, which is derived either from direct cultivation of the land by family labour, or from sharecropping arrangements.

Landlessness is a fact of the last sixty years of the history of Gisgis. In 1920, for example, there were no landless families in Gisgis, despite the fact that some of them did not have any licence for the land they farmed. Several factors facilitated the alienation of land from the peasants, such as excessive taxes imposed on farmers during the Second World War, indirect taxation later on and, today, usury, unfavourable price mechanisms, indebtedness and the high rate of growth of the population.

The majority of households, 133 out of 164 (81.1 per cent) have 50 *dönüms* or less. Given the type of agriculture and the low level of the productive forces in the village, these holdings can be considered small holdings which do not enable the family concerned to sustain itself, thus forcing its members to seek supplementary income elsewhere. Holdings between 50 and 200 *dönüms* may be considered medium-sized holdings. Income from such holdings would enable the holders to sustain a decent living and in some cases even to save some money. Of course, this category of 50 to 200 *dönüms* is not homogeneous within itself, and we are aware of the difficulty in subsuming someone with only 51 *dönüms* of land and someone else with 200 *dönüms* of land under the same category. In Gisgis most of the holdings (21 out of 31) in this category are around 60 to 100 *dönüms*, while holdings above 100 *dönüms* are not too numerous (7 holdings are between 101 and 200 *dönüms*).

The relatively rich farmers are able to save money and invest in more profitable spheres, such as transportation, commerce, shops, etc. For instance, Abdülkerim Üney owns 200 *dönüms* of land and co-owns a minibus which transports passengers between Gisgis, Ergani and Diyarbakır. He also engages in buying and selling grain and livestock. One of those with more than 100 *dönüms* of land is the only grocer in the village, Celal Pala, who owns 187 *dönüms* of land, which is worked by his wife and his son.

The data collected during the period of fieldwork also reveal that, in Gisgis, holdings consist of several fragments of land, vineyards, vegetable gardens and orchards. The 5,306 dönüms of total village lands owned by the villagers comprises 441 fragments of lands, vineyards, vegetable gardens and orchards. This fragmentation is due partly to the existing inheritance laws and partly to the peasants' desire not to be separated from their means of livelihood. Uncertain job prospects impel peasants to stick to their small piece of land as security.

It is clear from the above that the peasantry in Gisgis is not a homogeneous group of people, nor can it be seen to constitute one class. However, it can be analysed in class terms (1) and one of the constituents of an analysis of this sort is the study of the peasantry in terms of differentiation among its members. Having shown differentiation regarding landownership, we shall now attempt to demonstrate differentiation among the inhabitants of Gisgis concerning animal ownership. Furthermore, an attempt will also be made to denote the relations of production involved in animal breeding.

Animal Ownership in Gisgis

The distribution of animal ownership among the households of the village is shown in Table 17.

It is evident from our fieldwork that peasants tend to keep animals which are more useful for the reproduction of the household, unless they take animal husbandry as their main occupation. Oxen, cows and donkeys play a very important role in the reproduction cycle of the peasant family. Oxen are used as draught animals, while milk obtained from cows, and products made from the milk, like yoghurt, cheese, butter and çökelek (skimmed-milk cheese) are consumed by the household. Donkeys are one of the most essential animals for the peasant family, since they are used for transporting all sorts of commodities between the fields and the house.

The peasant families in Gisgis tend to keep cows and oxen rather than sheep or goats when they can afford to buy the former. Although they themselves do not keep many sheep and

TABLE 17 LIVESTOCK OWNERSHIP IN GISGIS

HOUSEHOLDS WITH:-	HOUSEHOLDS			LIVESTOCK		
	No.	PER CENT	CUM PER CENT	No.	PER CENT	CUM PER CENT
(i) COWS						
no cow	48	29.3	29.3	-	-	-
1 cow	28	17.1	46.4	28	10.7	10.7
2 cows	55	33.5	79.9	110	41.8	52.5
3 cows	13	7.9	87.8	39	14.8	67.3
4+ cows	20	12.2	100.0	86	32.7	100.0
Total	164	100.0	100.0	263	100.0	100.0
(ii) OXEN						
no ox	87	53.0	53.0	-	-	-
1 ox	21	12.8	65.8	21	15.8	15.8
2 oxen	56	34.2	100.0	112	84.2	100.0
Total	164	100.0	100.0	133	100.0	100.0
(iii) SHEEP						
no sheep	134	81.7	81.7	-	-	-
1-3 sheep	16	9.8	91.5	28	3.9	3.9
4-10 sheep	7	4.3	95.8	62	8.7	12.6
11-25 sheep	4	2.4	98.2	63	8.8	21.4
26+ sheep	3	1.8	100.0	563	78.6	100.0
Total	164	100.0	100.0	716	100.0	100.0
(iv) GOATS						
no goats	116	70.7	70.7	-	-	-
1-3 goats	31	18.9	89.6	42	13.8	13.8
4-10 goats	8	4.9	94.5	60	19.8	33.6
11-25 goats	5	3.1	97.6	63	20.7	54.3
26+ goats	4	2.4	100.0	139	45.7	100.0
Total	164	100.0	100.0	304	100.0	100.0
(v) DONKEYS						
no donkey	56	34.1	34.1	-	-	-
1 donkey	92	56.1	80.2	92	71.3	71.3
2 donkeys	11	6.7	86.9	22	17.1	88.4
3 donkeys	5	3.1	100.0	15	11.6	100.0
Total	164	100.0	100.0	129	100.0	100.0

goats, they have access to these animals through sharecropping arrangements. Despite the general tendency toward a preference to have cows rather than sheep and goats, some relatively rich families breed sheep and goats for commercial purposes. The high number of sheep and goats is due to this fact, which also explains the unequal distribution of sheep and goats among the village households.

Cows. Although cows are one of the essential factors in families' livelihood, 29.3 per cent of the families (48 out of 164) lack this essential constituent, while 20.1 per cent of the total families own 47.5 per cent of the cows in the village. Furthermore, if the first two categories are taken together, 46.4 per cent of the total families own only 10.7 per cent of the cows. The inequalities in the ownership of cows approximate to the inequalities in landownership.

Oxen. Unlike the case that some households have three or even five cows, the highest number of oxen owned by a single household is only two. This may be due to the fact that oxen are used only as draught animals and there are no families with lands so large that they would require more than one pair of oxen for tilling. Also, there is the fact that households in Gisgis with relatively large lands have recourse to renting tractors from other farmers in neighbouring villages to till their lands, on condition that their lands are suitable for the use of a tractor and if they can afford the rent charged. The households with one ox are usually relatively poor peasant households; they cannot afford to buy a second ox, nor do they think it would be wise to do so, given the small amount of land they have.

Sheep and Goats. As to ownership of sheep, Table 17 shows that the distribution is highly unequal. This is due to the fact that a few relatively rich households breed sheep for the market and that it is thought that it is more beneficial for the peasant family to keep one cow rather than having one or two sheep. However, a peasant family may come to own a few sheep through sharecropping.

If the peasant families are to choose between sheep and goats in terms of their usefulness they would prefer to keep goats, whose milk is highly valued by the peasants for making yoghurt and cheese. It is also cheaper to obtain a goat than a sheep. Goat's meat is also one of the most consumed meats in the Ergani district because it is much cheaper than lamb or beef. The ease of marketing makes goat breeding highly popular for some people in the area; however, the number of sheep is higher than that of goats in the area because lamb is more greatly desired than goat's meat in other areas, and so animal traders encourage peasants to breed sheep. However, it is not possible to say they are very successful in their attempts to encourage the breeding of sheep on a sharecropping basis, on the grounds that these arrangements may be very risky for the peasant family. This point will be touched upon when we deal with the forms of sharecropping arrangements in animal breeding in the next chapter.

Table 17 reveals that goats, which are a source of family sustenance, are unequally distributed among the households. For example, 5.5 per cent of the families own 66.4 per cent of all the goats in the village, while 70.7 per cent of the households own no goats at all. This inequality is also evident in the fact that the average number of goats per household is 1.9, while the nine families with the most goats have an average of 22.4 goats per household.

Donkeys are kept for use as a means of transport, and families with occupations other than farming did not have any donkeys. In the past, donkeys were more important for farming families. Crops produced in the village used to be transported on donkeys to Ergani, which is about 18 kilometres from the village, and/or to Çermik, about 17 kilometres away in the opposite direction from Ergani. Today, with the use of motorised transport, donkeys are no longer used for long distance transportation, although they are still important for farming families. The distribution of donkeys in the village during our survey did not reveal any inequalities of the kind we encountered with respect to sheep.

Landownership in Kalhana

Land is the main means of production in Kalhana, just as it is in Gisgis. The necessity for dealing with landownership patterns stems from the fact that this kind of analysis enables one to see at least some aspects of the relations of production. As we shall see, the distribution of land within Kalhana village is highly unequal; a situation which stems from the sixteenth century. The origins of landlordism in Eastern Anatolia have been dealt with above, and so it is unnecessary to tackle the problem with respect to Kalhana here, except to give a brief outline of the immediate history of the landownership in the village in order to shed some further light on the present situation.

In 1977, two families, Aydoğan and Gedikli, or rather off-spring of these two families, controlled between them 74.67 per cent of the total village lands (8,600 out of a total of 11,516 dönüms). The Gediklis are descendents of a local notable who was granted an ocaklık by the Ottoman sultan in the sixteenth century. Unfortunately, there is no data concerning this notable, and the account we relate here was told to us by several old men in the village during the course of our fieldwork. The reliability of the account is disputable but we do know that many local notables, tribal leaders and the like were granted lands by the Ottoman state during the sixteenth century and later and the account is in conformity with this historical fact.

We were able to obtain, from elderly people living in the area, information about landownership which dates back as far as the 1850s. Until 1907, one Lobud Ağa (born in 1834) controlled the lands of the whole village, the residents of which worked the lands as sharecroppers (yarıcı) and marabas. (2) Neither marabas nor yarıcıs had any rights to the land. The difference between maraba and yarıcı rests on the fact that the maraba was a worker with no means of production (oxen, plough etc.) who cultivated a piece of demesne land with the demesne's oxen and implements, using his family's labour and remunerated in kind, whereas the yarıcı was a peasant with farming implements and draught animals of his own, who used family labour in production.

Owing to the labour shortage in the area, a considerable part of Lobud Ağa's lands remained uncultivated. Lobud Ağa used force to keep the peasants in his village. Writing about the problems of Eastern Anatolia, Bozarslan refers to the period before 1920 as feudal and he describes the arbitrariness of the Ağas' behaviour in Eastern Anatolia:

> ... _ağas_ punished peasants in various ways: they beat them up, jailed them, even killed them. At that time (before the 1920s) _ağa_ or _bey_ meant a small sultan who could wreak his will (on the peasants) and was not answerable to anyone for his actions. Poor peasants! (Being so helpless they did not know what to do or whom to complain to.) They (the peasants) could not escape from the village since it involved danger. Because of the competition between _ağas_, escaping from the domain of one _ağa_ to that of another was considered almost equal to crossing the border of a country without a visa. That is why nobody could dare to endeavour this dangerous task. (3)

Centralised authority was so weak at the turn of the twentieth century that local _ağas_, especially the ones in Eastern and Southeastern Anatolia, and notables were enabled to become economically as well as politically powerful. Being one of the _ağas_ in the region, Lobud Ağa exercised his full power to exploit the peasants. He was infamous for his cruelty. When he died in 1907 the elder of his two sons, Hakkı Ağa, took over his position. The younger son, Mustafa Ağa (later Mustafa Gedikli) did not approve of his elder brother, the ağa-bey's behaviour in general. Hakkı Ağa was very spendthrift and granted the right to possession of some lands to many peasants in the area; he also sold a considerable part of his estate to Zakir Bey (whose account will be told later), after the abolition of the Ottoman land system in 1925. He did not mind selling his land very cheaply because first of all, owing to the technological backwardness of agriculture in the area the income from it was very low; secondly, there was an abundance of uncultivated land, due to the fact that there was a labour shortage.

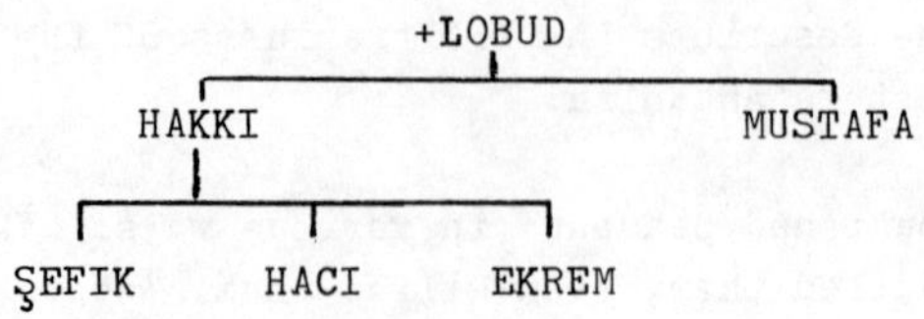

\+ This is not a complete family tree; it is included here to make it easier for the reader to see the relationships between the names which appear in the text.

Having been unhappy with his elder brother's extravagance, Mustafa took his share of about 1,000 *dönüms*, which he still has today, from the part of the estate remaining. Mustafa had married before he took his share of land from his brother, and he worked on the land controlled by Hakkı Ağa. He subsequently achieved one of his ambitions, by separating from his brother, but he never achieved his second and most important ambition, namely to have children. He says:

> I have always wanted to have children and my own farm, unfortunately God did not give me any children. I always could have modernised my farm if I had wanted to. I could have bought a tractor and ... I mean everything ... I consider these landless peasants as my own kids, let them cultivate my lands and earn their livelihood. These *beys* (he refers to the Güldoğan family) are infidels, they do not care about poor people, they only think about themselves. It was they who brought this blooming tractor to this village and caused all the unemployment and misery in this village. They are not Muslims, they are infidels ... Thanks be to God, I live quite

comfortably without a tractor and twelve families (he refers to his sharecroppers) earn their living under by auspices. I do not want to get richer; richer for what? For whom? Do I have any children to leave my property to? No.

Mustafa Gedikli is today about 79 years of age and does not work himself as he is quite content with the income he derives through his sharecroppers.

His brother's sons, Şefik, Hacı and Ekrem Gedikli inherited about 700 <u>dönüms</u> of land when their father died in 1943. Being the oldest of the brothers (20 years old at the time of Hakkı Ağa's death), Şefik Ağa became the head of the household. He resembled his father in terms of being a spendthrift and in a short period of time he became indebted to merchants in Ergani (both to grain merchants and to grocers). In return for his debts, he disposed of some lands and mortgaged some more. By the time the three brothers, Şefik, Hacı and Ekrem had separated their households they only had 300 <u>dönüms</u> of land left between them. Today, Şefik Ağa has even been reduced to being a sharecropper on his own land.

As to the Aydoğan family, they immigrated to Kalhana in 1915 from Çüngüş district where the head of the family, Zakir Bey, was one of the notables engaged in trade and usury. As a rich man, Zakir Bey did not have any difficulty in gaining the trust of rich Armenians who were also dealing with trade and usury as well as small scale production. In 1915, when the Armenians were expelled, and some were killed for rioting against the Ottoman state, some of the rich Armenians, personal friends of Zakir Bey and his trade partners, left their belongings with Zakir Bey on condition that they would get them back if they returned from wherever they were to be taken by the authorities. However, they never returned. With the expulsion of the Armenians the production of pottery and cotton cloth came to an end in the area, and of course in Çüngüş as well. Having lost his basis for trade, but with some precious metals and money hoarded away, Zakir Bey came to Ergani with his family and wanted to settle in Aşağı Balahur village. Realising that Zakir Bey had some cash, Hakkı Ağa, a relatively powerful landlord, would not let him settle in Aşağı Balahur village and persuaded him instead to settle in Kalhana, with the idea of getting some cash from him.

Aware of Hakkı Ağa's need for cash, Zakir Bey continuously bought land from him at very low prices. As we stated above, Hakkı Ağa did not care about land since there was an abundance of uncultivated land and a labour shortage. Zakir Bey not only bought land from Hakkı Ağa but also lent money to needy peasants, which resulted in the alienation of some peasants from their land. This process was continued, after Zakir Bey's death, by his sons. Until the 1960s they let the peasants cultivate their lands simply because of their own inability to cultivate the lands with the existing level of technology. Since the early 1960s, however, the Aydoğan family have been cultivating the lands with their tractor and have been expelling their share-croppers. Of course, this is not a smooth process. In fear of losing their access to the land, the peasants rebelled against the Aydoğan family several times in the 1960s. However, it was not difficult for the Aydoğans to suppress these various land seizure attempts with the help of the gendarmerie. (4)

We have digressed somewhat from our attempt to trace land-ownership in Kalhana village, and this much would seem to be sufficient to give an idea as to how the current inequality in landownership came into being. A few remarks about the data on landownership seem also to be necessary. The data were collected from three different sources: first through the application of a questionnaire - in this way household heads were simply asked to state how much land they owned; second, by going through tax office records in Ergani. This information seemed to be highly unreliable because the figures were based on the personal declarations of the landowners, who avoided giving the correct figures in order to evade high land taxes. Since no land survey has been carried out, the landowners were quite safe in declaring false figures. The third method was by referring to a reliable key respondent. Our key respondent was the village headman, whom we had known for fifteen years. The difference between the figures collected from the different sources reveal that landowners had given more or less the same figures in their answers to the questionnaires as they had declared to the tax office. The difference between the official figures and the figures obtained from the village headman is very great in the case of big holdings, and almost negligible in the case of small holdings. This is simply due to the fact that people with less than 50 *dönüms* of land are exempt from paying any land tax, while people with over 50 *dönüms* of land pay tax on that part in excess of 50 *dönüms*.

Table 18 demonstrates the highly inequitable distribution of land among the people living in Kalhana. This inequality can be said to be the result of a combination of two factors: the fact that the *yurtluk/ocaklık* system, based on big landownership, was legalised with the acceptance of private property in land in 1926, and the fact that continuous alienation of land from the direct producers has taken place. The fact that the estates of big landowners consist of numerous fragments of land reveals that many peasants have lost their lands totally or in part to the big landowners. Table 19 indicates the extent to which the big estates consist of fragmented lands.

In discussing landownership in Kalhana village it would be misleading to take into account only those people who live in the village. All the people who have land within the village boundaries should also be taken into consideration. However, even this treatment will not be fully illuminative for an investigation of the relations of production, since this would require the study not only of the relations between landlords and the people living in the village and working for the landlords, but also of the relations between the landlord village and the neighbouring peasant villages. The term peasant village is used here to indicate that land distribution among the inhabitants is more or less equal, farmers work on their own land with their own means of production.

The total land within the boundaries of the village is 11,516 *dönüms*, of which 10,014 *dönüms* are owned by inhabitants

TABLE 18 DISTRIBUTION OF LAND AMONG THE INHABITANTS OF KALHANA+

LAND OWNED (dönüms)	NUMBER OF++ HOUSEHOLDS	PERCENTAGE OF HOUSEHOLDS	TOTAL LAND (dönüms)	PERCENTAGE OF TOTAL
Landless	36	78.3	-	-
1-50	4	8.7	114	1.14
51-100	2	4.3	200	2.00
101+	4	8.7	9,700	96.86
Total	46	100.0	10,014	100.00

+ Calculated from the figures supplied by the village headman

++ Although the village headman was able to provide us with this information for all 46 households in the village, we were unable to obtain other data for two of the households whose heads were away from the village.

TABLE 19 LAND FRAGMENTATION IN BIG ESTATES, KALHANA

LANDLORD	TOTAL LAND (dönüms)	NUMBER OF LAND FRAGMENTS
Fuat Aydoğan	5,000	88
Hamdi Aydoğan	2,400	68
Havva Aydoğan	1,300	49
Total	8,700	205

TABLE 20 LAND OWNERSHIP WITHIN THE VILLAGE BOUNDARIES, KALHANA

LAND OWNED (dönüms)	NUMBER OF HOUSEHOLDS	PERCENTAGE OF HOUSEHOLDS	TOTAL LAND (dönüms)	PERCENTAGE OF TOTAL LAND
1-20	19	38.7	278	2.4
21-50	16	32.7	587	5.1
51-200	10	20.4	951	8.3
201+	4	8.2	9,700	84.2
Total	49	100.0	11,516	100.0

of the village. 1,502 _dönüms_ are owned either by the peasants from neighbouring villages such as Balahur, Malan and Keydanevleri, which are the labour sources for the landlord village, or by the absentee landowners, merchants, usurers and teachers, etc. The peasants from the neighbouring villages who have land in Kalhana work their own land, while the absentee landowners either give their land to sharecroppers to work, or rent it to a capitalist farmer, or to a peasant family. Even the inclusion of the lands within village boundaries owned both by peasants from the neighbouring villages and by the absentee landlords does not change the general picture of the distribution of the land in the village. Instead it indicates that 8.2 per cent of the landowning households control 84.2 per cent of the total lands owned in the village, while 92.8 per cent of the landowning families control only 15.8 per cent of the total lands owned in the village. These figures reach incredibly inequitable dimensions if we also take into account the number of landless farming families.

Differentiation, not only in landownership, but also in animal ownership, should be taken into account in illustrating the indicators of class affiliations, since products derived from stock constitute a part of the peasant family's means of reproduction and the main source of livelihood of some households who mainly engage in stock raising. Even a wage-labourer family may be able to have one or two sheep or goats to help the reproduction of the family. The raising of stock means different things to different households, depending on their class position.

For a capitalist household it is a business, aimed at enlarging production which is based on the appropriation of the surplus. The production is not in order to meet the consumption needs of the family, but to sell in the market in order to realise a profit, which is used partly to meet the expenses of the capitalist household (mainly for the acquisition of luxury goods), and partly in reinvestment for an extended production, in other words to produce more, and profit more, then reinvest more.

For a petty commodity producer family, the raising of stock

is both a business and a means to reproduce the household, the size of which varies in its demographic cycle over the years. Although production is for the market, the petty commodity producer's main concern is the reproduction of the family, not a profit. As to the peasant households, they produce different things, mainly for home consumption. The amount peasant producers sell in the market is determined by the cash needs of the family, as well as the amount saved.

It should be pointed out, however, that the above presentation in terms of petty commodity producers and peasants may lead us to the erroneous conclusion that these two categories are mutually exclusive, whereas in fact, in rural areas such as our two villages, it is possible to come across families reflecting the features of both the two types we have described here. For instance, in Kalhana there are some families producing cotton for the market and wheat for home consumption, and in Gisgis, too, there are families producing vegetables and grapes for the market as well as producing wheat and lentils for home consumption.

The same is true in stock raising. There are families raising stock for the market in order to reproduce themselves with the income derived from this, and there are also families raising stock to meet the family's needs, as well as families having a combination of the features of both these types.

Animal Ownership in Kalhana

The distribution of animal ownership among the households of the village is shown in Table 21.

Cows. The big landlords, who have 38 cows between them, raise stock for the market. Three of the landlords have employed one family to look after their animals. Their arrangements with animal caretakers are something between a wage-labour and a sharecropping arrangement. The case of Arif Başdemir can be taken as an example to illustrate the sort of arrangements made between the landowners and animal caretakers, who are mainly landless peasants.

TABLE 21 LIVESTOCK OWNERSHIP IN KALHANA

HOUSEHOLDS WITH:-	HOUSEHOLDS No.	PER CENT	CUM PER CENT	LIVESTOCK No.	PER CENT	CUM PER CENT
(i) COWS						
no cow	26	59.1	59.1	-	-	-
1 cow	7	15.9	75.0	7	11.3	11.3
2 cows	4	9.1	84.1	8	12.9	24.2
3 cows	3	6.8	90.4	9	14.5	38.7
4+ cows	4	9.1	100.0	38	61.3	100.0
Total	44	100.0	100.0	62	100.0	100.0
(ii) OXEN						
no ox	37	84.1	84.1	-	-	-
1 ox	3	6.8	90.0	3	27.2	27.2
2 oxen	4	9.1	100.0	8	72.8	100.0
Total	44	100.0	100.0	11	100.0	100.0
(iii) SHEEP						
no sheep	34	77.2	77.2	-	-	-
1-3 sheep	2	4.5	81.7	5	2.1	2.1
4-10 sheep	2	4.5	86.2	12	5.1	7.2
11-25 sheep	3	6.9	93.1	60	25.3	32.5
26+ sheep	3	6.9	100.0	160	67.5	100.0
Total	44	100.0	100.0	237	100.0	100.0
(iv) GOATS						
no goats	31	70.5	70.5	-	-	-
1-3 goats	5	11.4	81.9	8	5.6	5.6
4-10 goats	4	9.1	91.0	25	17.6	23.2
11-25 goats	2	4.5	95.5	42	29.6	52.8
26+ goats	2	4.5	100.0	67	47.2	100.0
Total	44	100.0	100.0	142	100.0	100.0

Arif Başdemir is 37 years old and the father of four children, who do not officially exist, since they have not been registered. (5) He was born in Kermukan, a village in the Maden district of Elazığ province. He was not sent to school since there was no school in his village and to go elsewhere was out of the question as his family could not afford it. For eight years, from the age of 10 until 18, when he was called up by the army, he worked as a shepherd, grazing the herd of a local landlord. Having finished his military service, he wanted to get married, which impelled him to seek work in Adana, where capitalist cotton production is dominant, in order to earn money for the başlık parası (bride-price). Being very poor, his family could not help him in accumulating the bride-price. In Adana he worked as a tractor driver on a farm, and saved TL5,000 in two years to pay the bride-price. He married when he was 23 and, after a period of four years of temporary work as an amele (unskilled worker in building and road construction), he moved to Migo village to work as a sharecropper for a landlord who owned the whole village, thinking that his standard of living would improve. He came to Kalhana village with his wife and three children in 1974 to work for the richest farmer, Zakir Bey, who died in 1976.

Arif is now working for Fuat Bey, the elder of Zakir Bey's two sons, and his job is to look after Fuat Bey's 80 animals, comprising cows, sheep and goats. The one-roomed house in which Arif and his family live, owned by Fuat Bey, is provided free of charge. Arif is paid TL6,000 per year in cash and is given a piece of land and some seed to cultivate on his own. However, this is not the case every year. For instance, Arif was complaining that at the beginning of the year Fuat Bey gave him 5.5 ölçeks of wheat and 2.5 ölçeks of lentils to cultivate on his own account but, when the harvest time came, Fuat Bey claimed half of the crop.

Since Arif is indebted to Fuat (he had to borrow TL5,000 from Fuat's father Zakir Bey when he first moved into the village) and is unable to repay his debt, he is tied to the village. Unless he pays his debt he cannot leave the village. This is in addition to the hopeless job prospects around the town of Ergani, which put him off the idea of leaving the village. In order to secure his place on the farm, Arif and his family feel obliged to comply with arbitrary orders from Fuat Bey, who, for example, would not let Arif work in irrigation for a few days to earn some supplementary cash. Although Arif's job, according to his verbal agreement, is to look after the animals and produce milk, butter and fettah cheese, and to deliver these to the landlord's house in Ergani, he also is asked to carry sacks and to load and unload trucks. His children are also asked to fetch water for the landlord's family when they stay in the village for about two months in the summer.

The conclusion to be drawn from this example is that, although animal caretakers may be paid a wage for the job they do, it is very difficult to call the relations between them and the animal-owners a capitalist relation of production. It is also difficult to draw a line between a wage-labourer and labourers of other kinds (sharecroppers, corvée labourers etc.), since the same labourer may be involved in different types of relations of production at the same time.

Oxen. As we mentioned before, the lands of Kalhana are very suitable for the use of agricultural machinery, since they are not stony. We also mentioned that big landlords having close relations with the government officials and, with the help of the state policy to give credits and assistance to wealthy farmers, have obtained agricultural machines which are rented out to the other farmers as well. The renting out of agricultural machinery gradually decreased the need for oxen to be used as draught animals. Thus there are only a small number (44) of oxen in the village.

Only four households have a pair of oxen, and three households have only one ox each. It was understood that the three households with one ox had had a pair in the previous year and had had to dispose of one ox for a variety of reasons such as the payment of debts, buying consumption goods, medicine, etc. The four pairs of oxen were all owned by sharecroppers who had at one time also thought of getting rid of their oxen but had changed their minds in the light of a 100 per cent increase in petrol prices in the summer of 1977. One of them told me: 'It is a good job that my wife did not let me sell our oxen. The _ağas_ were saying that they were going to raise the price of tilling the land by tractor from 30 to 50TL. My goodness! Nobody will be able to have their lands tilled by tractor.'

Sheep and Goats. Differentiation among the inhabitants of Kalhana village in terms of sheep and goat ownership is also the same in the case of Gisgis. As is evident from the table, 34 households have no sheep and 31 households have no goats. The number of families that have one to three sheep or goats is very small. For instance, only two families have sheep and five families have goats, in the category 1-3 sheep owned. These families are mainly poor families working as casual labourers. They use the milk of sheep and goats in the household and rarely sell dairy produce in the market, as the produce is not enough even to meet the family's needs. Some permanently employed people working as labourers or civil servants also keep sheep and goats for both home consumption and the market. Their wives and children look after the animals they own or sharecrop. The permanent employees are relatively well off since they have a stable income and their involvement in farming activities simply decreases the cost of living for them. They are subsumed under the categories of the groups of households with 4 to 10 or 11 to 25 sheep or goats.

Households with 26 or more sheep or goats are those of big landlords' families, who own 67.5 per cent of the sheep and 47.2 per cent of the goats in the village. The aims of big landlord families in stock raising are not to meet the needs of their families but to make more profit. For this reason, they employ labourer(s) on a permanent basis to look after their animals. Although only the head of the household is normally employed, the whole family has to comply with the wishes of the landlord, to work without payment, in other words as corvée labour. This is due to the competition between the workers and the landless village poor for a permanent income, and to the fear of being dismissed.

As we gathered from the case of Arif Başdemir, it is more profitable for the landlords to take advantage of the redundancy of the working force in the rural areas of Southeast Anatolia, and get involved in relations of production that do not have the features of typical capitalist/wage-earner relations as in industry. Instead, these relations carry the feature of both non-capitalist relations of production and wage relations.

Donkeys, as in Gisgis, though not as extensively, are used for the transportation of crops from the field to the house by producers who do not have tractors. There were twenty donkeys in the village during our fieldwork. Those households with access to land one way or another seemed to be the ones to have donkeys. Most of the landless casual workers did not have a donkey.

As a conclusion to this chapter, we can say that the pattern of distribution of land still carries the basic features of the past. Large estates and small peasant holdings still co-exist side by side. However, the relations of production have changed to a considerable extent, as we shall see in some detail in the following chapters. The requirements of the capitalist world market and of Turkish capitalism have forced the peasant household to engage in the production of commodities, (goods and labour), while the large estates have geared their production entirely for the market.

Notes to Chapter Five

1. As Lenin (1964) analysed the Russian peasantry
2. The name maraba comes from the term rubu, and means 'the one who receives one fourth of the crop'. For a detailed description of maraba see Chapter Six.
3. Bozarslan, 1966, 10
4. Similar sorts of land seizures and landlord-peasant disputes in other parts of Southeast Anatolia are dealt with by Yalman, 1971.
5. It is not common practice to register new-born children, since peasants have nothing to do with the state. Register-

ing a child with the population office requires one of the parents to go personally to the town centre and deal with the officials, who generally do not speak Kurdish. Furthermore, by not registering their children with the state, peasants avoid having to send their daughters to school and their sons to the army: military service is compulsory for boys aged between 20 and 22, and lasts for two years, but the boys' labour is very vital to the peasant household.

6. Relations Of Production Outside The Household

The household as an economic unit, a unit of reproduction of the peasant family, has responded to the requirements of the larger economy in different ways at different times in the development process of the larger economy. Although the relations of production in which the peasant households were involved have been different at different periods, one thing is certain: that the peasant household has been an integral part of the reproduction of the larger economy. This chapter will focus on the relations of production in which the peasant household in Eastern and Southeastern Anatolia have been involved from the establishment of the Turkish Republic (1923) onwards.

The conditions of peasant production are determined at larger levels (social formation and world economy) by ownership of means of production, market and credit mechanisms etc., but in most cases the actual process of production is organised by the peasant household. Therefore the peasant household, or at least the members of the peasant household, are involved in two sets of relations of production. First, relations of production outside the household, like landlord-peasant relations; and second, the relations of production within the household, such as control of the product of younger members by older members, etc. This chapter will concentrate on the relations of production outside the household and Chapter Seven on the relations of production within the household.

Historical Evolution of the Relations of Production

Our knowledge concerning the relations of production in Eastern Anatolia before the Republic is extremely limited, since there has been virtually no research on this subject. However, given the backward nature of agricultural technology and production, even in the 1950s, we can assume that the relations of production did not change with the declaration of the right of private property in land in 1926. What happened with the acceptance of private property in land was that de facto private ownership in land was confirmed by law, since those who produced an Ottoman tapu (title deed) were accepted as the real owners of the land.

Writing in 1934, I.H. Tökin states that, in the 1930s, in the Eastern and Southeastern provinces, the land and the other means of production of the peasants were the property of the tribal leaders, beys and ağas (landlords), (1) and despotism lay behind landlordism. (2) In the provinces of these regions, peasants not only cultivated the land, they also lived on the land of the bey and served as corvée labourer. Peasants had to do all sorts of things ordered by the landlord, (ağa, bey, etc.) as if it was their duty. If they refused to accept orders, the ağa would either expel them or mistreat them, (3) or would hand them over to the police for having committed a crime. (4)

In the 1950s, the peasants who worked on the landlords' land were called maraba or azab. The maraba was a direct producer who obtained a share of what he produced. Although in some places the maraba may have had his own land, he could not benefit from it. This was because either his land was not fertile or he was indebted to the ağa. In most cases, the maraba did not own any means of production; the ağa owned both the land and the implements and the maraba only had one rubu (one fourth of the crops). Azabs may be said to be agricultural labourers. The nature of relations of production engaged in by the *azabs* was described by Aras in the 1950s:

> Agricultural labourers in Southeast Anatolia are generally devoid of both land and capital. In other words they are poor people without any house or farm. For this reason the whole family prefers to take shelter on a farm than to find a temporary wage job. They would undertake the work given to them as a family (male, female and child members who are able to work will work together). (5)

Aras suggests that rural workers took the form of family labourers rather than individual labourers. This was very convenient for the landlords, who faced difficulties in finding a labour force. According to Aras, this form of wage labour should not be confused with sharecropping. However, *azabs* were more or less temporary wage labourers who were employed by the landlords under arrangements which were similar to sharecropping arrangements. *Azabs* would not only carry out agricultural work, but would also serve personally the landlord who supplied them with board and lodging. They were generally paid in kind, and sometimes they were allowed to cultivate a small plot of land on their own account, using the implements of the landlord, in lieu of receiving any payment. This way of cultivating the land on the worker's own account was called *ikramiye* (bonus) or *şekere* in the local dialect.

There were two kinds of *azab*. For instance, in Urfa province of Southeast Anatolia (one of the neighbouring provinces of Diyarbakır); there were two types of *azab*. The *sonbahar azabı* (autumn *azab*) was employed from the end of the harvest time (September) until April. He would prepare the land for cultivation and sow the seed. As a wage he would be given a plot of 10 *dönüms* and eight *timins* (6) of wheat seed. Sometimes two *timins* of this *ikramiye* may be barley. The *azab* sowed his *ikramiye* by using the farm equipment. The grain part of the harvest was divided into two equal shares, one for the landlord and the other for the *azab*. Some landlords would even ask for a further eighth of the harvest as the rent for the land. The ilkbahar azabı (spring azab) was employed for three months, starting in the beginning of April, in fallow works. He would be paid in cash, as well as being given board and lodging during his stay on the farm. (7)

There also existed a similar type of employment of workers in the Diyarbakır area, which was called şikarte. Here too, in order to tie the seasonal and permanent worker families to the farm, landlords would give them a plot of land, and some seed to cultivate on their own account. For instance, one worker would be given 240 kilos of wheat to sow on a plot of land provided by the landlord in return for his services over a period of nine months. The harvest was considered to be equal to 500 kilos of wheat and 500 kilos of barley, which was equal to the nine months' payment. The amount of sowing seed given to a three-month worker was 160 kilos of wheat. (8)

In addition to these arrangements, other kinds of sharecropping arrangements existed in the area. Writing in the 1950s, Aras tells us about the variety of sharecropping arrangements in Southeast Anatolia. The following account of these arrangements is based on Aras' work. (9)

(a) Yarıcılık: This is the basis of sharecropping: the landowner gives land, building and seed, in some cases also working capital if the peasant is unable to operate his land otherwise, and this debt is repaid either in cash or in kind, according to their verbal agreement. Other production expenses are the sharecropper's responsibility. Produce is divided into two equal parts, without first extracting the seed which had been provided initially. If the sharecropper is given any animal fodder during the year this must be paid back after the harvest.

(b) İcare: In this mode of operations, all expenditure for production belongs to the sharecropper except for land and buildings. This differs from yarıcılık as to the share of production expenditure, since the producer is not given seed by the landowner. Thus the landowner's contact with the land is reduced. The producer is free as regards the seed which will be sown and the agricultural method used. Because of these features, icare comes between tenancy and sharecropping. The share of the landowner varies between one-fifth and one-tenth in the icare mode. The lands which are given under the conditions of icare are generally poor and infertile. The land-tax is paid by the landowner, who sometimes takes one-twentieth of the produce as the 'right of title-deed'. Since there is no written agreement, the landowner can expel a peasant from his land. İcare exists mostly in the north of Eastern Anatolia.

(c) Cariyek: (quarter or one-fourth) This mode of operation is a kind of combination of yarıcılık and icare. Half the seed and equipment is provided by the landowner and the other half is provided by the sharecropper. Any other expenditure for production is provided by the sharecropper but the land tax is paid by the landowner. One fourth of production is given to the landowner, another fourth is given to the sharecropper, one sixteenth is the rent of the land and the rest is divided into two equal parts for the landowner and sharecropper. This mode of operation is not widespread, and is mostly found around Diyarbakır.

(d) Marabacılık: In this mode, all means of production belong to the landowner. The maraba lives only by his own strength. Each maraba is given 100 dönüms of land to cultivate; one-third or one-fourth of production is given to the maraba but no share is given from straw. The maraba also has to act as a servant to the landowner.

Despite the variety in types of arrangements between the direct producers and the landlords, one thing that emerges is that, in both azab and sharecropping arrangements, the peasant's household is the basic unit of production. The household, in order to reproduce itself, takes part in various relations of production. It is the level of development of the productive forces which enforces the above-mentioned relations between the landlords and the peasants. Owing to the low population density in the area, the landlords, who also held political power, mostly resorted to force to keep the peasants on their lands. (10)

Following the establishment of the Republic, it is understood that the economy was still to a large extent a closed agricultural economy, based on self-sufficiency, with very few relations with the market. Furthermore, in 1927 only 5 to 6.5 per cent of Turkey's total land area was under cultivation. For this reason, Turkish agriculture, especially that of Central Anatolia, is called 'oasis' type by P. Zhukovsky. (11) In a report presented to the Agricultural Congress in 1931, the general backwardness of the country's agriculture was described, and it was stated that the relation of the peasants to the market was only tied to the purchase of necessary consumption goods, such as sugar, paraffin, tea and coffee. (12) However, Tökin points out that, despite the dominance of a self-sufficient closed economy in Eastern, Southeastern and some parts of Central Anatolia, in Western and coastal parts of Anatolia, which had continuous relations with the world market and which were equipped with railway networks, the producers produced not for their own consumption but also for the market. (13)

In the period 1923 to 1950, not only small farms but also large ones were technologically backward. Large holdings used only 5 to 10 per cent of their lands as cultivable fields, the rest being used for pasture. (14) It was not until the 1950s that Turkish agriculture underwent a tremendous structural change. This was mainly due to the priority given to agriculture in Turkey's development attempts at the time. The number of tractors and combine harvesters increased dramatically. For instance, the number of tractors in Turkey rose from 17,000 in 1950 to 42,000 in 1960, 116,100 in 1971 and 243,000 in 1975. (1 With the state's help, middle and large landowners started to use agricultural machinery on their farms and to expel the sharecroppers from their lands. Kanbolat summarises the consequences of the mechanisation of agriculture in Turkey as follows:

(a) The enlargement of the cultivated area: Previously uncultivated parts of middle-sized and big holdings (which could be as large as 95 per cent of the total farm) became available for cultivation with the use of machinery. Stony parts, unsuitable for the use of machinery, were allocated for the use of sharecroppers. In this way middle-sized and large farms were converted into modern farms operating with machinery. An abundance of credit enabled some big landlords to accumulate capital and to seek to enlarge their holdings, either by renting new lands, or by annexing the state-owned pasture lands to their own holdings. (16) The figures available prove Kanbolat's point to be true. Cultivable lands rose from 6,628,000 hectares in 1928 to 13,900,000 hectares in 1948, 22,161,000 hectares in 1957 and 23,836,000 hectares in 1962. (17)

(b) The application of modern means of production: This increased the productivity of the labour force so that, whereas only two or three dönüms of land could be tilled in one day using a pair of oxen, with a tractor 70 dönüms of land could be tilled in one day.

(c) The production of commercial crops: This gained importance and areas used for this purpose were enlarged. (18)

(d) Rise of unemployed peasants: As a result of mechanisation in agriculture the number of unemployed people rose. The sharecroppers were freed from the means of production - the land - and had to sell their labour (19) in conditions of shrinking demand for labour.

Nevertheless, despite these changes, the household as an economic unit, a unit of reproduction of the peasant family, has stubbornly persisted in Southeast Anatolia. Largely due to its adaptability to the new situations it has encountered throughout these changes, the peasant household has remained a vital factor in the functioning of the rural economy of the region. This was partially due to the wider integration of the region into the Turkish social formation which helped bring about the play of new factors like marketing and credit mechanisms. The conditions of these market forces and credit mechanisms are, of course, determined at the national and international levels, and will be discussed in some detail in later chapters. At this stage it suffices to note that the specific structures generated by such factors consolidated the existing duality in landholdings. As a result, the peasant household has remained the basic unit of production, as can be seen from the following discussion.

Relations of production vary in Eastern Anatolia according to the nature of the farm in which they occur. Different sets of relations of production occur in small family farms and in big semi-capitalist farms respectively. By semi-capitalist farm we refer to a large estate, the main object of which is to accumulate capital, and in which various forms of labour are used, such as wage labour, seasonal labour, unpaid labour, etc. In a capitalist production unit the main components are the capitalists, who are the owners of the means of production, and the wage-labourers, freed from all the property ties. The relations between these two are of an economic nature, based on a contract. However, in the big estates of Eastern Anatolia the relations between the workers and the owners of the estate are not purely economic. In some cases other types of relations, such as debt peonage, patron-client relations, etc. may also be involved. Of course, in some cases the relations between workers and landlords may also take purely economic forms.

In order to illuminate the relations of production in Gisgis and Kalhana, we shall attempt to describe the relations of production both outside and within household economic units, based on data collected in our fieldwork. We shall then try to show the relations and interactions between the two sets of relations. It must be stated, however, that the analysis we are about to undertake is mainly relevant for those families who have access to land and it is divided into two chapters: relations outside the household being discussed in this chapter.

Relations of Production Outside the Household

Given the uncertain employment possibilities outside agriculture, peasants always try to have access to a piece of land from which they can earn a living, or at least part of a living. If they do not have any or sufficient land to secure their livelihood, they engage in various relations of production. Wage labouring, sharecropping and tenancy are the main types of relations the peasants may engage in. (20) The members of the household may engage in all of these relations of production, either at the same time or in different periods of the year. Sharecropping is widespread amongst peasant households around Ergani, and the data pertaining to land use in the two villages under consideration will illustrate this point.

Land use in Gisgis

The forms of land use in Gisgis are shown in Table 22.

TABLE 22 LAND USE IN GISGIS

LAND USE	DÖNÜMS	PERCENTAGE OF TOTAL
Cultivated by the owner	4,111	77.5
Given to sharecroppers	1,082	20.4
Uncultivated	113	2.1
Total	5,306	100.0

It should be pointed out that the uncultivated lands are mostly in very small fragments, the cultivation of which would not be beneficial at all, and that some uncultivated lands are extremely stony or hilly.

It is evident from Table 16 (p.116 above) that at least 81.1 per cent of the families do not have enough land to reproduce themselves. Sufficiency of land for the reproduction of the family, of course, will depend on the fertility of the land, size of the family, level of development of the productive forces, etc. There are, therefore, major difficulties involved in defining the amount of land necessary for the reproduction of the family. For instance, the answer given to the question 'How much land do you think is necessary for a decent life?' revealed that it was very difficult to arrive at a consensus among the peasants. It became evident that 'a decent life' was itself a vague concept, because it meant different levels of standard of living to different people with different expectations.

Nevertheless, families with 50 dönüms of land or more were considered relatively well off in the village. Therefore, 31 families (18.9 per cent of the total) may be said to have had enough land for their reproduction cycle according to Table 16. The remaining households have to look for supplementary income. If they want to derive some supplementary income from farming, they have either to engage in sharecropping arrangements or to work as agricultural workers, or both. However, the limited possibilities of finding work as an agricultural labourer or as a labourer in the vicinity of the village or in the town forces peasants to enlarge their holdings by resorting to sharecropping arrangements, and so to seek a living by engaging in farming.

From Table 23 below it can be seen that the less the amount of land owned, the more peasants are inclined to seek work outside farming. For instance, only 20 per cent of the landless families engage in farming, whereas 83.9 per cent of families with 51 dönüms or more engage in farming.

TABLE 23 FARMING FAMILIES BY LAND OWNED, GISGIS

LAND OWNED (dönüms)	NUMBER OF FAMILIES	NUMBER OF FARMING FAMILIES	PERCENTAGE OF TOTAL
Landless	40	8	20.0
1-10	33	16	48.5
11-20	12	6	50.0
21-50	48	39	81.3
51+	31	26	83.9

The landless families who cannot find work outside agriculture work as sharecroppers. Two aspects of sharecropping seem to be important. First, with the land obtained through sharecropping arrangements the size of the holding comes closer to the amount which will render more productive use of labour, draught animals and tools, and therefore increase the household income; second, through sharecropping arrangements a part of the product of the direct producer is appropriated by the owner of the land. Generally, in sharecropping arrangements the landlord provides the seed and the land, and the sharecropper works the land with his draught animals and tools, using family labour. The crop is shared on a fifty-fifty basis, and the straw is also equally shared between the landowners and the sharecroppers.

In most cases the sharecropper is also responsible for the transportation of the landlord's share from the field to the landlord's house. This is done using donkeys as a means of transport. If the landlord is resident in the village or in the neighbouring villages, the sharecropper or his son would take the crop to the landlord's house. If the landlord is an absentee and lives in the town, the crop would be transported on the only lorry, which carries goods and crops as well as passengers, between the town centre and the village. The cost of transportation may be shared by the landlord, depending on their verbal agreement.

If the landowner himself is a farmer, he may ask his sharecropper to help him for a few days in his farming. Although this is not a very widespread practice, knowing that to refuse help to the landlord would mean the loss of access to land, sharecroppers comply with the requests of the landlord. This kind of practice occurs more widely in the villages where big landownership is dominant and access to land is more difficult, the case of Kalhana village can be given as an example.

Land fragmentation makes it extremely uneconomical to cultivate the land. That is why some of the families with little land seek work outside agriculture (see Table 8 , p. 90), which leaves their lands available for sharecroppers. However, those who cannot find work outside agriculture remain as dwarf farmers, seeking a supplementary income which in some cases is obtained through sharecropping. The cross-tabulation of land ownership with sharecropping given in Table 24 shows the relations between the amount of land owned and the amount of land sharecropped by the families in Gisgis.

TABLE 24 LANDOWNERSHIP BY SHARECROPPING IN GISGIS

LAND SHARECROPPED (dönüms)		LAND OWNED (dönüms) NIL	1-10	11-20	21-50	51+	TOTAL
None	(1)	32	23	7	33	23	118
1-10	(2)	2	4	2	6	-	14
11-20	(3)	2	3	3	5	-	13
21-50	(4)	4	3	-	4	8	19
51+	(5)	-	-	-	-	-	-
Total No. of Families	(6)	40	33	12	48	31	164
Total No. of Sharecropping Families	(7)	8	10	5	15	8	46
Total No. of Farming Families	(8)++	8	16	6	39	26	95
Ratio	(7):(8)	100	62.5	83.5	38.5	30.8	48.4
Ratio	(8):(6)	20	48.5	50.0	81.3	83.9	57.9

++ This column is derived from Table 23

Table 24 shows that there is a negative correlation between landownership and sharecropping. For example, all the landless farming families have sharecropping arrangements (100 per cent), while only 30.8 per cent of the farming families with 51 or more dönüms have sharecropping arrangements. The fact that the percentage of sharecropping families within the 11 to 20 dönüms category is higher than the percentage of families in the category of 1 to 10 dönüms seems to be contradictory to our claim that there is a negative correlation between landownership and sharecropping. This may be explained by the fact that the less land people have the less likely it is that they will stay as farmers. (See Table 24 , line 10)

Furthermore, there is not much difference between having no land and having, say, about 5 <u>dönüms</u>. That is to say, a piece of land as small as 10 <u>dönüms</u> would not yield an income sufficient to maintain a family and, furthermore, most of the peasants with 10 <u>dönüms</u> or less do not have a pair of oxen to enable them to cultivate more land. Landowners would not give their lands to someone without any draught animals. Those with 20 <u>dönüms</u> are more likely to stay as farmers, and to have at least one ox or a pair of oxen, than those with no land or very little. From the landowner's point of view, a family with a pair of oxen is more desirable than one without. Therefore, peasants with 10 to 20 <u>dönüms</u> and a pair of oxen are much more likely to find land to sharecrop than those with less land and only one ox.

Land use in Kalhana

Compared to those of Gisgis, the lands in Kalhana are more fertile and are used to their full extent. There are no stony fields in Kalhana. Table 25 indicates land use in the village in terms of whether the land is worked by its owner or is share-cropped or rented out.

TABLE 25 LAND USE IN KALHANA

LAND USE	DÖNÜMS	PERCENTAGE OF TOTAL
Cultivated by the owner	9,031	78.4
Given to sharecroppers	1,865	16.2
Rented out	620	5.4
Uncultivated	-	-
Total	11,516	100.0

The category 'cultivated by the owner' includes the lands of both large and small farms, the latter being the more numerous. The sharecropping category includes those lands given to the sharecroppers both by the big farmers and by absentee landowners.

The third category comprises land rented out by the owner. The difference between the sharecropping and renting categories lies in the nature of the arrangements made between the owner and the tenants. In the sharecropping category the landowner shares the risk of the investment in case of crop failure, since his share consists of half the crop in return for seeds and the field provided by him, and he also has the right to interfere in decision-making. The share that he receives as payment in kind may, therefore, be termed 'absolute ground rent'. As to the renting of land, although it is not a very widespread practice in Southeastern Anatolia, as it is in the Çukurova and Aegean regions, the landowner lets the farmer use his land for a certain period of time, usually one year, in return for a certain fixed payment in cash. He is not concerned with the production process, nor with the yield of the crop. The farmer who rents land has to find the seed himself, and has to bear the total loss in case of crop failure. The rent the owner receives may be called 'capitalist ground rent', in the sense that Marx uses the term in Capital. (21)

Although the existence of rented land is considered an indication of capitalist farming, the non-existence, or rather non-dominance of land-renting of this kind does not exclude capitalist development in agriculture. The existence of capitalism in agriculture should not be reduced to the existence of certain elements such as wage labour, renting land for rent in cash, etc. What should be done in the study of capitalism in agriculture is to try to establish the extent to which capital dominates labour. Capitalism in agriculture can make use of labour other than wage labour, as is shown by Banaji in the case of India, and by others in the case of Latin America. (22)

We pointed out that giving land to sharecroppers and renting land out differed from each other in Eastern and Southeast Anatolia, and the reasons for giving land to sharecroppers varies according to the nature of the village where the land is situated. With the danger of overgeneralising, we may conclude that, in the villages where there is no excessively unequal land distribution, the reasons may be: (i) the land is too small for a family to sustain itself and so they have found an alternative source of income; (ii) in order not to divide a farm into marginally small pieces, relatives may decide to let one family cultivate the land on a sharecropping basis; (iii) the landowner may be engaged in a permanent and more remunerative job; (iv) the landowner may not be fit enough to work his land himself.

In landlord villages, however, where large farms are dominant in the village, the landowners give their lands to sharecroppers because it is more beneficial for them in the long run. In this way landowners tie the peasants to the land in order to reduce their expenditure on labour during peak seasons. Our two villages can be given as examples of these two trends. We have seen the case of Gisgis previously, now we shall examine the case of Kalhana concerning sharecropping.

In Kalhana the main crops are, in order of importance, cotton, wheat and lentils. They are produced for the market as cash crops by the big farmers. Cotton production especially, and to a lesser degree lentil production, require a high number of workers at harvest time. To find workers in the peak season is very difficult and costly. As we have seen in Table 18, p.128, 36 households out of the total 46 households in Kalhana village (78.3 per cent) are landless. Although the prospects of finding jobs in the towns are very poor, there is no reason for the landless poor to stay in the village, apart from the nearness of the village to the town centre. The solution the landlords have found to the prospect of a shortage of labour is to tie the landless poor to the land by giving them access to the land. This is done by means of sharecropping arrangements which are considered beneficial by both landlords and the rural poor alike. From the point of view of the rural poor, the sharecropping arrangement provides a basic source of income and sometimes, if they come from elsewhere, even a place in the village in which to live. Furthermore, since the amount of land sharecropped does not necessitate the year-round labour of the household in order to cultivate it, some male members of the family, in many cases the household head, are also able to leave the village to seek a supplementary income, working the land and working as cotton pickers at harvest time.

It is also beneficial from the landlord's point of view, in the long run, to give some land, especially the relatively infertile parts, to landless poor or to poor peasants with little land, for this leaves a sizeable number of potential workers in the village, at the same time as it enables them to a certain extent to impose their will on the sharecroppers. For instance, they give their lands to those who guarantee a certain number of people, including women and children, to work in the peak seasons as cotton-pickers, who are normally paid in kind. Such a worker could not earn more than the equivalent of TL40 per day, while a day-labourer would get about TL150 to TL200 per day. This is because such workers are entitled to one-twentieth of the cotton they pick instead of a wage. On average a worker can pick 60 to 70 kilos of cotton per day, which leaves him with between 3 and 3.5 kilos of cotton. The price of cotton on the market was TL10 per kilo in 1977, which means that such a worker could earn as little as TL30 to 35 per day. Furthermore, most of the cotton pickers are unable to market their share of the cotton, thus being obliged to sell at a lower price (TL8 to 8.5 per kilo) either to cotton merchants or to others able to take the cotton to the head office of Çukobirlik in Elazığ. In Kalhana, only big landowners are able to transport their cotton to Elazığ, which is 100 kilometres from the village.

From the above it appears that landowners not only benefit from the cheap labour force kept in the village, through sharecropping arrangements, but they also reduce their expenditure on the labour force by paying in kind and also taking advantage of the inabilities of the workers to market the goods they have earned. However, if we take a sharecropping arrangement on its own and try to calculate the landowner's benefit or loss in comparison with the situation where he cultivates the land on his own account, we end up with the conclusion that the landlord may incur a loss in absolute terms. Let us take an example to illustrate this point.

Since the landlords give lands of 10 to 50 dönüms to sharecroppers we thought it would be appropriate to base our example on a 20-dönüm piece of land. The village headman provides us with our example, and the figures were arrived at by careful calculations made together with the headman. Our example in no way constitutes an absolute example, valid for every other sharecropping arrangement, nor is it an absolute representation of various sharecropping transactions taking place in Southeast Anatolia. For the cost of production will vary from field to field, depending on the fertility of the soil, the nature of the inputs (fertiliser, labour, etc.) and on the equipment used. However, we thought that an example of this sort would help to indicate whether sharecropping arrangements are more beneficial to the landowners or not, when taken in isolation from the other involvements surrounding it.

The village headman is a landless peasant who earns his livelihood sharecropping about 200 dönüms of land consisting of several fragments. Admittedly, 200 dönüms is unusually high for a sharecropper, but being the headman of the village places him in an advantageous position. This is due to the fact that, in order to obtain fertiliser from the Agricultural Office or credit from the Agricultural Bank, the confirmation of the village headman is required. For these reasons landlords favour him in giving him lands for sharecropping, and they also use him in recruiting wage labourers. So much for the headman's relations with the landlords, let us now come to the point.

Muhtar Seydo, (23) the village headman, rents a tractor to till the land and a combine harvester for the harvest. In Kalhana 20 dönüms of land are sown with 10 ölçeks of wheat (1 ölçek of wheat equals 35 kilos of wheat). At the time of our calculations, one kilo of wheat was TL2.90, so for 20 dönüms of land 350 kilos of wheat, costing TL1,015 were sown. Rented tractors would cost TL30 per dönüm to till the land, so the total cost of tilling 20 dönüms would be TL600. A combine harvester would cost TL25 per dönüm giving a total of TL500 for 20 dönüms, and the total cost of fertiliser would be TL600, on the basis of a requirement of 300 kilos of artificial fertiliser for 20 dönüms at a cost of TL2 per kilo in 1977. The productivity of the wheat in Kalhana varies from threefold in poor soils to tenfold in good soils. Muhtar Seydo informed us that the field in question would never yield more than sevenfold, so we thought it would be appropriate to take a yield of sixfold for our example. Accordingly, the total harvest would be 2,100 kilos bringing a total return, gross, of TL6,090. Transport costs were 10 kuruş per kilo (100 kuruş make 1TL) so the total cost of transport to the state-owned buying station, Toprak Mahsulleri Ofisi (Office of Soil Products) amounts to TL210. We should also add TL200 for the cost of loading and unloading, to the total costs.

		TL
The total costs are thus:	Seed	1,015
	Tilling	600
	Harvesting	500
	Fertiliser	600
	Transport	410
	Total	3,125

From the sale of 2,100 kilos of wheat at the price of TL2.90 per kilo, a total of TL6,090 would be secured, and the net income from this is thus TL2,975 for the landlord.

In the case of sharecropping, the landlord only has to supply seed and half of the fertiliser; that means a capital outlay of TL1,315 (TL1,015 for seed, TL300 for the fertiliser). He will also have to bear half the cost of transport, i.e. TL205, so that his total expenditure will be TL1,520 and the remaining costs are borne by the tenant, i.e. a total of TL1,605. In the end, the two parties will receive half of the total selling price, i.e. TL3,045 each. The landlord's total profit is therefore TL1,525. This figure is considerably less than the TL2,975 of the previous calculation. In absolute terms the landlord seems to be on the losing end of the sharecropping arrangement. However, this is not the case if the benefits brought by the other aspects of sharecropping are taken into consideration, namely the fact that sharecropping arrangements render it possible for a large labour force to stay in the village and for the landlords to take advantage of this labour force in the several ways described previously.

It was not possible to make a cross-tabulation to show the relationship between landownership and sharecropping, as we have done in the case of Gisgis, owing to the fact that the sharecroppers in Kalhana, with the exception of two households, did not own any land at all. The amount of land owned by the two exceptional families hardly warrants their being called landowners: one of the families has four <u>dönüms</u>, while the other has ten. In Table 26 we give the names of the household heads and the amount of land sharecropped by them.

TABLE 26 SHARECROPPERS AND SHARECROPPED LAND IN KALHANA

NAME OF HOUSEHOLD HEAD	AMOUNT OF LAND SHARECROPPED	AMOUNT OF LAND OWNED
Seydi KAVAL	200 dönüms	4 dönüms
Mustafa ÇETIN	400 "	nil
Ömer CIVELEK	30 "	nil
Ramazan KAVAL	50 "	nil
Hüseyin ASLANOĞLU	70 "	10 dönüms
Halil YOLDAŞ	20 "	nil
Izzet GÜÇLÜ	100 "	nil
Fahim GÜÇLÜ	30 "	nil
Halil ERGIN	25 "	nil
Recep ERGIN	20 "	nil

Three families seem to have very large amounts of land to sharecrop. Seydi Kaval is the village headman and, because of his position, he is favoured by the landlords. As to the other two, namely Mustafa Çetin and Izzet Güçlü, the lands they sharecrop are mostly in other parts of the district, rather than in the village itself. Since they are both tractor owners (Mustafa Çetin is sole owner of his tractor, while Isset Güçlü is co-owner of his tractor, with some of his relatives), they are in a favourable position for access to the lands of absentee landowners who prefer to have their lands cultivated with agricultural machinery and modern technology, rather than by the use of draught animals and more backward methods. Most of the other sharecroppers sharecrop the lands of three big landlords in the village. Ten households work as sharecroppers in the village, that is 21.7 per cent of the total village households.

Sharecropping arrangements are not the only way to keep the labour force in the village. As we stated before, 36 families are landless in the village, 8 of which work as sharecroppers. What about the rest of the landless people? Why should they stay in the village? As we shall see in Chapter Ten, the rate of migration out of the village is very high. Those remaining in the village are both natives of the village and peasants from other areas who have settled in the village. Although some of the settlers do not have any access to land, they do at least have somewhere to shelter. They are the poor of other villages who could not survive in their home villages. To migrate to the towns would bring them greater misery and suffering. Seasonal job prospects in the village, as agricultural workers, and the closeness of the village to the town centre, are the main driving forces behind the applications of rural proletarians to the big landlords for shelter on their farms. In the village centre all the big landlords have some sort of accommodation, one or two roomed houses, built of mud bricks (kerpiç). A whole family may live in the same room with their animals. The prospect of whether or not a family will remain in the village depends upon their relations with the landlord. The head of a settler family may go to the town centre or Elazığ to seek a job, mainly in building construction, while the rest of the family work in the cotton fields.

Sharecropping in animal breeding and caretaking

Sharecropping in both animal breeding and animal caretaking has long been practised in Eastern Anatolia. Giving animals to sharecroppers for breeding and raising is practised in two different ways: either it is implemented together with land sharecropping or it is practised on its own. (The latter type is practised mainly by nomadic families who tend flocks of sheep and goats as sharecroppers).

Sharecropping agreements are of a verbal nature, based on mutual personal trust. Arrangements are made for a certain period of time, the minimum period being three years, while the maximum varies according to the arrangements made between the owner and the sharecropper. The period usually starts in September, or at the end of the lactation period, and finishes in the same month after the agreed number of years has elapsed. The terms of sharecropping arrangements vary according to the place, type of animal, age of animals and the conditions of the two parties involved. Below, we shall attempt to point out some widespread forms of sharecropping arrangements prevalent in Diyarbakır province in Southeast Anatolia. This classification, it should be pointed out, is in no sense exhaustive. (24)

(a) <u>Sharecropping in young animals</u>: Lambs, calves and kids, under one year old but no longer lactating, are given to sharecroppers to look after until their first birth-giving year. The sharecropper is entitled to use the first year's milk and, at the end of the lactation season, the whole lot, including breeding animals and their young, are divided into two equal shares. The sharecropper is also expected to bear all the costs of raising and maintaining the animals.

(b) <u>Sharecropping in sheep and goat breeding</u>: Two types of arrangements are apparent:

i) A number of animals whose ages are recorded are given to a sharecropper for three years. The sharecropper gives 8 kilos of cheese and 8 kilos of butter for every 10 sheep or goats giving a live birth. If, according to their agreement, the sharecropper is to give only butter, in that case the amount is 1 kilo of butter for each animal giving a live birth. The total sum obtained from the sale of male lambs, old animals, goat's hair and wool is shared by the owner and the sharecropper on a fifty-fifty basis. The total costs of breeding and maintaining the animals are borne by the sharecropper. At the end of the three years, the same number of animals with the same ages as those handed over to the sharecropper at the beginning is taken out from the herd by the owner, the rest are then shared equally. In this way, the number of animals given to the sharecropper as capital is a fixed number, and any decrease is out of the question. Any loss in the fixed capital has to be compensated by the sharecropper. This form of sharecropping arrangement is highly risky for the sharecropper, who is in danger of losing even his own animals in the event of disease or other natural disasters.

ii) The owner hands over a certain number of animals to the sharecropper on the condition that the sharecropper owes the owner a certain amount of money, fixed according to the existing market prices of the animals in question. As in the first type, the amount of cheese and butter to be provided by the sharecropper is stated in the verbal agreement. The money obtained from the sale of male lambs, ewes, goat's hair and wool is taken by the owner without being shared, in payment of the original debt. When the value of the capital is totally paid up, the sharecropper becomes entitled to have half the herd. Any loss or damage is met by both sides, unless it is due to the negligence of the sharecropper, and any other expenses are met by the sharecropper.

Apart from these two forms of sharecropping arrangements, it is possible to find a third, less widespread type, in which the two sides attempt a sharecropping arrangement by providing capital animals (sheep and goats) in a certain ratio. The side which undertakes the care of the animals is considered to be the sharecropper. The herd comprises a number of animals provided by the owner and by the sharecropper at a ratio of two to one. Expenses are met by the sharecropper, the owner is given <u>niv kilo</u> (half a kilo) of butter for each animal which gives a live birth. The income derived from any sales is shared equally between the two sides. At the end of the third year of the arrangement, the herd is divided into two between the two sides if they wish to end their arrangement.

<u>(c) Sharecropping in cattle raising:</u> There are several sharecropping arrangements in cattle raising, similar to the ones in

sheep raising. The following prominent types can be distinguished:

i) The cattle to be given to the sharecropper are evaluated in money terms and the sharecropper agrees to pay half of the amount evaluated as his debt. All the expenses pertaining to the upkeep and raising of the animals are borne by the sharecropper. Two to eight kilos of butter, depending on the milk productivity of the animal, is given to the owner for each animal giving a live birth. At the end of the agreed three years, capital animals and their young are shared equally between the two sides.

ii) The sharecropping arrangements take place by combining the cattle of the two sides to the agreement. As is the case in sheep sharecropping, the owner provides two cows for each one from the sharecropper, and the rest of the conditions pertaining to the agreement are the same as those mentioned for sheep sharecropping.

iii) A three year-old cow (which has previously produced young) is given to the sharecropper in the autumn. The sharecropper looks after the calves born from the capital animals until they are three years old and gives one three year-old cow for each of the capital animals to the owner, the rest being shared equally. The owner gets four kilos of butter for each cow which gives a live birth. This type of sharecropping is called _dolaşma_ (literally: going round) among the peasants.

From the above analyses, we can conclude that, despite the changes in the relations of production in which the peasants are involved over a period of time, the peasant household as a unit of production has remained the same. This is despite the fact that the relations of production in which members of a peasant household are engaged vary from different types of sharecropping arrangements to wage labour relationships. For, while the large estates try to increase productivity by using machinery, thereby releasing most of their ex-sharecroppers, the peasant household, in order to reproduce itself, is forced to seek supplementary income. This is possibly because the division of labour within the peasant household allows its male members to go out to work for a period of time: a situation that will be examined in the next chapter.

Notes to Chapter Six

1. Tökin, 1934, 176
2. Tökin, 1934, 177
3. Bozarslan, 1966, 10
4. Tökin, 1934, 178
5. Aras, 1956, 24-25
6. One timin equals 24 kilos of wheat
7. Aras, 1956, 25
8. Idem
9. Aras, 1956, 59-62
10. Bozarslan, 1966, 10
11. Zhukovsky, 1951, 128 and 131
12. Tökin, 1934, 22-23
13. Tökin, 1934, 29
14. Köylü, 1947, 120-121
15. State Institute of Statistics: Summary of Agricultural Statistics, relevant years
16. Kanbolat, 1963, 23-24
17. State Institute of Statistics: Summary of Agricultural Statistics, 1967
18. Kanbolat, 1963, 24
19. Kanbolat, 1963, 42
20. Long, 1975, 270-271 mentions a similar trend in Peru
21. See Marx, 1974, III
22. For India, see Banaji, 1977a; for Latin America, see Duncan and Rutledge, 1977, especially the articles by Kay, Martinez-Alier, Cardoso and Taussig
23. The village headman is called Muhtar Seydo (Headman Seydo) or Topal Seydo (lame Seydo) by the villagers; his real name is Seydi Kaval.
24. This classification owes much to Aras, 1956

7. Relations Of Production Within The Household

The very nature of the organisation of production in the peasant household enables the larger structure (urban capitalism) to take advantage of the surplus labour created by the extensive use of female labour. It is this female labour which makes it possible for a part of the household labour force to be released from the production which takes place in the household economy. In turn, the larger structure forces the household to organise its production in such a way that a surplus labour force will be available. At the level of the peasant household production unit, this production process materialises through a division of labour by age and sex, and through subordination of women and the young by men and elders respectively. In this chapter we shall see, in the light of our fieldwork data, how this division of labour within the household takes place in Gisgis and Kalhana.

Division of Labour Within the Household

The household is the basic economic unit in both Gisgis and Kalhana, regardless of whether it consists of a nuclear or an extended family, and agriculture constitutes the primary source of income of the majority of the households in both villages. Those families who have a piece of land to cultivate form work groups on a patrilineal basis and all the members of a family, including the women and children, either work together in the same field or work in different fields at the same time. The head of a household controls the agricultural activities as well as the land and its products. Members of the family occupy different positions in relation to one another depending on their seniority and sex, and a complex set of relations of production takes place among the members of the family. All the members are subordinate to the head of the family if the family contains only the head, his wife, his married and unmarried son(s) and unmarried daughter(s). If the family also includes retired parents, the head of the family (the oldest son) cannot have power over his parents, but he will have power over the other members of the family, including his junior married and unmarried brother(s). At the expense of being descriptive, an attempt will be made through detailed studies of several different households to outline different combinations of relations of production within the household economic units. Through the study of various households we shall aim to identify the different ways which govern the unity or fission of the families as economic units.

In the case of a family consisting of a husband, his wife and their unmarried son(s) and daughter(s), the husband is the head of the household organising the process of production. It is he who decides what is to be produced, and who will do a particular job in the field, though there is a general pattern of division of labour among the members of the family, depending on such factors as age and sex. (Division of labour by sex has varying significance according to the position of the family in the social class differentiation. We shall come to this point later, when we discuss the importance of female labour in the reproduction of the household and the significance of female labour for capitalism.)

The head of the household may send his grown-up son(s) (fourteen years old or more) to nearby towns such as Ergani, Elazığ, Diyarbakır, etc. to work in building construction. This takes two forms: either the son leaves the village on his own, taking with him his bed, consisting of a döşek (a kind of mattress made of a sack filled with old clothes and rags and flattened into the shape of a mattress), a yorgan (home-made quilt) and a yastık (pillow), and sleeps on the building site; or he joins a team of duvarcıs (masons) and ameles (unskilled labourers), organised by a duvarcı ustası (master mason), who has a verbal contract with the man for whom the building is being constructed. The owner of the construction organises the building process through the duvarcı ustası, who mediates between the ameles and the owner. The wages to be paid to the ameles are decided between the usta (master) (1) and the owner. The usta is completely free in recruiting his workers and in deciding the amount of wages each worker will receive. Generally, the usta appropriates the difference between the amount of money received from the owner of the building construction and the amount of money given to his workers. In the event of an amele questioning this practice, he would simply be dismissed, and it is not surprising to hear that in some cases the usta disappears with the wages.

Young workers, aged between 14 and 17, are usually paid the lowest wages. If the worker is young and he has come to work on his own, without joining a group, he is at the mercy of the owner of the building site. He may be made to work longer hours and be paid less, and may even be refused pay if the building site owner is dishonest and realises that the boy is without protection. This is exemplified in the case of Mehmet Çok, who had been sent by his father to work in Elazığ. He notes that:

> I could not find any work for five days. The money I had was going very fast, although I stayed in the attic of a cheap hotel with some other ameles and ate nothing but a loaf of bread a day. On the fifth day I was picked out by a man, from the amele pazarı. This is where all the ameles gather at about 5 o'clock in the morning in the hope of being picked out by someone who needs a labourer. As there are a lot of ameles seeking

work only the strong and big, and those who accept low pay are chosen. At least half of the *ameles* would wait until 9 o'clock without being chosen, and then they leave the *amele pazarı* with disappointment, thinking of their hunger. Anyway, I was picked out by a man whom I did not like at first sight. He said he would give me 35 lira for half a day's work. We took a passing lorry to go to his place, which was about 15 kilometres out of the town. I was to carry straw from a nearby field to his house, but the work was at least two days' work for one person. By 2 o'clock I asked him to pay me for my half day's work but he said I had to finish carrying the straw first, otherwise he would not pay. I had no alternative but to continue in order to get my money. Towards evening he came and said there was no hurry to finish the work, I could continue the following day. I could stay the night with him and he would pay me the following day, with some extra money if I stayed there with him. I did not like his way of smiling at me. I was very frightened - he was much bigger than me, he could do whatever he wanted to me. When I saw a passing lorry I ran like hell and waved to the driver to stop. Luckily he stopped and picked me up. I was frightened and ashamed. I did not tell anybody anything. The following day I was picked out by an *ustabaşı* (chief master-labourer) from the market place, and worked with him for about two weeks without being paid. The *ustabaşı* kept saying the building site owner had not paid him, so we had to wait. I had borrowed money from other workers, and from a grocer who comes from my village. At the end of the second week we heard that the *ustabaşı* had been paid by the building site owner but he had already disappeared with the wages of six workers by the time we heard of the payment.

We have stated that the head of the family may send his son(s) to town to work in order to earn supplementary income. Of course, his decision to send a son to work outside the village is dependent on the age of the son and the labour requirements of the family. If the sons are not grown enough to be sent out to work, and if the wife can cope with the farm work with the help of the children, then the head of the family may go out of the village seeking work himself.

Sons, if they are not sent to school to become teachers or imams (Islamic clergy who lead public worship), in most cases remain subservient to their father until his death or retirement. If the family does not have any land, or only very little land, the father may release his son, in order for him to establish a separate household. Otherwise, the father would direct his sons and control the products of their labour, as well as any payment they might receive from non-agricultural work. Marriage, which necessitates a payment in cash or in kind to the father of the girl, and military service both play an important role in the dependence of sons on their fathers. The başlık money (the sum paid to a bride's father by the bridegroom's family) varies between TL1,000 and TL100,000, and so it is impossible for a young man, the product of whose labour has been controlled by his father, to break his relations with his father if he wants to get married. Furthermore, two years of compulsory military service between the ages of eighteen and twenty consolidate the dependence of the son on the father. First, soldiers are not paid, and have to be supplied with some money by their families; second, when they finish their military service they join the army of unemployed, so the very limited job prospects force them to return to their villages at the end of their two years of military service. Had they been able to work in an income-bearing job for two years, the village youth might have been able to save some money towards their marriage başlık payment.

Married sons generally stay within their fathers' household if they want to have access to land. When they decide to establish a separate household, they have to find a way of sustaining their family. However, there are cases where the father lets his sons, or some of his sons, establish separate nuclear families, and gives them a piece of land to cultivate on their own account, but in most cases the members of the sons' families would work for the grandfather in peak seasons.

In the event of the father's death, the eldest son takes over his function, and all the other members of the family work for him, and he also determines the labour process. The extended family may split into nuclear family units if some of the brothers think that they contribute more to the family's subsistence than the others. They may ask to split, but the final decision is taken by the senior male member of the family. The split becomes easier if the senior brother has fewer children than his brothers, and thinks he produces a surplus which is then consumed by the children of his younger brothers. In the case of the father's retirement, the eldest son takes over his function, and organises the process of the production with his father's consent. The father's consent, in such cases, is especially vital in the event of the extended family splitting into nuclear families.

From the above discussion, which was based on fieldwork data, we can conclude that, in the peasant households of Southeast Anatolia, heads of the households enjoy almost complete dominance over the other members of the family. This applies to matters of production, products, disposal of the products, distribution of the products, organisation of work, etc. It should be pointed out, however, that the male-oriented nature of the above discussion does not in any way imply that women are not an important constituent part of the family labour process. On the contrary, as will be shown below, female labour is central to the whole process; central, in that it permits male labour to engage in seasonal migration and thereby provide the household economy with the additional income necessary for its reproduction. In other words, despite the importance of the male in the decision-making process of the household's reproduction, it is female labour which constitutes the basis.

Female Labour in Gisgis and Kalhana

In the majority of micro-level studies of Turkey, we come across a common feature: the underestimation or total neglect of the importance of women's labour for the subsistence of the family. In some of the village studies, like that by Güçbilmez (2) for example, the division of labour by sex is completely left out, while in others the labour contribution of women is reduced to housework and is considered marginally important in terms of the family's subsistence. (3) Moreover, none of the micro-level studies has yet tried to relate the importance of women's participation in agriculture to the development of capitalism and to the accumulation of capital in rural Turkey. Rural communities in these studies are taken mainly as separate isolated units, and the nature of the relations of production within village communities and their relations with wider economies (national, and world capitalist economies) are simply excluded from the analysis. The analysis would be more meaningful if it were located in a wider context and given a wider perspective.

While capitalist development in agriculture proletarianises the peasantry, the insufficient development of industry in underdeveloped countries does not allow the proletarianised peasantry to be absorbed within the industrial sector. The combination of the lack of access to land, high population growth and limited employment opportunities in industry has a stimulating effect on the semi-proletarianisation of the peasantry.

Meillassoux argues that, in underdeveloped countries, rural communities are being taken advantage of by capitalism, which does not assume its social security function. Capitalism uses the rural communities as a source of cheap labour:

> ... once people are compelled to undertake wage earning activities in order to pay taxes, gain some cash, if the capitalist system does not provide adequately for old age pensions, sick leave and unemployment compensations they have to rely on another comprehensive socio-economic organisation to fulfil these vital needs. Consequently, preservation of the relations with the village and the familial continuity is an absolute requirement for the wage earners ... (4)

It is the 'super-exploitation' of the labourer and his kin group that accounts for the cheap labour in underdeveloped countries. (5) Since land in Turkish rural communities is controlled by individual families rather than by whole communities the role of the reproduction of labour power falls upon families. Women have a very important part to play in the reproduction of the labour force, and of the subsistence foodstuffs for the family's consumption. In Turkish rural areas it is generally the male members of the family who leave the farm to earn additional income, and it is the women who stay behind in the village to look after the children and do the bulk of the agricultural work. This division of labour by sex contributes to capital accumulation by lowering the wages the capitalists have to pay, and helps sustain the reproduction of the household unit.

In what follows, an attempt will be made to analyse the relationship between the agricultural division of labour by sex and the differentiation of the peasantry in Kalhana and Gisgis villages. In doing so, we shall try to show that rural seasonal labour migration is very much related to the degree of the women's participation in agricultural production. Nevertheless, prior to proceeding with this discussion it is necessary to outline the method adopted in collecting and classifying the data.

In the questionnaire used during our fieldwork, the majority of the answers given by the heads of households to the question 'What is your wife's occupation?' was evhanımı (housewife). Only 1.5 per cent of the adult women in the village of Gisgis and 1.4 per cent in Kalhana were considered rençber (farmer). It became clear that the uniformity of the answer 'housewife' stemmed from the way the question was posed. Although rural women have dual occupations, as rural workers (whether paid or not) and as housewives and mothers, and although their work contributes to the sustenance of the family, in a patriarchal society such as that of Gisgis and Kalhana, their prime responsibility is considered to be towards their home and children.

A different methodological approach was adopted in our

detailed census headed 'Operation Sheets'. The first of the operations sheets, the 'Field Operation Sheet', was used to collect data on labour performed in different fields cultivated by the household. This sheet was organised in such a way as to enable us to record the type of work done by each member of the household and by each non-household labourer, be he wage labourer or exchange labourer, and it also enabled us to see the amount of time spent by each participant in the field. Twenty-two households were studied in detail, for a period of six months. They were visited once a week for the purposes of a detailed survey, as well as being observed daily. Of course, the difficulties arising from the distances between the fields of the families made it impossible to visit each family every day. However, each family was generally observed in the field once every three or four days for a period of two to three hours. In addition, each family was interviewed in depth.

Furthermore, a stratified sample was used for farm analysis and villagers were stratified according to the amount of land they owned and the positions they had in the production process. Although no strict delimitation is possible, a crude grouping served our purposes. The <u>first</u> groups consisted of landless families and those with land up to 10 <u>dönüms</u>. These people are not only unable to make a living from the land they farm, but also earn the main part of their income through wage labour. The <u>second</u> group consisted of those who had 10 to 25 <u>dönüms</u> of land. These may be called small farmers, who derive their living mainly from the family farm, whether market-oriented or not. Even in this group, however, and irrespective of whether any other members of the family are working for wages or not, the heads of the households have to find additional sources of income outside the farm, either in agricultural work or in non-farming activities; for instance, as coffee-house owners, pedlars or even as mine-workers. The <u>third</u> group may be called small independent farmers who have 26 to 100 <u>dönüms</u> of land. This delimitation may not hold true for Gisgis, where the land is rocky in some places. In this category the heads of households are completely engaged in farming operations on their own farms.

In many cases, and especially in Kalhana, during the summer, temporary employment of paid labour becomes necessary. This does not mean that other members of the family do not seek work as wage labourers on others' lands at times when there is not enough work for everyone on the family holding. The fourth group, who may be called medium farmers, have 100 to 500 dönüms of land and employ hired labour in the months of greatest activity. Wage labour by members of the family is less frequent in this group. The fifth group, which does not exist in Gisgis, but which dominates agriculture in Kalhana, is the large farmers who have more than 500 dönüms of land. Family labour is not used on these farms; the land is worked by agricultural wage-earners, sharecroppers and, to a limited extent, by corvée labour.

Since the majority of lands in the last category are utilised by the owners through the employment of wage labourers, we may call these holdings capitalist holdings. Furthermore, since the lands belonging to these capitalist landlords and given to sharecroppers are cultivated by peasant families - including landless peasants - they are analysed under the first two groups. It would not, therefore, be too misleading if we were to leave out the last group from our analysis concerning the role of peasant women in the accumulation of capital in general.

Although we have defined four groups (excluding capitalist farming) in terms of landownership and the role played in the production process, in reality it is difficult to draw a clear-cut line between the groups. Furthermore, it is possible to reduce our four-fold classification into a three-fold classification: poor peasants, middle peasants and rich peasants. In that case we could consider the first two groups together, that is, under the category of poor peasants, with the third group coming under the middle peasant category and the fourth group as rich peasants. As we stated earlier, our simplistic classification cannot overcome the difficulties involved in defining the groups and determining the families to be subsumed into these groups. However, in accordance with our crude classification, twenty-two families were studied in detail. The distribution of households was as shown in Table 27.

TABLE 27 NUMBER OF SELECTED HOUSEHOLDS BY LAND OWNED

GROUP	NUMBER OF DÖNÜMS	NUMBER OF HOUSEHOLDS SELECTED GISGIS	KALHANA
1	0-10	4	3
2	11-25	4	0
3	26-50	2	1
4	51-100	2	1
5	101-500	2	1
6	500+	-	2
Total		14	8

Our purpose in this section, however, is to try to observe a tendency in the accumulation of capital towards the utilisation of rural female labour. A few detailed studies, therefore, will be indicative of the general process of capital accumulation and of the contribution of women's labour to this process.

CASE STUDY I: Efrahim Çatal was born in Gisgis in 1926, one of three children of a poor peasant, Apo Çatal, who had 20 *dönüms* of land. As a small boy, Efrahim worked as a shepherd, grazing the family's two sheep and one goat, and he also helped his parents in the field from the age of 10, watering the vegetables and carrying water from the fountain to the field or to the house. When he was 16 he was married to his uncle's daughter, Kezzo, who was then 19. The young couple lived with Efrahim's parents until he was called to do his national service at the age of 20. His wife and first child, Ibrahim, stayed with his parents while he completed his two years military service. When he returned, he worked on his father's land for four more years and, in the meantime, his second and third children were born. He realised that it was becoming more and more difficult for them to earn their living from his father's 20 *dönüms* of land.

Although in some years they were able to find a small plot of land to sharecrop, it was still very difficult to survive on the amount of land they were able to cultivate. The size of the family had doubled in ten years, with his wife and children, and later his brother's wife joining them too. He and his brother Hasan worked as labourers in building construction in Ergani for one or two months a year; however they could not save much, since they had to support themselves in the town.

With encouragement from his wife, Efrahim dared to ask his father's permission to establish his own household, and permission was granted without any fuss. Efrahim was hoping that he could find a plot of land to sharecrop but he could not. As a last resort, he applied to Hasip Ağa, the owner of Zengetil village in Ergani district, who had about 7,000 dönüms of land. Hasip Ağa housed the family, let them sharecrop 6 dönüms of irrigated land, where they grew vegetables, and gave them 30 ölçeks of wheat (1 ölçek equals 35 to 36 kilos of wheat, so about 1,080 kilos in total), in return for the services of the whole family. They were totally at the disposal of Hasip Ağa, who made it seem that by accepting Efrahim and his family into the village he was doing them a great favour. Given the lack of work opportunities existing in the area, the big landlords were able to impose their will upon the peasants. The ağas could even go as far as to use their hizmetkars (service men, like Efrahim) as a security force against their enemies. Owing to land disputes and other social causes, there were always clashes between powerful ağas, who could use their peasants (most of them being indebted to them) as security forces. Efrahim said: 'In order to secure your future you have to comply with the orders of the ağa; if you don't want to see your children in misery, dying of hunger, you have to say "Evet Ağam" (Yes, my master).'

Efrahim and his family stayed in Zengetil for five years and then left for Gisgis, following the death of his father. As the oldest son he took over control of the land but, after a few years, his feeling that he was mainly working to provide subsistence for his brother's children made him decide to divide the land between himself and his two brothers. Ever since then he has worked his own land (almost 7 dönüms) as well as share-cropping some land. At the age of 30 he lost his wife because of an unknown illness (apparently cancer) and married his present wife, Emine, who was 17 at the time of her marriage. For the last 10 years Efrahim has been going to Adana to work in the cotton fields as a seasonal wage labourer, where he would work for three to three and a half months in the cotton fields as a hoer and cotton picker.

The contact between the capitalist farmers of the Çukurova region and the seasonal workers is made through the elçis, the local agents of the farmers. Each year, capitalist farmers, who are also named ağa, but whose relations with their workers are entirely different from those in Southeast Anatolia, send telegrams to their elçis in the region. The elçis' function is to contact the workers who are willing to go to the Çukurova region. The workers are transported in big lorries, loaded to their full capacity with the workers and sometimes their wives and children, as well as their so-called beds and necessary cooking equipment. Each lorry is loaded with at least 30 to 40 workers, and the cost of transport is met by each worker. After ten to twelve hours of exhausting travel, the lorry arrives at Adana.

The workers stay in tents for the whole period they work there. There is no written contract between the workers and the employers, and in fact the workers and employers never come face to face. Their relations are mediated by the elçis. There is no social security, nor health facilities for the workers, most of whom suffer from malaria, which is endemic in the area. Those workers who are ill or not fit enough to work lose their job. Otherwise they work from 6 o'clock in the morning until 6 o'clock in the evening, with one hour's break at lunch time. Food has to be provided by the workers themselves. The eleven hours of work was remunerated by TL63 in 1977 (TL33 was equivalent to £1 sterling at that time, so they were paid the equivalent of £1.90 per day). This was the rate for hoeing, whereas for cotton pickers a piece-work system was in operation. For one kilo of cotton picked, workers were paid one lira. According to Efrahim, a strong worker could only pick an average of about 60 kilos of cotton in a twelve-hour day.

Efrahim's family in 1977 consisted of six people: himself, his wife and four children - his first son from Emine, Recep (17 years old), his elder daughter Nuriye (14), his younger daughter Leyla (12) and his younger son Ahmet (9). The other children from his first wife had already married and left home by the time of the interview. For the past couple of years, Efrahim had taken his son Recep with him to Adana to work as a cotton picker. He said: 'I am getting old. If it were not for Recep I could not have earned enough money last year'. Although he was only 51 he looked much older, and very weak. Nevertheless, he was still able to work, even if not as productively as in the past.

In 1977, Efrahim owned 7 <u>dönüms</u> of land and sharecropped 15 <u>dönüms</u>. The owner of the sharecropped land was a school teacher who had inherited the land from his father and did not have the time or the intention to cultivate it himself. The family grew wheat, lentils and vegetables, mainly tomatoes, green peppers, aubergines, cucumbers and onions. On the sharecropped land, wheat was planted and 5 <u>dönüms</u> of the family land was used for lentils. The rest was reserved for growing vegetables. The family owned one ox, one sheep, one donkey and several chickens.

Since Efrahim owns only one ox, he has to make an arrangement with another villager who also has an ox, in order to be able to make up a pair to till the land. As soon as he returns from the Çukurova region in mid-September, he tills the land with an ox-drawn wooden plough. It takes him about 12 to 15 days to prepare the 20 <u>dönüms</u> of land for planting, with the help of his son Recep. The actual sowing of the wheat and lentils takes five days. While male members of the household are engaged in tilling and cultivating, the females would do the weeding by hand. Usually the planting of wheat and lentils is completed by the end of November. In addition to the usual, everyday housework tasks, female members are also responsible for collecting wood, bringing meals to the field workers, and fetching water from the village fountain.

During the cold and snowy winter, which lasts from December until the middle of March, male members of the family spend their time in one of the two village coffee houses, drinking tea, smoking cigarettes and playing cards. Efrahim does not participate in the latter activity, for he does not like to play cards, but his son spends whole days playing cards or backgammon. Since playing cards in front of one's father is considered disrespectful, Recep and Efrahim are careful not to frequent the same coffee house in the village.

In contrast to the adult male members of the family, adult female members of the family are always busy. Their day starts with feeding the animals, preparing breakfast (generally lentil soup with bread, or tea and bread), fetching _tezek_ (dried animal dung, prepared in the summer for use as fuel for cooking and heating), and lighting the fire. The day is filled with activities such as making bread, knitting socks and jumpers, mending clothes, cooking lunch and dinner, washing up, fetching water from the fountain in the middle of the village and so on. Most of the peasant women are engaged in these daily activities all through the year, except for some special activities necessitated by different seasons, such as heating the house in the winter.

The second half of March and the first half of April is the season for planting vegetables. Vegetable growing is a hard task, requiring constant attention. It takes 6 to 7 days for Efrahim and his son Recep to hoe two _dönüms_ of land. The weeding is done by the women, by hand. The field is divided in _mişers_ (areas of land 3 x 5 metres), and a space of about one metre is left between _mişers_ so that it is possible to walk between them. Also, very shallow canals are made between the _mişers_ to regulate the irrigation. One corner of each _mişer_ has an exit into the canal, which can be opened, or blocked with shovelfuls of mud. Some _mişers_ are not planted initially, instead they are reserved for the replanting of the seedlings pulled up from the previously planted _mişers_ in the process of thinning. This thinning out and replanting of the seedlings is done by hand by women (wife and daughters). The irrigation of the vegetable plots, daily, or on alternate days, is carried out by women and/or young boys. Once the irrigation canals have been opened by the men, and the *mişers* are organised in such a way, as shown below, it is a simple although time-consuming, task to water the plants. The simple irrigation system designed and implemented by Efrahim is shown in Figure 6.

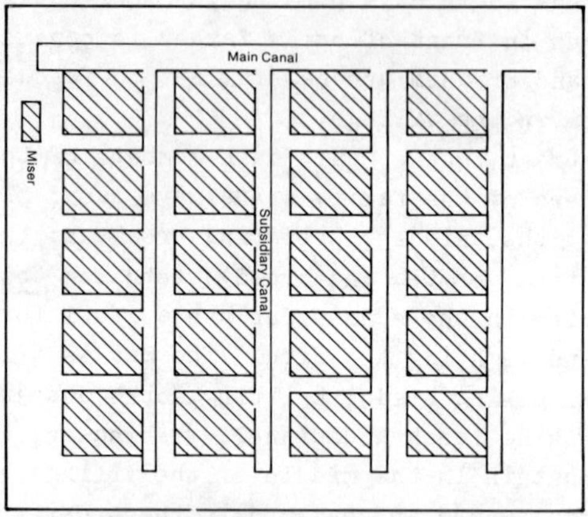

Fig. 6. Efrahim's irrigation system

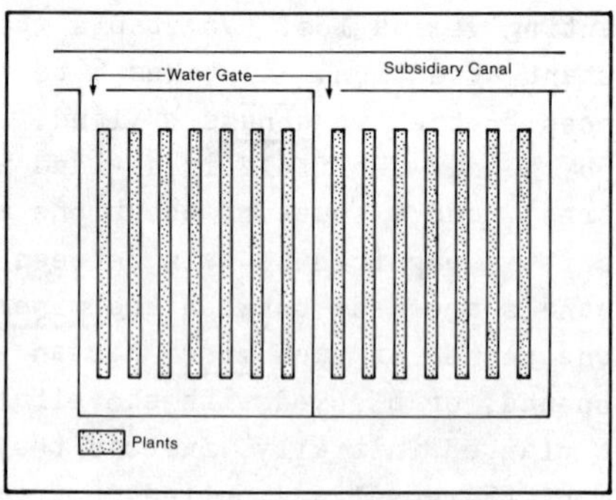

Fig. 7. Design of a *Mişer*

The water is collected in a simple small pond, built in front of a natural water source. The pond is filled overnight, otherwise the amount of water from the tiny stream would not be sufficient for irrigation needs. The water in the pond is allowed through a vertical L-shaped hole, the upright section of which is blocked with a long thick piece of wood which can be held out of the water. The amount of water allowed through is then regulated by pulling the piece of wood upwards. If the vegetables are to be watered,all the other exits to the other fields have to be blocked with mud. The main canal is about 20 centimetres deep and 30 centimetres wide. As we mentioned before, each <u>mişer</u> has an entrance for water, and is designed in such a way as to enable the water to reach all the plants by running along all the small subsidiary canals which follow the line of the long sides of the oblong <u>mişers</u>. Vegetables are planted in the middle of the distance between these small canals, about 20 to 25 centimetres apart. Generally tomatoes, peppers and aubergine plants are planted between canals, on ridges. The design of each <u>mişer</u> in Efrahim's vegetable garden was as shown in Figure 7 (as it was for the general pattern in the village too).

Irrigation is carried out by women, sometimes helped by young male children. Since water is very precious, the irrigator has to be very careful not to let water overflow the canals and <u>mişers</u>. This is done by regulating the amount of water released from the pond. Irrigating the vegetables took Efrahim's wife at least 3 to 4 hours a day. Irrigation is usually done between 3 o'clock and 7 o'clock in the afternoon/evening and, towards the completion of the task, Efrahim's wife would rush home to prepare the evening meal, leaving the final responsibility of irrigation to Nuriye.

In mid-April, having prepared the vegetable garden and sown the vegetable seeds, Efrahim leaves for Adana, with Recep too during the past two years, to work in the cotton fields as a hoer. The hoeing season in the Çukurova region lasts from April until mid-June, or the end of June in some places. While Efrahim and his son are away, all the productive activities of his household, as well as housework, fall upon the female members of the family, though they may be assisted by their young son (9 years old) in tasks such as fetching water from the fountain, or attending to the transportation of vegetables from the field to the house on a donkey. Once the vegetables start to mature, at the end of May and beginning of June, Emine is faced with two more tasks: picking the ready vegetables and marketing them. Vegetable picking is done in the late afternoon and early evening, between 6 and 8.30 p.m. Since it is very hot during the day, an early picking would cause the vegetables to rot. Collected tomatoes are put into big wooden boxes, which weigh about 20 to 30 kilos each when full. Peppers and aubergines are put into large sacks. Wild purslane, which grows around the fields, is put on the bottom and on the top of the sacks to protect the vegetables. Boxed and sacked vegetables are then transported to the house on donkeys, late in the evening. The following day Emine and the children would get up at about 4.30 a.m. to transport the previous day's collected vegetables to the köy meydanı (the centre of the village) to load onto the only lorry which transports both vegetables and passengers between the village and Ergani town.

In the summer, each morning at about 5 o'clock, those peasants who want to sell some vegetables, grain, or cheese etc. in the town, would load their goods onto the lorry and board the lorry themselves. The marketing of the vegetables is mainly done by men, who prefer to go to the town, rather than staying in the village. However, during the summer, quite a lot of the male labour force is away from the village, thus making it necessary for the women to take the goods to the market. Having sold the vegetables to a grocer, Emine buys the things necessary for the household, such as salt, soap, margarine, paraffin, etc. and returns home, either on the lorry or by dolmuş (a minibus which runs between certain fixed destinations, and for which the fare is shared between the passengers). So we can add marketing and shopping to the other activities performed by women.

All through the summer, at least one of the female members of the family spends one or two hours of her time each day in collecting mayıs (fresh cow dung). The collection of mayıs is done by hand. Bucketfuls of dung are carried home and there moulded into flat round shapes to be left in the sun to dry, ready for future use as fuel. The shaping of the mayıs is also done exclusively by female members of the family, mostly by daughters or daughters-in-law.

The cutting of grass and weeds on the hills around the village is also done by women, between the end of May and the end of June. Sickles are used to cut the weeds, which are then collected in heaps. Emine and her two daughters, Nuriye and Leyla, and the youngest son Ahmet, would leave home at about 5 a.m. to go to the hills to cut animal fodder. The cutting continues until about 1 p.m. when it becomes too hot to continue, and then restarts at 3 p.m. The long grass, when cut, is twisted into long pieces which are then plaited by two people working together. The plaiting of grass for drying is always done in pairs. At about 4.30 p.m. Emine would return home with the first donkey-load of fodder, taking Ahmet with her. It is Ahmet's job to transport the fodder from the place where it is being collected to the house. In the meantime, his mother would be preparing the dinner and doing other housework. When it has dried in the sun, the fodder is stored in the ground floor of the house, which is used as a barn for the animals.

July and the first half of August is harvest time for wheat and lentils. In some years, at the beginning of July, Efrahim comes back from the Çukurova region to help in the harvest, if they are sharecropping some land in that year. Otherwise he stays in the Çukurova region, seeking temporary employment as an amele (working in building construction) for there is no demand for hoers after June. During our fieldwork, in 1977, he had returned from the Çukurova region.

Efrahim's family reap their wheat and lentils using scythes and sickles. Combine harvesters are not available in the villages where there is not big landownership. The owners of the combine harvesters come from Yozgat and Adana to lease their machines to the big landlords. Using these machines on small plots necessitates moving the machine from one field to another which takes up a lot of time, something the owners of the machines are not very keen on.

While Efrahim and Recep reap the wheat with scythes, Emine and sometimes Nuriye join them with sickles, which are much easier to use, but less efficient in terms of the amount that can be cut at one stroke. The younger children, Leyla and Ahmet, either collect mayıs or çalıçırpı (literally: sticks and thorns) at this time, or they may be sent to the vegetable garden to look after the garden or to weed or collect some vegetables.

It takes about 8 to 10 days for Efrahim and his family to reap 15 dönüms of wheat and 5 dönüms of lentils. The threshing of wheat used to be done simply by renting a threshing machine, which would be brought by its owner to the back of the village at a certain date, for a few days. All those who wanted to have their wheat threshed would bring their wheat to the field where the patoz (thresher) was situated. There were two types of threshing machine in the area at the time the fieldwork was carried out. One type did not separate the wheat from the straw, it would only grind the wheat stalks, and the wheat would come out at the other end mixed with straw. The other type of machine would separate the straw from the wheat. Use of the first type of machine necessitates winnowing the wheat. Passing the wheat through the threshing machine requires quite a number of people working to ensure that the process continues without stoppages until the whole lot is finished. At least six people are needed to bring the wheat and feed it into the machine regularly and to collect the separated wheat, etc. Relatives, neighbours and friends all give each other their mutual assistance when they have wheat to thresh in a patoz. This mutual aid is called imece.

However, the use of the patoz in most of the rural areas which depended on renting them declined drastically in the summer of 1977, owing to the fact that petrol prices rose 100 per cent after the government stopped subsidising petrol. The increase in the price of petrol was reflected in the prices of everything. Of course, the price of renting agricultural machinery took its share as well. Prior to the increase in the price of petrol, the rent for the use of a patoz for an hour was

TL125 in Ergani, and this went up to TL300 per hour after the petrol price rise. Since the floor prices fixed for food products by the government were not increased at the same rate as the prices for other items, including petrol, the peasants producing mainly for home consumption were not able to meet the requirements of the price increase. They immediately reverted to using old traditional methods in agriculture, which did not cost them anything.

Efrahim was one of those who could not afford to rent a threshing machine; as he said: 'Do you think I do not know it is much easier to have your wheat threshed in a patoz? Of course I do. Unfortunately I am helpless, I cannot afford it. Never mind, I have plenty of time; God does not like idleness.' He implied that wheat-threshing is a time-consuming operation. Once reaped, the wheat has to be collected by hand. The threshing floor is prepared by women. A flat part of the field is chosen and a round area of 10 metres diameter is cleared and wetted with water, then flattened with a heavy cylindrical roller and left to dry. The wheat is transported to the threshing floor by donkey. The bundles of wheat are prepared by female labour and loaded onto donkeys by male labour. Bundling and loading are not exclusively female or male tasks respectively, as males and females may help each other in these activities. The wheat is gathered into the middle of the threshing floor and separated by means of a döven (flint-studded threshing sledge), drawn by a pair of oxen. Generally, young boys would keep an eye on this operation, which is play-like for them, as they sit on the threshing sledge as it is pulled by the oxen.

Winnowing is carried out by males, using wooden forks. While Efrahim and Recep take the winnowing in turns, Emine and her daughters sieve the course bits which gather at the edge of the winnowing heap. When the wheat has been totally separated from the straw the landlord is invited to the field to attend the measurement of the crop. In Efrahim's case, one of the relatives of the landlord represents the landlord, who is an absentee. The wheat is measured by a kind of bucket, called a çap, which holds about 9 kilos of wheat (4 çaps equal 1 ölçek). The measured wheat is poured into sacks by women and transported to the house.

Once the crop has been harvested, the male members of the family are released from all sorts of duties. Efrahim and Recep spend their time in coffee houses until mid-September, when they set off for the Çukurova again, for the cotton picking, which lasts for three to four weeks. The end of the harvest signals the start of new types of work for the female members of the family, as they are now engaged in preparing foodstuffs for the winter.

Wheat and foodstuffs made from wheat constitute the main diet of peasant families in Southeast Anatolia. The preparation of foodstuffs made from wheat falls completely upon the women in rural areas. The foodstuffs include _bulgur_ (cracked wheat), _doğme_ (boiled and pounded wheat), _cücük_ or _yarma_ (fine cracked wheat, used for making soup and various kinds of cracked wheat rissoles, _bulgur köftesi_). We shall describe the preparation of the above-mentioned foodstuffs as observed in Efrahim's family, although the same process was observed as it was carried out by many women in both villages. However, I believe that by confining our description to one case we shall be able to indicate satisfactorily the general trend that women are the ones who are responsible for the bulk of the production and processing of the foodstuffs consumed by the peasant family.

Efrahim's wife, Emine, and their daughter, Nuriye, fill sacks with the required amount of wheat and load them onto the donkey to take to the main fountain, situated in the centre of the village. The wheat is washed there in _leğens_ (huge bowls), then boiled and spread on large cloths to dry in the sun for a few days. When the boiled wheat reaches a certain dryness it is pounded in a _soku_ (large stone mortar) which takes about 5 to 6 kilos of wheat at a time, using a _tokmak_ (big wooden mallet). The boiled and pounded wheat is then winnowed to separate the chaff from the grains, which is called _dövme_ at this stage, and becomes _bulgur_ when it has been cracked in a special hand operated wheat-cracking machine. Coarsely cracked wheat is separated from finely cracked wheat, which is called _cücük_ or _yarma_, by sieving.

Preparation of the dried vegetables, pickles and tomato

paste are other processes carried out by women in readiness for winter use. In almost every house in both villages aubergines (their middles scooped out) and green peppers are dried in the sun, ready for use in preparing dolma (stuffed peppers and aubergines).

So far, we have described the activities in which rural women play an important part in the reproduction cycle of peasant and semi-proletarian families, by taking Efrahim's family as an example. This has indicated that women do play a very important and decisive role in the reproduction of the peasant and semi-peasant families who provide a significant part of the seasonal labour force used by rural and urban capitalism.

Our first family studied here in detail was included under the grouping 'poor peasants'. We have shown that it is the women who, by shouldering the bulk of the productive work (production of the foodstuffs as well as the labour force), made it possible for some of the male members of the household to go out of the village for a period of time, to seek additional income, in order to assure the reproduction of the household. If it were not for the women's work in the village the whole reproduction process of the household would be distorted, and with the low wages obtained in return for seasonal work the workforce could not continue to function as it does at present. We shall now have a look at another farm, which may be subsumed under the category 'small independent farm', in order to see the extent and significance of women's labour in the reproduction of the household in this category.

CASE STUDY II: Mehmet Şerif Ece's holding consisted of 70 dönüms of unirrigated and 20 dönüms of irrigated land in Gisgis, and he owned 70 dönüms of the total 90 dönüms he was using in 1977. The other 20 dönüms which he sharecropped belonged to his brother. There were two cows, a pair of oxen, a pair of unweaned calves, one lamb and three donkeys on his holding. As agricultural tools he owned one plough, seven sickles, one scythe, three spades, three hoes and a winnowing fork.

He inherited 10 dönüms and bought the other 60 dönüms with

the money he saved when he was working as a stoner, breaking rocks in the village environs and carving huge stones into cubic pieces, then selling them to be used in building construction. Today he does not work as a stoner because it is a very hard job, requiring great physical strength. He now derives most of his income from agriculture, but also from buying and selling livestock.

Out of 90 dönüms total land, 15 dönüms of irrigated land were reserved for kavak (poplar wood, used in building construction), which constitutes one of the sources of cash for Mehmet Şerif's household, and 5 dönüms of irrigated land were planted with vegetables. As to the 70 dönüms of unirrigated land, the division was as follows: 15 dönüms under wheat cultivation, 15 dönüms under lentils, 5 dönüms of küşne (a kind of vetch, used as animal fodder), 5 dönüms of barley (also used as animal fodder), and the remaining 30 dönüms were left fallow.

Mehmet Şerif's family consisted of eight people: himself (52 years of age), his wife Perihan (42), his sons Zeki (23), Ömer (17), Ramazan (12), Hasan (10), his daughter Hatice (7) and his daughter-in-law, (Zeki's wife) Hüsna (20). We shall try to indicate briefly what sort of activities the women members of the family perform as their part in the division of labour within the household economy. In order not to be repetitive, we shall not give all the details of the tasks performed by members of this family where they are more or less the same as those performe[d] in Efrahim's family. Instead we shall give a list of tasks performed mainly by women, or participated in to a great extent by women (see Table 28).

Mehmet Şerif sends his two older sons to surrounding towns (Ergani, Diyarbakır, Elazığ) to work as ameles in building construction, to earn some cash in order to meet the family's needs, and to save some money. In this way he was able to save enough money to build a small house at the back of his house, which he usually rented to the commander of the village gendarmerie, and it was here that we stayed during the fieldwork, since the sergeant acting as commander of the village gendarmerie at the time had not brought his family to the village and so stayed in the gendarmerie headquarters. Once the ploughing of the land is completed, Zeki and Ömer set off for the towns in search of work. Although they would come home once a month or so for a few days, they stay in town for a total of about 5 to 7 months a year, generally between April and October. However, they may stay in the village for about a month between April and October if they cannot find work in the towns, or if they are desperately needed in the village to help the family in agricultural work. For instance, when a number of poplar trees are to be sold, at least one of the boys is asked to return to the village in order to fell the trees. The bark of the poplar tree has to be peeled off in order to prepare it for use in building construction. This task is done mainly by women and children, using sickles. Although the work is not very difficult, it is very time-consuming; it may take one person a couple of hours to remove the bark from one tree.

All the housework is done by the daughter-in-law. This includes milking the cows, feeding the animals (sometimes), cooking the meals and the bread, washing the clothes, washing up, collecting firewood and fetching water from the fountain (sometimes this is done by Ramazan or Hasan, the two youngest sons). The mother-in-law mainly directs the daughter-in-law in carrying out the housework. There is a great deal of co-operation between Perihan and Hüsna, her daughter-in-law, in the preparation of foodstuffs for the winter.

In Mehmet Şerif's household, as in most of the households in the village, ploughing the land is entirely a male task, but in harvesting male and female members of the household take a more or less equal share in the work. In secondary jobs related to the harvest, such as preparing the threshing floor, sacking the grain, transporting the hay and grain, storing the hay and straw etc., the women do more work than the men.

In Table 28 we show the particular tasks performed by the different members of the family. The table is divided into four parts, to enable us to see if a particular task is carried out exclusively or partly by the male, female or child members of the household. In the first part of the table all the tasks done exclusively by women are listed. In the second part, the tasks done by women with the co-operation of other members of the family are listed. Of course it is very difficult to determine to what extent a task is done by one individual or another, so this list should be borne in mind when considering the third and fourth lists relating to tasks performed by men and by the children respectively. The aim of the second grouping is to indicate the participation of women in the tasks listed, and also to show who else might contribute his labour. This is indicated by the letter 'M' for adult male, 'C' for child under 14 years of age after each task listed, to show their participation with women in each task. Where 'M' and 'C' are indicated together, this denotes the participation of either male, or child, or male and child labour in this particular task, as well as female labour. On any particular single occasion, such a task may be carried out by only women, or only men, or only children, or by a combination of any two, or all three of these. The list is in no way exhaustive.

TABLE 28 TASKS PERFORMED BY THE MEMBERS OF A HOUSEHOLD

1 TASKS DONE EXCLUSIVELY BY WOMEN	2 TASKS PERFORMED BY WOMEN AND OTHERS (M=Male, C=Children)	
Looking after and nursing children	Reaping crops	M
Washing clothes etc.	Transporting crops to the threshing floor	MC
Washing up	Collecting firewood	C
Washing and spinning wool	Fetching water	C
Knitting socks and jumpers	Collecting animal dung	C
Mending clothes	Shaping and drying animal dung	C
Cleaning the house	Cutting hay	C
Whitewashing the walls (once a year)	Plaiting hay	C
Making bread	Transporting hay to the village to dry	C
Cooking meals	Going to the mill	M
Milking the cows		

TABLE 28 (Continued)

Making yoghurt
Making white cheese
Making butter
Heating the house
Vegetable planting
Watering vegetables
Vegetable picking
Thinning vegetable seedlings
Washing wheat
Boiling wheat for *bulgur*
Sewing the sacks
Dispersing wheat on sheets to dry
Collecting up the dried wheat
Hollowing out peppers and aubergines
Stringing up peppers and aubergines to dry
Pickling vegetables
Making or repairing earth oven (*tandır*)
Making *pekmez* (boiled grape juice)

Shopping	M
Marketing vegetables and dairy produce	M
Weeding	MC
Pounding wheat	M
Measuring grain harvest	M
Sacking grain harvest	M
Threshing grain harvest	MC
Winnowing	M
Loading grain harvest onto donkeys	M
Unloading grain harvest from donkeys	M
Removing the bark from poplar trees	MC

3 TASKS DONE EXCLUSIVELY BY MEN

Tilling the land
Cutting wood (for firewood)
Cutting poplar trees
Doing building repairs
Tool repairs
Carrying heavy loads
Marketing surplus grain
Marketing poplar trees

4 TASKS DONE EXCLUSIVELY BY CHILDREN UNDER 14

Watching to make sure that birds and animals do not harm the vegetables and crops
Grazing the animals
Taking meals to workers in the fields and bringing back the dirty dishes
Looking after younger sisters and brothers

TABLE 28 (Continued)

Work outside the village
Nightwatch in the harvested fields until the whole crop has been transported to the house

The foregoing analysis suggests that, being unable to reproduce itself with its own production, the peasant household seeks supplementary income from outside. The division of labour by age and sex within the household frees some of the male members of the household for outside work. As Meillassoux suggests, capitalism takes advantage of the labourers whose subsistence needs are met partly by the household. In this way, capitalism avoids paying for the workers' social security, old age pensions, sick leave etc. Women's labour within the household plays a vital role in the reproduction of the labour force, and one which is taken advantage of by capitalism.

We have just said that the peasant household is not able to reproduce itself with its own production. By this we do not mean that the peasant household production is small in quantitative terms. In most cases the amount produced by the household would be enough for its reproduction if a part of the product was not expropriated by various means. However, the conditions of household production are determined externally. Expensive inputs, unfavourable market conditions and credit mechanisms all play important parts in the impoverishment of the peasant household. In the next two chapters we shall see how the credit mechanisms and market forces operate in a manner that continuously transforms the viability of the household economy.

Notes to Chapter Seven

1. The word usta (master) in Turkish becomes ustası when used together with the word duvarcı (mason), for grammatical reasons.

2. Güçbilmez, 1972
3. See, for example, Akşit, 1967; Berkes, 1942; Erdentuğ, 1956, 1959; Yasa, 1954, 1961, 1966
4. Meillassoux, 1972, 103
5. Meillassoux, 1972, 102

8. Credit Mechanisms

Turkish agriculture is predominantly characterised by small-scale production. The exploitation of these small producers does not take place through the capital wage-labour relation but through other mechanisms, some of which we shall encounter in the cases of Kalhana and Gisgis villages. Small producers are no longer isolated from market relations; they are dependent on the market either in selling their goods or in buying some of the items they use at home. Therefore, although the main aim of the household as an economic unit is to reproduce itself, the requirements of the wider economies, in terms of what to produce and how much to produce, have to be taken into consideration. This is, of course, due to the fact that these households are not self-sufficient units.

Capitalism needs sources to accumulate and develop and, of course, agriculture and agricultural producers are sources which contribute to this development. But, in order for capitalist accumulation to take place, in the strict sense, the direct producers must be separated from the means of production, and the owners of the means of production must be separated from the wage labourers. Of course, this definition of capitalism leaves aside small commodity producers such as those who characterise the social structure of Gisgis and Kalhana. How are we going to understand the small producers' exploitation by capital? Initially it is necessary to differentiate between various kinds of capital, namely industrial capital (production capital), merchant capital, finance capital (banking capital), and usurers' capital, in order to understand the ways in which these small producers are exploited.

In this chapter, we shall concentrate on the credit mechanism in Turkey in general, and its manifestations in the Diyarbakır-Ergani region in particular. We shall then try to situate the small producers in the credit mechanism in the Diyarbakır-Ergani region in the light of data collected during the summer of 1977 in Gisgis and Kalhana villages.

Organised Credits in Turkey

Agricultural credit in Turkey may be categorised under two headings, differentiated by the sources from which the credit is obtained: organised agricultural credit and unorganised agricultural credit. The organised credit agencies are Ziraat Bankası (Agricultural Bank), Tarım Kredi Kooperatifleri (Agricultural Credit Co-operative) and Tarım Satış Kooperatifleri (Agricultural Sales Co-operatives). (1) In fact the state-owned Ziraat Bankası acts as a supervisor for the two groups of co-operatives and, as a result, the three organised credit sources are inter-related organisations. Given the limited organisational networks of the Tarım Kredi Kooperatifleri and Tarım Satış Kooperatifleri, the Ziraat Bankası can be considered as the only organised source which gives credit to the farmers. The Ziraat Bankası, established in 1888, apart from its ordinary banking activities, is mainly engaged in providing agricultural credits in order to achieve the targets summarised by Atasagun. (2) These targets are 'to complement the existing capital of farmers in order for them to run their farms, to increase and improve their production, to help them to obtain land or enlarge their holdings and to facilitate and increase the marketing and selling of agricultural goods'. (3) Furthermore, it is stated in the Charter of the Agricultural Bank that small farmers and their needs will be given priority in the provision of credits. (4) The types of credit which are available to the farmers can be summarised as follows: (5)

(a) Working Credits: The credits given to farmers in order to complete the elements of the working capital are of two types, differentiated by their place of use and duration: management credits (çevirme kredileri) and equipment credits (donatma kredileri). The management credits are those credits designed to help farmers meet their expenses in buying animal fodder, seed, seedlings, fertilisers, weed-killers and insecticides, in paying agricultural labourers employed in production, in expenses incurred in the breeding of poultry, bees and silk-worms, in the production of animal fodder from their fields and communal pastures (mera and çayır) and in the care and upkeep of livestock. The duration of the management credits is one year. The equipment credits are those credits designed to extend and strengthen agricultural holdings through the provision of agricultural tools of any sort, movable assets for the farm, such as small machines and other equipment, working and draught animals as well as bees, etc., or through increasing the supply of such items. The duration of equipment credits is up to five years, according to the value and durability of the equipment in question, or the lifespan of the animals.

(b) Verimlendirme and Iyileştirme Kredileri (Productivity-raising and Improvement Credits): These are designed to raise the productivity of crops and improve the types of crops. The duration of these credits is up to 20 years.

(c) Arazi Edindirme Kredileri: These credits are aimed to endow producers with land. They are credits extended to those wishing to enlarge their holdings or to centralise their scattered small fields. Again, the duration of these credits is up to 20 years.

The agricultural credits extended by the Agricultural Bank can also be categorised into three groups, according to the way in which the repayments of the credits given are guaranteed. Credits may be given to the farmer in return for the mortgage of his lands, or in return for the pledge of his crops and other movable properties, or they may be given in the case of joint sponsorship of the farmers for each other.

Nevertheless, it should be pointed out that, although the Agricultural Bank aims to help small producers by providing credit and agricultural machinery, big farmers seem to be the main beneficiaries from the implementation of the bank's credit policy. This can be substantiated when we outline some aspects of the general structure within which this policy is operated.

Turkey was expected to give priority to agriculture and become a food and raw material supplier for Europe, according to the Marshall Aid Plan. The Democrat Party government adopted this policy and implemented it. (6) This was in no way unexpected, since the Democrat Party had been created as a reaction to the Republican People's Party government's scheme of land reform with the collaboration of big landlords, notables, and the commercial bourgeoisie. (7)

The tractors provided by Marshall Aid were given out to farmers on credit. As a result, the number of tractors rose to over 40,000 in 1955, from 961 in 1936, 1,750 in 1948 and 31,415 in 1952. The number of combine harvesters rose to 6,000 in 1956 from 104 in 1936 and 994 in 1948. The credits given by the Agricultural Bank grew greatly, from TL50 million in 1940 to TL235 million in 1948, TL1,212 million in 1953 and over two billion Turkish lira in 1957. (8) The prices of agricultural products were also raised, by 16 per cent for wheat, 23 per cent for sugar beet and 47 per cent for cotton in the 1951-1955 period. (9) William H. Nicholls, a member of the World Bank Mission who advised that agriculture should be given priority, evaluated this development in 1955 and noted: '25,000-27,000 farm families (one per cent of the total farming families) directly benefitted from the implementation of the policy of mechanisation in agriculture'. The average annual income of these families is possibly more than TL15,000 and these families received 25 per cent of the total agricultural credits, whereas 2.5 million small farmers could not directly benefit from this policy. (10)

By 1965, credits given by the Agricultural Bank had risen to 5,551 million Turkish lira. (11) It was the big and medium sized farmers who benefitted from the increased credits. The benefit of the small-holdings from such a credit policy has remained very limited, and insignificant. Aksoy points out that only one-third of agricultural holdings made use of Agricultural Credits in 1965. (12) A report by the Turkish Workers' Party shows the highly unequal distribution of agricultural credits. According to the report, fifty per cent of the holdings which have access to Agricultural Bank credits receive TL300 or less, an amount of money which can in no way assist production; 37 big holdings receive TL625,000 each. This unequal credit distribution became even more acute during the late 1960s. (13)

The fact that small-holdings are dominant in Turkey and suffer in unfavourable credit conditions plays an important part in the process of social differentiation in the rural areas. Thus small producers and poor peasants are pushed into the arms of usurers for two reasons: first, the total amount of agricultural credit in Turkey is far from meeting the demand; between 1963 and 1969, despite the 275 per cent rise in the total agricultural credits extended, only 35 per cent of the demand for agricultural credits was met. (14) Second, as indicated above, the credits extended to agriculturalists are unequally distributed and favour big and medium sized farmers.

Not only big and medium farmers are given large amounts of credit, but merchants also somehow manage to get sizeable agricultural credits. For instance, in Izmir some merchants who have nothing to do with agricultural production and whose only relation to agriculture is as sales representatives for agricultural chemicals, receive hundreds of thousands of Turkish lira from the Agricultural Bank's special schemes. In an office opposite the agricultural chemical shop, the merchant then engages in usury, giving credits at 40 per cent interest for three months. (15)

Furthermore, farmers are asked to produce the title deeds to their lands in order to be given agricultural credits by the Agricultural Bank, and they are also requested to find a merchant to sponsor them. In Turkey the inadequacy of cadastral surveys, excess of formalities, arbitrariness in giving credit to small landowners, inconvenient debt repayment time, and difficulties in postponing the date of repayment are all very important factors in leading to the practice of usury. As a result, merchants and big landlords who get credits easily from the Agricultural Bank act as usurers, lending money at high interest rates. (16)

It should be noted that most of the credit given to producers is used for consumption needs. This is primarily due to the fact that the amount received is too small to be spared for agricultural production and is therefore spent on the immediate consumption needs of the family.

Until now we have tried to see the activities of the Agricultural Bank in terms of types of credit, credit extension and the significance of credit for the different strata of agricultural producers. Earlier, we mentioned that, besides the Agricultural Bank, there were other organisations extending agricultural credits, though under the control of the Agricultural Bank. We shall now briefly mention the other organised credit sources.

Tarım Kredi Kooperatifleri are under the strict control and trusteeship of the Agricultural Bank in terms of their establishments and functions. (17) The aim of these co-operatives is: to improve and increase the production of their members, to make production profitable for their members, to prevent their members from being exploited by usurers by providing them with cheap production credit, agricultural inputs and machinery, and thereby to enable them to be strong against internal and external competitors. (18)

Despite their good intentions, the Tarım Kredi Kooperatifleri have great difficulty in achieving their aims, for a number of reasons. First, they depend on the Agricultural Bank for their money supply. The share of agricultural credits in the total credits in Turkey is very limited and is insufficient, yet a considerable amount of the agricultural credits is given to Tarım Satış Kooperatifleri for buying up agricultural products from the producers. The amount allocated by the banks as production credits is 13 to 14 per cent of the total agricultural credits, and from this 13 to 14 per cent the Tarım Kredi Kooperatifleri obtain a part as their share to distribute among their members. (19) Second, the Agricultural Bank does not give sufficient credit to the Tarım Kredi Kooperatifleri. Third, organisational problems play a significant part in the failure of the Tarım Kredi Kooperatifleri. Usurers, merchants and intermediaries, for example, play a very important role in the local organisations of these co-operatives, and receive most of the credits. (20)

As to the Tarım Satış Kooperatifleri, these are not credit distributing organisations. Their aim is to help their members by marketing their products and each year they buy up certain products from the producers at prices determined by the government. The money to buy the products is obtained from the Agricultural Bank. Nevertheless, lack of facilities and delayed payments force the producers to sell their products to merchants and in some cases the co-operatives play the role of intermediary between the producers and the merchants. As we are not directly interested in the agricultural sales co-operatives we shall not go into the details of the mechanisms of their operation. (21)

Unorganised Credits in Turkey

Unorganised credits are those credits extended by individuals to those in need of cash. The provision of private credits is regulated either by traditionally accepted norms or by personal relations. These private credits are of two types: one is given by merchants and usurers with interest, and the other is obtained from relatives, friends and neighbours, without interest. The first type is called tefeci kredisi or murabaha kredisi (both terms refer to credits extended by usurers) and is extended by those who take usury as their occupation. The usurers, in most cases, are merchants and landlords at the same time.

Tefeci credits can be categorised into two groups (22): credits extended in cash and credits extended in kind. Producers resort to the money-lenders when they need cash to meet their production expenses (the purchase of seed, animals, agricultural machinery and labour power) or consumption expenses (food and clothing), or to repay their debts (to a bank or an individual). The money-lenders are usually those merchants who engage in the buying and selling of agricultural export products. Before the harvest they give money to needy producers in return for their harvested products, either at a predetermined constant price or at a price which is a predetermined amount lower than the market prices at the time of the harvest. The prime motive for the usurer is to take advantage of the difference between the prices. In some places, if the produce is sold before the harvest at a constant price, which is usually lower than the market price, a certain amount of interest is added to the initial amount of money lent. Then the amount of crops equivalent to the total sum of the initial loan, plus interest, is calculated. The indebted person has to take the agreed amount of crops to wherever the creditor wishes it to go. If the producer for some reason fails to hand over the crops, he has to pay his debt in cash at the highest market price for the crop in question, plus interest for the days beyond the original date of payment agreed upon. In these cases, small producers usually end up selling or mortgaging their lands or joining the ranks of the rural landless, rural proletariat, sharecroppers or casual labourers. The second type of credit extended in cash by money-lenders involves the mortgaging of movable property (such as jewellery, gold and silver ornaments, etc.). If the initial loan, plus the interest is not paid when it falls due, the money-lender appropriates the mortgaged goods. This is a very widespread method of usury in Turkey.

As to the credits given in kind, the basis of these credits is that the needy producers are supplied with goods instead of with money, and the debt is repaid either in kind or in cash. These credits are of two types: materials necessary for production and materials necessary for direct consumption.

Economically weak holdings need seed, working animals, small agricultural tools and agricultural equipment and under abnormal conditions (crop failure and such like) these needs become more intense. The production needs of hard-up small producers are usually met by the rich producers and landlords of the same village or neighbouring villages, or by the town merchants, who engage in buying and selling these goods on terms more or less similar to those for selling on credit. The mode of repayment varies according to the type of goods advanced. If the agreed repayment is to be in kind, a certain amount is added to the original amount, and if the repayment is to be in cash, again a certain amount of interest is added to the original sum.

The consumption goods obtained on credit by producers comprise foodstuffs that are not produced by the producers themselves, such as oil, salt, sugar, paraffin and margarine, or clothes and shoes. These goods are obtained from the village grocer, town grocer, drapers in nearby towns and shoe-makers or shoe-sellers.

The contracts between the creditors and the producers are verbal and do not involve formalities or any sort. Village grocers, in particular, do not hesitate to provide villagers with the goods they need at prices much higher than the usual market prices. The total debt is usually repaid at harvest time, and the payment may be in cash or in kind. If, for some reason, the debt is not paid at all, or only partially paid, the debt may be transferred to the following year, with one year's interest added.

So far we have tried to give a general view of the credit mechanisms existing in Turkey. Of course, it is not possible to discover everywhere in Turkey all the forms of credit mechanisms described above. However, it is possible to see some of the above-mentioned mechanisms or combinations of them in different regions of the country. We shall now turn to our area of fieldwork, to see how credit mechanisms operate there. By describing individual cases we hope to discern general tendencies in the area.

Organised Credits in Ergani

In the course of our fieldwork, it became clear that both organised and unorganised credit mechanisms were in operation in Ergani. Furthermore, in some cases, credit given by the Agricultural Bank acts as a catalyst for usurers' exploitation because in Southeast Anatolia big landlords and merchants receive the lion's share of agricultural credits, whereas small landowners get very little from the Agricultural Bank. Farmers from Gisgis, for example, received credits of between TL300 and TL10,000 according to the fieldwork data (Table 29).

TABLE 29 CREDITS RECEIVED FROM THE AGRICULTURAL BANK

AMOUNT (TL)	NUMBER OF PEOPLE	AMOUNT (TL)	NUMBER OF PEOPLE
300	15	3,500	10
500	28	4,500	4
800	11	5,000	3
1,000	10	7,500	2
1,500	20	9,000	1
2,500	14	10,000	2

In theory, the amount of credit received is determined by the amount of land owned, number of animals owned, type of crop grown and so on. In practice, however, apart from the factors listed above, factors such as political affiliation, nepotism, and the amount of the bribe offered to the official in charge are also very effective in the allocation of credits. Credits given to small producers are in no way enough for them to be useful in production and most of the credits received by the small farmers were used in meeting the immediate consumption needs of the family. In addition to buying food and clothes, the credits were also spent on such things as medicine, building construction, opening grocery shops, wedding ceremonies, circumcision ceremonies, setting up in business as a pedlar (*çerçi*) and repayment of debts etc.

Mecit Güzey, of Gisgis, had a crop failure a few years ago and he could only produce 25 *ölçeks* of wheat, which was 40 *ölçeks* less than his family (comprising himself, his wife, son, daughter-in-law and six grandchildren) needed. He borrowed TL2,500 from the Agricultural Bank at 9 per cent interest. This was a short-term working credit, but, instead of using the money for production purposes, Mecit bought wheat. When the repayment date came round a year later, he did not have the money to repay his debt of TL2,775 and nobody in the village would lend him money. He had to resort to borrowing TL2,500 from the village grocer at TL125 interest per week.

At this point it should be noted that the short-term (one year) borrowing mechanism works as follows: producers are lent money for one year and at the end of that time they repay it with interest. Within a week of repayment the borrowers are allowed to borrow the same amount again. The short-term credits are 'frozen' credits, in that the borrower borrows money from somewhere in order to repay the bank's money, in order to be able to borrow the same amount again. In fact, what the borrower is doing is simply paying interest to the bank each year on the same frozen amount, and the money-lenders take advantage of the inability of the borrower to produce the necessary amount to repay the bank.

In Mecit's case, what he does is to pay TL350 each year to the Bank as interest, without getting any credit at all, apart from the initial credit which was spent on food. So each year Mecit has to produce TL475 worth of surplus in order to meet the interest requirement from the bank and the money-lender. If he fails to do so, he will have to find alternative solutions such as selling his land, animals and equipment. This is an example of the way in which national finance and local usury articulate together to appropriate the surplus produced by the peasant household.

It should also be pointed out that, in some parts of Eastern Anatolia, some *ağas* use the people who live in their villages as a means of obtaining more credit. We ourselves did not come across this sort of mechanism in the Diyarbakır-Ergani area, but

Bozarslan describes it as follows:

> The *ağa* takes his villagers to the bank and registers them. When the money (credit) is distributed to them they are given two to three hundred lira each. The villagers get the money from the bank, putting their mark on the documents by finger printing, and they hand over the money to the *ağa* as soon as they come out of the bank. The *ağa* plays this trick on virtually everybody in his village. It is the villagers who are indebted to the bank, and it is the *ağa* who pockets the money. It is up to the goodness of heart of the *ağa* whether he repays the money or not when the repayment is due ... (If the *ağa* does not repay) the bank will get the money from the villagers. (23)

In this example, the villagers are in fact sharecroppers on the *ağa*'s lands. In the case of the *ağa*'s failure to repay the debts, the villagers are doubly exploited: first, as sharecroppers they have to do without a part of their crop; second, they have to pay the interest on the money borrowed by the *ağa*. However, the mechanism described by Bozarslan seems to be rather exaggerated. Can the *ağa* use the same mechanism for everybody? And more than once? Would the villagers not rebel against such blatant exploitation?

Now let us consider another example of the Agricultural Bank's mediation, albeit unintentionally, in the exploitation of needy producers. Until very recently, the Agricultural Bank used to mediate between the producers and the *Ziraat Dairesi* (Agricultural Office) in the provision of artificial fertilisers. The Agricultural Bank pays the Agricultural Office for the amount of fertiliser it gives to the producers and the amount is determined by the area of land owned and the type of crop cultivated. The producers are thus indebted to the Agricultural Bank without any cash transaction having taken place and before they obtain the artificial fertilisers. Since most of the producers are in need of cash to meet their consumption needs, and they are mostly not familiar with the use of artificial fertilisers, they would sell the fertilisers to a merchant at a lower price than they bought it. The merchants in turn would sell the fertilisers to other producers who, for various reasons, could not get fertilisers from the Agricultural Office through the mediation of the Agricultural Bank. They may not have large enough lands to make them eligible for obtaining fertilisers from the Agricultural Office; they may already be indebted to the Agricultural Bank, which would not give them more credit, owing to the fact that the working credits given to farmers were frozen; they might believe that the corrupt bank officials would not give them any credit; (24) they may be tired of the bureaucratic nature of the transactions which may take weeks or even months.

At the time of our fieldwork, the Agricultural Bank had already stopped giving fertiliser credits and the producers had to pay promptly for the fertilisers if they wanted to obtain some. Most of the small producers did not even try to get any fertilisers from the Agricultural Office since they did not have the necessary cash for the purchase. However, the merchants who also engage in buying and selling fertiliser still find other ways of obtaining supplies of fertilisers. Officially it is illegal to buy and sell fertilisers and certain other agricultural chemicals which are distributed by government agencies.

Nevertheless, there were three merchants in Ergani engaged in the buying and selling of fertilisers illegally. One of them was getting fertilisers from the Agricultural Office by bribing the officials, while the other two were buying it from the producers. The three merchants have grocery shops in Ergani town, and have very close relations with some of the producers, who are dependent on these grocers for some of their food supplies and are indebted to them. The merchants ask some of their indebted clients to get fertiliser for them from the Agricultural Office. The merchants were paying TL200 per ton and were able to gain TL1,500 from the sale of that amount.

Of course, not everybody could get fertilisers from the Agricultural Office, since it requires the official confirmation of the village headman as to whether or not the applicant has a certain number of <u>dönüms</u> of land. This is because no cadastral survey has been carried out in the village and the muhtar's (village headman) approval is considered sufficient for the allocation of artificial fertiliser. Those small producers who cannot obtain fertiliser from the Agricultural Office are left at the mercy of the merchants, who were charging TL2.5 for one kilo of fertiliser when the official price was around one lira. This is particularly so in the case of the small vegetable producers, who only need about 20 to 50 kilos of fertiliser. They cannot get such a small amount from the Agricultural Office, and have to buy it from the black market.

In some cases, the big landowners themselves sell fertilisers to small producers from neighbouring villages, or to their sharecroppers, at a price higher than the officially declared prices. For instance, Zülfü Ağa of Gözlü village in the Ergani district is able to get many tons of fertiliser from the Agricultural Office because he owns large areas of land (about 10,000 dönüms) and is friendly with the officials. He uses some of the fertiliser on his farm and sells the rest to the neighbouring villagers who cannot get it from the Agricultural Office. They are quite happy about this situation because they are thus saved from the drudgery of transporting the fertiliser from the town to the village. Furthermore, and more important, they can buy it from the ağa by instalment. Zülfü Ağa also gives some of his relatively less fertile lands to sharecroppers, who bear the cost of production, the only thing provided by Zülfü Ağa being the seed. At the beginning of the agricultural year, Zülfü Ağa agrees to give his lands to sharecroppers on the condition that they will use artificial fertilisers in production. Since the sharecroppers do not own any land or only very small amounts, they cannot get fertilisers from the Agricultural Office. Even if they had enough land to make them eligible to obtain fertiliser from the Agricultural Office, it has to be approved by the village headman, who himself is under the strict control of Zülfü Ağa. So, eventually the sharecroppers have to apply to Zülfü Ağa to buy fertilisers on credit. Zülfü Ağa doubly benefits from all these transactions, to the detriment of his sharecroppers. First, he gets half of the crops without doing any work in their production; second, he gets a part of the sharecroppers' shares as the difference between the price he initially pays for the fertilisers and the price he charges his sharecroppers. Of course, he also benefits from the increase in production resulting from the use of fertilisers.

The Agricultural Bank not only appropriates a part of the surplus or of the necessary production of the producers in the form of interest, but it also paves the way for some to exploit others by way of its credit policy. We have already stated that the big landowners receive the lion's share of the credits. This is also evident from the data collected from our fieldwork. We mentioned that the credits given to the producers from Gisgis village ,where small landownership is dominant ,ranged from TL300 to TL10,000. In Kalhana, where big landownership is dominant, landlords receive a sizeable amount of credit, not only as working credits but also as equipment credits. For instance, the credit allocation for Fuat Aydoğan was TL500,000; for Hamdi Aydoğan it was TL750,000; for Havva Aydoğan it was TL100,000. These figures are astronomical compared with the TL300 which was received by some of the small producers.

Big landlords do not use all their credits in agriculture; they sometimes invest them in more profitable areas, such as transport, commerce, etc., and they sometimes engage in usury. This latter aspect allows them to tie the poor peasants to the farm so that they can make use of their labour in the peak season. For instance, in Kalhana most of the landless rural poor were indebted to one of either Fuat, Hamdi or Havva. Also, Hamdi and Fuat engage in other sorts of activities besides agriculture. Fuat is the owner of the only two petrol stations in Ergani, his father had taken over one of them from a relative before his death, having realised the lucrative nature of being an agent for British Petroleum. Fuat opened the second petrol station, with the credit received from the Agricultural Bank, a few miles outside the town, on the main highway between Diyarbakır and Elaziğ, which links them to Ankara and Istanbul. As to Hamdi, he became a partner in a small building construction company with the credit he received from the Agricultural Bank for the purposes of opening a chicken farm in Kalhana. (25)

Of course, these examples are related to the misuse of large scale agricultural credits. Relatively small amounts of credits are also misused. For instance, Celal Pala borrowed TL4,500 from the Agricultural Bank and used it to open a grocery shop in Gisgis, and Abdülkerim Üney used his TL9,000 credit to pay the advance on a jointly owned minibus, to transport passengers between Gisgis, Ergani and Diyarbakır.

From the above we can conclude that agricultural credits are not sufficient to be used in production and they are unequally distributed among the farmers. Furthermore, small producers are left at the mercy of merchants, usurers and big landlords in terms of credits, seeds and fertilisers, etc.

Unorganised Credits in Ergani

The credits extended by those other than organised institutions take two forms: credits in kind and credits in cash. The relations between the producers and the merchants (grocers) play an important role in the credit mechanism in Ergani district. All through the year, small producers and the village poor are in need of both cash and consumption goods, and village or town grocers supply the consumption needs of the producers' or the village poor's families. The prices are fixed by the grocer, and of course are much higher than market prices. At the end of the harvest, the producer has to give his produce to the grocer at a price lower than the market price. The village poor pay their debts with the money earned from working as casual labourers, either in building construction, or in agriculture, working as cotton pickers and hoers in the Çukurova region. The price of the product is fixed by verbal contract before the grocer will supply the producer with consumption goods. The producer's exploitation by the grocer is two-fold: first, he pays more for the goods than their market price; second, his products are sold at a lower price. Under these conditions small producers can never repay their debts to the grocer, and the unpaid amount is transferred to the following year. In the long run, the small producer has to sell his land and other assets (draught animals, household utensils, etc.), and becomes impoverished, searching for work for his family's subsistence.

In 1977, the village grocer in Gisgis, Celal Pala, was supplying some of his clients with consumption goods such as sugar, macaroni, salt, cigarettes, paraffin, etc. on credit. The repayment was agreed to be fresh vegetables (tomatoes, peppers and aubergines), melon, grapes, eggs and butter, all at prices lower than current market prices. For instance, he would accept tomatoes, peppers and aubergines at a price one lira lower than the market price in Ergani. He had arranged with some grocers in Ergani to supply them with fresh vegetables, and he made about TL0.75 per kilo of vegetables simply by transferring them to the town. Since he is the only grocer (the other had just closed down) in the village, most of the peasants have to shop from him. It is a fact that in some parts of Turkey, as in Ergani, people will do their shopping from the same grocer in the town all the time, and sometimes the people of a whole village will do their shopping from the same grocer. (26) For instance, most of the villagers of Kalhana, Malan and Aşağı Balahur villages shop from the same grocer in Ergani.

Sometimes credits in kind end up with a pledge mechanism. When the indebted person cannot repay his debt, he pledges his land to the creditor for a certain period of time (generally for four to seven years), during which the creditor has usage rights to the land. In return, the owner does not pay interest on the amount he owes to the creditor. If the loan is not paid back in due time, the creditor has the right to sell the land to recover his initial loss. Of course it is impossible for the producer to repay his debt under these conditions, and he ends up by losing his means of production. In most cases, during the pledge years the merchant gives the mortgaged land to its real owner to cultivate on a sharecropping basis. Because of his indebtedness to the merchant, the producer is reduced to the position of a tenant on his own land. He has to hand over at least half his produce to the merchant. The producer not only loses his land at the end of the mortgage period, but also his labour is exploited and his product extracted from him during this time.

In Gisgis, A.K. Üney and his partner also deal in the

buying and selling of grain, mainly wheat. Since most of the producers in Gisgis have reserved a part of their farm for vegetable production, some of them are unable to produce enough wheat for their home consumption. A.K. Üney and his partner bring in lorryloads of wheat to sell on credit in the village. Payment is made, either in kind or in cash, at the time of the harvest. The rate of profit is between 50 and 100 per cent. If the payment is in kind, at harvest time the debtor has to deliver one and a half times as much wheat as he borrowed initially.

Around Kalhana region, the villages of Kalhana, Malan and Aşağı Balahur grow cotton as a cash crop. Cotton merchants in Ergani give credit to those who need cash to pay their agricultural labourers, to rent tractors or to buy seeds, artificial fertilisers, etc. Since the credit supplied by the Agricultural Bank is very limited for small producers, they apply to the merchants and usurers, who are in most cases one and the same people, for credit and other facilities. Repayment of debts takes different forms. Sometimes it is paid in cash, with interest varying from 50 to 200 per cent. Sometimes it is paid in kind at a price fixed by the merchant-usurer, much lower than the normal price for the goods in question. In this case, the producer has to hand over his product to the merchant-usurer at the merchant-usurer's place, generally his store. The type of crop to be grown is sometimes decided by the merchant-usurer, who does not control the means of production. Although household labour, and to a certain extent wage-labour, is used in the actual production process, merchant capital controls the production, for it provides an initial sum of money and receives products, the value of which is greater than the initial money invested.

In this example the risks in production are borne by the owner of the land. The merchant-usurer does not concern himself with the fate of the production. He is only concerned with the money he has loaned, and its interest. However, there are certain cases in which merchants take on half of the risks involved, by becoming a partner of the landowner. The merchant pays rent for the land, and gives seed to the owner, thus entitling the merchant to receive half of the crop produced. All the other costs of production are borne by the actual owner of the land. If a loan is received by the owner of the land, then the interest mechanism becomes operational. At harvest time, the merchant gets half the crop plus a part of his partner's share for the loan made. The price of the partner's share is pre-fixed by mutual agreement, at a level generally lower than the market price.

Apart from the mechanisms described above, which involve either credit in kind or repayment in kind, or both, usury also exists in the area. Usurers advance credits at high interest. Among the many reasons for which one may apply to usurers in the area, the principal reason is in order to buy necessary consumption goods for the family. Dowry payment, wedding and circumcision ceremonies, crop failures, having son(s) in the army, illnesses, natural disasters (such as earthquakes) and house building are among the other major reasons for resorting to borrowing from a usurer.

The rural poor, who have no land and choose to set up in business as *çerçi* (pedlars) also undergo certain exploitation through credit mechanisms. *Çerçi*s are those people travelling between remote villages and the town, selling small kitchen utensils, glasses, buttons and such like. If the *çerçi* does not have the initial capital to set up the business, he either applies to a wholesaler in the town or to a usurer (*faiz ağa*). The *çerçi* commutes between the town and the villages for nine months of the year, on a donkey or mule, then he loses a part of any profit he makes in interest payments. If he makes a loss, he still has to repay his debt with interest; usually he ends up selling his small plot of land or his house or household utensils. (27)

We can conclude that a part of the peasant household's surplus is drained away through credit mechanisms (organised/unorganised). In order to be able to produce this surplus, the peasant household has either to lengthen the working period or to reduce the level of consumption. This is referred to by Bernstein (28) as 'simple reproduction "squeeze"'.

Commoditisation of the peasant household production pushes the peasant household more and more into the exploitative arms of the merchants and usurers. Of course, international and home markets play a decisive role in the determination of the type of commodities to be produced by the peasant household. In order to appropriate a part of the surplus produced by the peasants, the larger structures regulate the prices of these products. In the next chapter, we shall attempt to show how the market mechanism is used in the expropriation of the surplus produced by the peasant household.

Notes to Chapter Eight

1. See Hassan, 1970
2. Atasagun, 1977
3. Atasagun, 1977, 83
4. Iloğlu, 1968, 1-11
5. The information concerning types of agricultural credits is derived from Sayın, 1969, 17-19 and 43
6. Cem, 1970, 437 and 439; Halil, 1968, 191; Avcıoğlu, 1968, 401-402
7. Avcıoğlu, 1968, 351-358; Cem, 1970, 387-388. See also Yerasimos, 1976, III, 1344-1346
8. Avcıoğlu, 1968, 402
9. Okyar, n.d., 8
10. Nicholls, 1955. See also Kanbolat, 1963, 19 for the effect of mechanisation on agriculture following the 1948 decision to give priority to agricultural development.
11. Aksoy, 1969, 72
12. <u>Idem</u>
13. Türkiye Işçi Partisi, 1968; Aksoy, 1969, 73
14. See Hassan, 1970, 90
15. Koç, 1969
16. For a similar assessment, see Mülayim, 1968 and Bozarslan, 1966, 42-46 for the working of the credit mechanism and the significance of <u>ağadom</u> in Eastern Anatolia.
17. For the development of co-operatives in Turkey, see Mülayim, 1967, 18-24 and 91-109
18. Dinçer <u>et al</u>., 1969, 54
19. Hassan, 1970, 93

20. Hassan, 1970, 94
21. For this point, see Hassan, 1970, 95-98
22. This categorisation is mainly derived from Atasagun, 1977, 96-116. For a similar approach, see Hassan, 1970 and, for a descussion of an earlier period, see also Tökin, 1934, 146-151
23. Bozarslan, 1966, 44-45
24. This last case is true for other parts of Turkey as well. Kıray, 1964, 62, for example, states that the villagers would not go to the banks for credit, believing that 'the bank helps those whose ship floats, not those whose ship rolls', i.e. the bank helps those whose business goes well, not those who are in trouble.
25. See Chapter Four, p.
26. Kıray, 1964, 61-63 indicates the same tendency in the Ereğli region
27. Bozarslan, 1966, 42
28. See Bernstein, 1977, 64-65

9. Marketing Structures

Marketing goods produced by the villagers plays an important role in the reproduction cycle of the peasant family and in the reproduction of the relations of production they are involved in. Market relations help us to gain a deeper understanding of relations between direct producers, merchants, landlords and the state. In this chapter, we shall attempt to explain how the marketing of agricultural goods is organised at the level of Turkish social formations and then move to the fieldwork to see manifestations of this general situation at local levels.

Marketing Structures in Turkey

As in most of the underdeveloped countries, the agricultural sector accounts for a decisive part of the gross national product in Turkey. In its efforts to industrialise or to speed up industrialisation and development, the state apparatus pays particular attention to the policy of transferring resources from the agricultural to the industrial sector. In order to achieve this, a price regulation system has been developed in Turkey.

There are doubts about the extent to which this policy is successful in transferring resources from agriculture to industry, and we shall see later that it is merchant capital which benefits from the agricultural price policy rather than industrial capital. Furthermore, not only does agriculture comprise a major part of the Gross National Product but it is also the main source of foreign currency earnings, which are crucial for the development of Turkey's industry, the working of which depends to a large extent upon the importation of oil, raw materials, intermediate goods, technology and know-how. In 1977, for example, 59.4 per cent of total export earnings came from the export of agricultural goods. Although this percentage dropped to 37.3 in 1982, it still constitutes a major part of export earnings (see appendix Table A.4).

The four most important export crops are hazelnuts, cotton, tobacco and dried raisins. The government, each year, declares 'floor prices' for the most important crops other than some fruits and vegetables. The state buys most cereal crops through its agency Toprak Mahsulleri Ofisi (Office of Soil Products) and most export crops through state-backed agricultural sales co-operatives such as Çukobirlik, Antbirlik, Tariş, Fiskobirlik, etc. It should also be pointed out that the 'floor prices' policy has gradually enlarged its spheres of influence since the 1960s. The number of crops with prices fixed by the government was only six or seven in 1963; by 1975 it had risen to nineteen - wheat, barley, sweetcorn, cotton, raisins, dried figs, sunflower seeds, unhusked rice, pistachio nuts, sugar beet, hazelnuts, sultanas, tea, tobacco, wool, olive oil, livestock and silk cocoons. A point of interest is that all the crops added to the list by 1975 were those non-cereal crops. (1)

When the year's price of a particular crop is fixed, several factors are borne in mind by the government. For instance, the price of wheat in most years is fixed above world prices because the rural masses play an important and determining role in elections. Political parties, in order to gain votes and maintain popularity among the rural population, fix high prices for cereals, which are mainly consumed within the country. This policy seems to be paradoxical. On the one hand the government tries to speed up industrialisation through new investments that are accumulated in the hands of industrialists; on the other hand, by fixing high prices for wheat they raise the cost of living of the working class, since wheat and wheat products are the staple diet in Turkey. This, in turn, enforces the working class to seek higher wages, thereby hindering capital accumulation in the industrial sector.

Would the ever-strengthening Turkish capitalist allow such things to take place? Of course not. What happens is that the state ensures that the price of bread is kept low. The mechanism is as follows: Toprak Mahsulleri Ofisi buys the wheat from the producer at the fixed price, which is higher than the world price. Then the Toprak Mahsulleri Ofisi, in accordance with the law, hands over the wheat, ten kilogrammes per person, to local administrations, which act as co-ordinators between the Toprak Mahsulleri Ofisi and the wheat mills. This transaction is made at a subsidised price much lower than the market price, the loss being carried by the state treasury. The total cost of such agricultural price support schemes rose from some TL550 million in 1950 to TL5,900 million in 1971. (2)

The champions of the price support policy have been claiming that, through this policy, they have been protecting low-income groups in both rural and urban areas. By keeping down the price of bread, the cost of living of the urban poor is reduced and, by giving a high price for wheat, the income of small farmers is increased. This is far from being a convincing argument. It is obvious that the high price policy is one of the reasons for the high rate of inflation in Turkey, and it is the people with low incomes who are most affected by the inflation. As for the rural areas, it is still less likely that the small producers benefit from this policy. It cannot be denied that some producers benefit from the implementation of the price support policy for wheat, but the question is whether or not small producers benefit from this policy and, if not, then who is the beneficiary? Only those who produce more wheat than their consumption needs, in other words those who have a marketable surplus of wheat, benefit from the high price of wheat. (We shall see that small farmers in Gisgis and Kalhana do not sell wheat in the market, rather they buy a proportion of their wheat.)

The question of who is selling wheat seems to be crucial in understanding who benefits from the high price policy. Therefore it is vital to examine the distribution of holdings that are concerned with the production of wheat. According to the results of the Agricultural Census carried out in 1963, there are two million wheat-producing holdings. Of these, 5.5 per cent produce 32 per cent of the total wheat and, cumulatively, 18.5 per cent of the total holdings produce 53.5 per cent of the total wheat. This shows that only a small minority of the wheat producers are positively affected by this policy.

However, in 1979 the existing government seemed to be following a different policy, in accordance with the conditions laid down by the International Monetary Fund. Increasing economic difficulties, especially the shortage of foreign currency, led the government to seek financial help from international organisations. One of the conditions laid down by the International Monetary Fund was that the Turkish government should not follow an inflationary price policy of subsidising agricultural goods. The first thing the government did was to declare that the Toprak Mahsulleri Ofisi was to cut down the provision of wheat by 50 per cent, and also the subsidisation of the price of wheat was stopped. No longer could the flour factories obtain cheap wheat from the Toprak Mahsulleri Ofisi, and so they had to find wheat in the market. This boosted the market price of wheat.

What followed was that the price of wheat in the world market rose by about 30 per cent, to $200 per ton in 1979, owing to a bad harvest in the USSR which is the biggest wheat producer and importer in the world and which had to buy 25 million tons of wheat from the USA. (3) Seeing the possibility of exporting some wheat, the government declared a very low floor price for wheat, 420 kuruş per kilo, while the world price for wheat was about 700. Another measure taken to secure foreign currency through the export of wheat, and to prevent the merchants from benefitting from this policy, was to prohibit the export of wheat by anybody other than the Toprak Mahsulleri Ofisi. However, things did not go as the government planned. The wheat merchants offered 430 kuruş per kilo and collected the wheat from the producers' store. Milliyet, a daily newspaper, reported, on 24 July 1979:

> ... producers in Kirklareli do not give their wheat to the Toprak Mahsulleri Ofisi. They prefer the merchants since this saves them expenses.

and continued:

> Since the government has declared the floor price for wheat to be 420 kuruş, merchants have been buying wheat at 430 kuruş from the producers' store ...
>
> When producers take their wheat to the Toprak Mahsulleri Ofisi the price of wheat drops to 400 kuruş from 420 kuruş, owing to factors like weighing charges, the degree of humidity of the crop, cleanness of the crop, etc. In addition to which, the need to queue for a number of days urges the producers to sell their wheat to merchants. In contrast to the situation in the Toprak Mahsulleri Ofisi, merchants go to the producers and, without charging them anything, they pay them 430 to 440 kuruş according to the condition of the wheat.

The above is but one example. Similar developments have taken place all over Turkey, as verified by statements given by Toprak Mahsulleri Ofisi officials. For instance, Toprak Mahsulleri Ofisi Istanbul Regional Directorate declared that, until 26 July 1979, they could only buy 36 thousand tons of wheat, whereas they had purchased 450 thousand tons by the same date in the previous year. Authorities of the Istanbul Directorate stated that: 'We were expecting to buy about 700 to 800 thousand tons of wheat this year. Unexpectedly we have only been able to buy 37 thousand tons so far'. (4) The daily paper Cumhuriyet also states that, in other regional directorates of Toprak Mahsulleri Ofisi such as Ankara, Afyon, Konya, Iskenderun and

Diyarbakır, the amounts of wheat sold to the Toprak Mahsulleri Ofisi had fallen considerably in comparison to the previous year. The worst hit region was Trakya, where some people spread the rumour that 'this government is about to fall, the coming government will give a better price for wheat - 470 kuruş is too low. Even the merchants offer 455 to 460 kuruş for a kilo of wheat. Towards the winter the price of wheat may go up to 800 kuruş'. (5) In the same article, Cumhuriyet stated that, despite all the rumours, the Toprak Mahsulleri Ofisi authorities had emphasised that there was to be no price rise for wheat. This was confirmed by the Inter-Ministerial Economic Co-ordination Committee (Bakanlıklararası Ekonomik Koordinasyon Kurulu), which discussed the question of giving a premium of 50 to 100 kuruş per kilo of wheat to those who had sold and those who were going to sell their wheat to the Toprak Mahsulleri Ofisi, and decided against this plan on the grounds that merchants had already bought considerable amounts of wheat from the producers. A decision to give 50 to 100 kuruş premium per kilo would enable the merchants to make huge profits by selling to the Toprak Mahsulleri Ofisi the wheat they had already bought from the producers. (6)

Despite all their good intentions, the government could not resist the merchants' insistence that the price given for wheat should be raised. Having insisted that there was not going to be a rise in the price of wheat, the government suddenly changed its mind. This occurred under pressure from the merchants, whose interests are strongly represented in parliament. On 13 September 1979, the government announced that those who had sold their wheat to the Toprak Mahsulleri Ofisi would get 80 kuruş premium per kilo, and those still to sell their wheat to the Toprak Mahsulleri Ofisi in the future would also benefit from this implementation. (7)

Through this change of policy, the government acted as a bridge in the transfer of value from the producers, mainly small producers, to the merchants. It was only small producers who had sold their wheat to the merchants, for they could not afford to store their products. This was because, first, they needed cash for their immediate needs; second, they were mostly indebted to merchants and landlords, banks, etc.; and third, either they had nowhere to store their produce or their stores were not suitable for keeping the produce in good condition. The small producers sold their crops to merchants because merchants were offering more than the Toprak Mahsulleri Ofisi at that time. On the other hand, big landlords, who in some cases are also merchants, were in a position to stock their produce. Moreover, having close contact with the officials, and also being able to follow market movements, they were in a position to know that there was going to be a rise in the price of wheat. We may, therefore, conclude that the state plays an intermediary role in the exploitation of the small producers by merchants and big landlords.

So far we have looked at the state's price policy concerning wheat. We shall now briefly examine the effects of the price policy followed by the government in terms of other important crops, such as cotton, hazelnuts, tobacco, etc. While doing this, we shall also try to draw attention to some of the relations of production in which the producers of these crops are involved, which would directly or indirectly affect the distribution of these crops and the circulation of moneys involved in the marketing of these crops.

In fixing the price of agricultural goods, the government seems to have been following a policy which would urge the producers to produce export crops. If we look at the rate of increase in the support prices for various crops, we shall soon realise that export crops are favoured in comparison with others.

There seems to have been a huge increase in the support prices between 1978 and 1979 if we just look at the figures. However, this is not the case, as Kafaoğlu writes:

> Compared with last year the price of cotton in the world (market) has risen by 30 per cent. Given the fact that prices in Turkey have gone up generally by around 40 per cent, the price of cotton should have been raised by 82 per cent. Coincidentally, the support price given by the government has been kept at the same level. Any price below that would have been unjust. Yet it looks as if

the price of cotton in the world conjuncture is going to go up. Therefore the price of cotton could have been declared slightly higher than the current support price. (8)

Kafaoğlu goes on to say that world prices for raisins and figs were more than 55 per cent higher than the previous year's prices. Then, taking into consideration the existing level of price rises in Turkey, he calculates that the price increase should be around 117 per cent in these two crops. The difference between the government fixed prices and Kafaoğlu's calculation is negligible, knowing that world prices are likely to continue to rise.

Furthermore, despite the fact that, in comparison with cereals, export crops are favoured by the government in their price policy, the prices given for these crops are not high enough to meet the increasing expenses of the growers. For instance, support prices given to four commercial crops (cotton, tea, sugar beet and hazelnuts) are lower than the production prices in some years. (9) A question arises: Would the producers benefit if the government gave higher prices than the current internal and world market prices? The answer is both 'yes' and 'no'. 'Yes', for those who have control over their production process and own their land; 'no', for those who own insufficient or no land, who are indebted to merchants and landlords, who cannot find credits to run their farm and therefore lose their surplus to merchants.

Many studies have shown that small producers, who are devoid of credit, fertilisers and other facilities, are exploited by merchants. A few examples will clarify the way in which small producers are exploited at the level of marketing. Research based on the data obtained from the Ministries of Monopolies and of Commerce reveals that producers are working for the mediators. In 1964, export merchants bought 90,394 tons of tobacco for TL611 million, of which TL600 million had been obtained from the Central Bank, and the average price paid for the tobacco was TL6.76. Merchants claimed that they had spent TL 3.28 per kilo on storage, processing, etc., though the study emphasised that these expenses would not exceed TL2.00 per kilo. Including TL3.28 per kilo as expenses, one kilo of tobacco would cost the merchant TL10.04, while the average export price of tobacco was TL12.60 per kilo. The total profit of the merchants was TL231,408,640. This amount was shared by 100 export merchants, each of whom made an average of TL2,314,000 profit. (10)

It should also be pointed out that half of the 450,000 producers sold their tobacco to export merchants. According to the ministries mentioned above, the average production price for tobacco in 1964 was TL6.20 per kilo. The producers, therefore, parted with their tobacco for a 10 per cent profit, namely TL 0.56 per kilo. The profit of the 227,000 families who did sell amounts to TL50,620,000 from the sale of 90,394 tons of tobacco. This should be contrasted to the TL2,314,000 average profit made by each merchant and examined in the context where the average annual profit of the tobacco producers is TL223. (11)

A similar case can be observed for the cotton producers. According to a study based on data obtained from the Regional Agricultural Research Institute and Söke Agricultural Technicians Office, the price of production for cotton per _decare_ in the case of land owned by the farmer is TL249, while the income received per _decare_ is TL333.90. In return for his labour, therefore, the producer receives TL84.90 per _decare_. However, a farmer of 50 _decares_ of land can obtain only one fourth of his credit requirements from the Bank and Co-operative and inevitably resorts to borrowing from usurers. For this reason, the burden of interest amounts to TL66.60 per _decare_, leaving the farmer with a profit of TL16.30 per _decare_, or TL815 annual profit. Had it not been for the interest due, his annual income would have been TL4,242. (12)

Following a report that the usurers avoid income tax in Söke, the tax inspectors reported as follows:

> The richness of the Aegean crops directly accrues to the usurers. Usury is very widespread in the Aegean region .. The mechanism is as follows: agricultural credits are insufficient and are given to influential _ağas_ and merchants. The needy producers have no alternative but to apply to usurers. Banks other than the Agricultural Bank issue credits only on condition that the merchant's

> guarantee is secured. Taking advantage of this, the usurers open credits to producers with interest varying from 40 to 200 per cent. The average rate of interest is about 87 per cent. Söke produces TL120 million worth of cotton per year. Despite a requirement of TL59 million of credit in Söke the banks only provide TL10 million at the most. Under these conditions usurers find incredible freedom of the movement in the area. (13)

A similar point is made by Mülayim:

> Hundreds of thousands of farmers have to sell their cotton, whose floor price is about TL2.20 to 2.30, before the harvest, at TL1.30 to 1.70 per kilo. It is these usurers/mediators who ruin the Turkish peasants, and who were declared 'the enemies of the Turkish peasants' by the Tarsus farmers. It is perfectly clear that the problem the cotton producers encounter is not that of raising the floor prices by a few *kuruş*, but rather that of being able to obtain the declared prices. (14)

The mechanism of exploitation of the cotton producers from production to exportation is concisely described by Selçuk:

> (1) the expenses in irrigated cotton farming total about TL300 to 325 per *decare*, excluding land rent, and TL250 to 300 in unirrigated farming. The credits distributed by the Agricultural Bank are TL115 per *decare*, i.e. one third of the expenses, which is insufficient.
>
> (2) ... The government intentionally does not open the cotton market until very late in the year. The agricultural sales co-operatives (Çukobirlik, Tarış and Antbirlik) cannot get the money from the government in time to buy cotton from their members, or the government deliberately avoids giving the money to the co-operatives.
>
> (3) Each year, while on the one hand the rumour is spread to the effect that cotton production is going to be

plentiful, and therefore quite a number of people will not be able to sell their cotton, on the other hand the cotton exporters spread another rumour that the price of cotton has gone down in the world market.

(4) Having thus been panicked, the masses of producers are left at the mercy of cotton-gin owners and intermediaries. Co-operatives and Unions are not on the horizon yet. The cotton is acquired by underhand means at less than its value.

(5) To these should be added the part played by the usurers who buy the crop before it is ripe, giving credit on the condition that the producer signs a sales contract before the harvest, thus enabling the usurer to obtain the crop at below its market value. (15)

The inability of the state and the state-backed co-operatives to buy up the whole production also forces the producers to sell their crops to merchants and usurers. For instance, Milliyet newspaper reports that the Çukobirlik, which buys cotton in accordance with the government's support price policy, can only buy 30 per cent of the harvest and the rest is sold to intermediaries. In the same article the leader of the Farmers' Union is quoted as saying:

> Cotton producers are very weak in facing the intermediaries. The producers who queue for days to sell their cotton are selling it at well below its value in order to avoid transport costs and to repay their debts. The fixed floor prices do not mean anything at all for the producers. (16)

Hazelnut producers also encounter similar difficulties. We shall not go into the particular details of how the hazelnut producer is affected by the price support policy, since this subject has been well documented elsewhere. (17)

As a conclusion from the above, we may say that, unless the inequalities among the producers in terms of the conditions of production are overcome, a price policy would not be beneficial to small farmers. The inequity in land-human relations paves the way for the unequal distribution of the resources which are transferred from non-agricultural sectors to the agricultural sector. The poor become poorer, while the rich become richer. The inequalities between the poor and the rich are intensified through the state policy. The agricultural credits are insufficient and small producers have no, or very little access to these credits. In order to meet their credit needs, small producers have to accept the terms laid down by the merchants and usurers, which leaves them with no alternative but to sell their products at below the floor prices, either before or after the harvest. The price policy does not help the producers at all. It is the merchants and usurers who benefit from it.

Marketing Structures in Diyarbakır

Diyarbakır province is a commercial centre for a number of surrounding provinces, such as Mardin, Siirt, Bitlis and Van. Commerce in the province is mainly based on agricultural products, livestock and livestock products which are produced within the province. However, the existence of quite a number of wholesalers, who act as bridges between industrial centres such as Istanbul and Adana and the surrounding relatively small provinces, contributes to the importance of Diyarbakır as a business and commercial centre in the Southeast. Tables 30 and 31 show that Diyarbakır is a very vital commercial centre. In Table 30 we see the items imported into Diyarbakır from other places and in Table 31 the items exported from Diyarbakır to other provinces are listed.

A comparison between the two tables reveals that Diyarbakır province plays an intermediate role as a commercial centre. Most of the goods brought into the province from other regions are sold to the neighbouring provinces. Of the exported goods it is mostly agricultural ones which are produced within the boundaries of the province. Apart from the agricultural products, oil, which has been extracted since 1961 by Shell and Turkish Petroleum, has been an important item in the economy of

TABLE 30 GOODS IMPORTED BY DİYARBAKIR PROVINCE IN 1969

TYPE	VALUE (million TL)	TYPE	VALUE (million TL)
Textiles	160	Lorries	5
Drapery	50	Glass	5
Fuel oil	50	Tea	5
Margarine	40	Luxury goods	5
Cement	20	Shoes	3
Timber	20	Carpets and mats	3
Iron	20	Electrical goods	3
Construction materials	10	Vegetables and fruit	3
Motor vehicle parts	30	Dried fruit	3
Agricultural tools	25	Olives	2
Intoxicants	25	Olive oil	2
Medicine	20	Soap	2
Sugar	10	Furniture	3
Books and stationery	3	Flour	2
Coal	5	Other	16

Total value of goods imported: 550,000,000TL

Source: Cumhuriyetin 50 Yılında Diyarbakır: 1973 İl Yıllığı

TABLE 31 GOODS EXPORTED FROM DİYARBAKIR PROVINCE IN 1969

TYPE	VALUE (million TL)	TYPE	VALUE (million TL)
Textile and drapery	140	Medicine	10
Minerals and unrefined oil	140	Rice	10
Grocery	50	Sugar and sweets	5
Intoxicants	40	Fuel and cooking equipment	5
Construction materials	40	Luxury goods	5
Grain	40	Silk and silk products	3
Livestock	40	Gall-nut and gum tragacanth	5
Livestock products	30	Other soil products	5
Melted butter	5	Tobacco	5
Margarine	30	Dried fruits	2
Agricultural tools	15	Shoes	2
Motor vehicle parts	15	Vegetables and fruit	2
Fuel oil	10	Books and stationery	2
Confectionery	10	Other	14
Melon and watermelon	20		

Total value of goods exported: 700,000,000TL

Source: Cumhuriyetin 50 Yılında Diyarbakır: 1973 İl Yıllığı

the province. The importance of oil for the province derives from its work provision for the local people. In 1972, for example, Shell employed more than 150 local people. (18) The oil extracted from 35 wells in Diyarbakır is pumped to Iskenderun through pipe lines. The daily amount of oil pumped to Iskenderun was 45,000 barrels which accounts for 53 per cent of the total oil extraction in Turkey. (19) However, in short we may say that the goods sold to other regions mainly comprise oil, grain (wheat, barley, rice and millet), pulses, livestock, livestock products (butter, unprocessed leather, wool, intestines, etc.), shelled nuts (almonds and walnuts), melons and water melons.

Of the goods produced within the province and transported to other places, about 70 per cent go by road, the remainder by rail. (20) According to the book Diyarbakır in the 50th Anniversary of the Republic, 800 to 1,000 vehicles come and go in and out of Diyarbakır each day. Although the province centre is well connected with other parts of Turkey, we cannot say the same thing for the road network within the province. Compared to the 357 kilometres of state roads (of which 276 kilometres are asphalt, 61 kilometres stabilised and 20 kilometres graded earth without drainage) there exist 488 kilometres of provincial roads, of which 284 kilometres are stabilised and the rest are earth roads. As for the village roads, Diyarbakır is poorly equipped. Within the boundaries of the province there are 1,856 inhabited places (this includes villages, mezras and koms) of which only 362 are connected with the nearest town by road. Of the total 1,378 kilometres of village roads, 544 kilometres are graded roads and 834 kilometres are hard surfaced (kaplama) roads. (21) Of course, the lack of suitable roads makes it extremely difficult for the inhabitants of these places to transport their goods to the market. Even in the villages with road links, it is very expensive and burdensome for small producers who have only very little marketable produce to take their crops to the market. This leads this type of producer to sell his crops at a lower price to a middleman in the village, or to a middleman who comes to the village.

Marketing Structures in Gisgis and Kalhana

In this section we shall deal with the extent of commercial relations in which the people of Gisgis and Kalhana are engaged. One way or another, all the households in the two villages are engaged either in buying or in selling, or in both activities. However, the degree to which the households are engaged in market relations varies considerably. In the case of grain, and especially wheat, 47 of the 95 farming families in Gisgis had no surplus to sell in the market. Given that wheat and lentils constitute the basic diet of peasant families in the area, and that most of the holdings in the village are smaller than 50 dönüms, it is hardly surprising that half the farming families do not have any marketable grain. In some cases small farmers have to buy grain for their own consumption needs. The cash for this is obtained either by selling vegetables and fruits or by working as seasonal wage labourers. Those who have a marketable grain surplus are faced with three alternatives: (a) to sell the surplus to the Toprak Mahşulleri Ofisi (Soil Products Office) in Ergani; (b) to sell it to allafs (grain merchants) in Ergani; (c) to sell it within the village.

Although it is possible for the small producers to sell their grain to the state-owned Toprak Mahsulleri Ofisi, in practice this is almost out of the question. During our fieldwork, the Toprak Mahsulleri Ofisi Ergani agency had only three officials to deal with the buying of the grain produced in the whole district. The agency had one weighing station and no store. With the help of a few porters, the grain was weighed, priced and stored in the open air by the three officials. Since the weighing and unloading process took quite a while, there were queues of lorries waiting to be unloaded. During the peak season, it may be necessary to queue for as much as three or four days. Furthermore, the transportation fee for lorries was TL500 per day. Given that the floor price for wheat was TL2.80 per kilo in 1977, waiting three days in the queue would cost the producer 535 kilos of wheat, which means 10 per cent of a lorry-load (considering that a lorry would carry a load of 5 tons of wheat).

Apart from the difficulties arising from the lack of organisation and facilities in the Toprak Mahsulleri Ofisi Ergani agency, the attitude of the officials towards small producers forces them to sell their crops to crop merchants. What was happening was that the Toprak Mahsulleri Ofisi officials were giving lower prices than the officially-declared prices to those who had less than a lorryload of grain, by the ruse of claiming that the quality of the grain was below standard, or saying that there were strange materials mixed with the grain. So, under these and similar pretexts the small producers were given TL2.40 to 2.50 per kilo, and they also were charged a certain amount toward the cost of unloading.

On the other hand, the allafs were offering 10 kuruş more than the Toprak Mahsulleri Ofisi officials, buying the wheat at between TL2.50 and TL2.60 and then handing it over to the Toprak Mahsulleri Ofisi at TL2.80, which was the officially declared price. This collaboration between the Toprak Mahsulleri Ofisi officials and the allafs caused a considerable degree of discontent amongst some of the small producers who sent hundreds of protest telegrams to the General Directorate of the office in Ankara. Nothing was done about this, however, because the law allows the officials to give low prices to substandard crops. The term 'standard' is too vague to define, thereby allowing the officials to behave arbitrarily in valuing the product of the unprotected small producers.

Some producers either prefer to, or have to, sell their wheat within their village. The village merchant in Gisgis pays less than the market prices for the grain and sells at a higher price than the market price. When he buys within the village, he deducts a certain amount for the transport cost, as if he had transported the grain to the town market. When he sells the crop, he adds a certain amount on top of the market price, as if he had brought the grain from the market. This is the case when the payments are in cash. In the event of a purchase by instalment, an interest of 30 to 50 per cent is also added to the bill. Since the production of grain in Gisgis is very susceptible to weather conditions, most of the small producers are affected in bad harvest years. In order to survive, borrowing or buying wheat from the village merchant becomes inevitable for those who do not have any stock supply. What the merchant does is to buy cheaply from those who are indebted to him and sell expensively to those who are in need. Of course there is also buying and selling among the peasants without any interest, but this is very limited in its extent.

Although some vegetables and fruits (melons and grapes) are consumed by the peasant families, most of them are sold in Ergani town centre. In this sense we can say that the vegetables and fruits are the most important commercial crops grown in Gisgis. Vegetables picked during the night are transported to the town early in the morning, at about four o'clock, by the only village lorry, which is somewhat antiquated and which carries passengers, fruit, vegetables and animals at the same time, between the village and Ergani: a distance of 18 kilometres. In Ergani there is no market system where the direct producers can sell their goods direct to the consumers. The vegetables are bought up by early-rising grocers, who sell them in turn to the consumers. In some cases, particular vegetable producers have to give their vegetables to particular grocers to whom they are already indebted. The grocer supplies the peasant all through the year with necessary consumer goods, in return for which the peasant has to supply the grocer with a certain amount of vegetables all through the summer at a fixed price, which is usually lower than that which the peasant would have been able to obtain in the market had he not been indebted to the grocer.

Apart from a few households who have a number of livestock, the average peasant family does not usually sell dairy products in the market. Milk, cheese and yoghurt are rarely consumed by the peasant family. When there is a pound or so of butter in excess of family needs it might be sold, and this takes place mostly within the village. For those who have a large number of livestock, cheese, butter, yoghurt, livestock, wool and mohair constitute some of their marketable commodities. Ergani is the main market for these goods. However, livestock is sometimes sold in Diyarbakır, where the demand for animals for meat is much higher than in Ergani. Unless the farmer has quite a number of animals, making it worthwhile to bear the transportation costs, he would not take them to Diyarbakir which is 78 kilometres from the village.

The above discussion for Gisgis is more or less applicable to the peasants of Kalhana village. The most important difference between the two villages in terms of marketing is that the majority of the villagers of Kalhana do not have access to any land. Thus their relations with the market involve only the action of buying, rather than buying and selling. Households with no access to land or livestock take part in market relations as consumers, not as producers. However, when we say that they do not engage in selling activities we only mean the selling of commodities produced by the household. We, of course, exclude labour power as a commodity which is sold by household members.

Another important difference between the two villages in terms of marketing stems from the nature of the distribution of the means of production and from the nature of the land. Big landownership, easy access to credits and machinery, coupled with the possibilities for irrigation, allow the cultivation of commercial crops such as cotton and sugar beet. Since agriculture is accepted as a business by the big landlords, whatever they produce constitutes exchange value, rather than use value. That is why they force their sharecroppers to grow more profitable crops like cotton whenever possible. Cotton has no use value for the sharecropper, who would prefer to grow wheat instead. So he sells his cotton in order to buy wheat. What we should like to emphasise is that the small producers of Kalhana are more market oriented than their counterparts in Gisgis, owing to the fact that the whole village is oriented to commercialised agriculture by virtue of the control exercised by the big landlords.

The cotton produced in the village is mainly marketed in Elazığ, where the main buyers are the _Çukobirlik_ and the Elazığ cotton thread factory. The _Çukobirlik_ does not buy cotton from those who are not members, but all the big cotton producers are members of the _Çukobirlik_. The small producers who only produce cotton irregularly, in alternation with other crops such as cereals and lentils, and who are unable to meet the membership requirements, do not become members of _Çukobirlik_.

For membership it is necessary to apply to the district officer or regional representative of Çukobirlik and, in addition, the candidates have to prove that they have been holding a tenancy to the land for at least ten years. Failing that, they must show a copy of the cadastre, proving the freehold of their land. The small producers cannot meet these membership requirements, owing to the fact that either they have not been tenants for the last ten years, or they have no cadastral proof to present. However, the big landlords can easily meet the requirements and benefit from the facilities provided by the Çukobirlik.

At the end of the harvest, the small producers, being unable to take their cotton to Elazığ, which is about 106 kilometres from the village, hand over their cotton either to big landlords or to cotton merchants, who provide the producers with credit in return for their cotton at a lower price than the market price. The difference between the market price and the price small producers get accrues to the big landlords, or to the merchants.

The same can be said for sugar beet. The main buyer is the Elazığ sugar factory. The small producer of sugar beet, either by his own choice or by the landlord's imposition, is not usually in a position to be able to transport his crop to Kezin railway station, where the representative of the Elazığ sugar factory buys the sugar beet. Again, merchants or relatively well-off producers play an intermediary role, appropriating a part of the small producer's production.

It is very rare for Kalhana households with only one or two animals to sell dairy products. It is those with quite a number of animals who sell both livestock and dairy products.

As we stated earlier, both villages are dependent on the market for some of their consumption needs, and for most of the things they use for production. The basic consumption goods bought by the Gisgis villagers include sugar, salt, paraffin, margarine, macaroni, matches, cigarettes, etc. and these are mainly obtained from the village grocer, who sells these items for cash or by instalments, or by bartering. The only items the grocer would normally purchase from his customers are cheese, butter and eggs, which could be sold daily within the village, mainly to the teachers, health officials, midwife and gendarmerie sergeant, as well as to some of the villagers. This is despite the fact that the basic production of the village is vegetables; they have to be marketed elsewhere. All other consumer goods, like clothing, chairs, woven carpets, etc. and agricultural tools such as sickles, hoes and spades, are bought in Ergani. Some items, like plastic plates, cotton thread, aluminium kitchen utensils may be obtained from the çerçis (itinerant pedlars) who travel from village to village on donkeys or mules, selling or bartering all sorts of goods. It is mainly women who make transactions by bartering.

There is no village shop in Kalhana, but there are two pedlars living in the village, travelling between the town and nearby villages, selling all sorts of odd things, as well as some consumer goods such as sugar and cigarettes. Kalhana villagers are more dependent on the market than Gisgis villagers because 67 per cent of the families during our fieldwork did not have any access to land. Most of the people have to buy all their consumption needs from somewhere. Since the landless people generally do not have ready cash to buy their staple food, wheat, they apply to one of the big landlords to obtain wheat on credit. The debt is usually paid in labour. However, not everybody can get wheat on credit from the landlords; some are left to solve their problem by themselves.

Again, most of the consumption goods are bought in Ergani. However, the landlords, being concerned about the quality and the type of the things they consume and use, very often make a trip to Diyarbakır, Ankara or Istanbul to obtain their needs. They usually obtain their luxury goods, such as televisions, cars, carpets, ornaments and furniture from Diyarbakır if it is possible. Otherwise they do not hesitate to use the excuse to make a 'small trip for a break, to get away from this boring and suffocating environment', in the words of Fuat Aydoğan.

The arguments put forward in this chapter complement those of the previous chapter. The peasants are urged by the state to produce for the market, but they are not given the necessary implements and credits for this. The amount of credits given to small producers has been extremely insufficient, and thus the peasants have been left at the mercy of merchants and usurers. The inability of the state to organise necessary marketing conditions has resulted in the exploitation of the small producers by the merchants and usurers. The floor price policy has been far from beneficial to the small producer. Being continuously exploited and indebted, the peasant household has either lost its means of production or resorted to what we may call 'self exploitation'. In order to survive, the peasant household lengthens its working periods and seeks supplementary income. It is this need to earn some cash outside the household which forces some of the members of the household to migrate from the village, permanently or temporarily. In the following chapter, we shall deal with this migration question in Gisgis and Kalhana.

Notes to Chapter Nine

1. Varlier, 1978
2. Ramachandran, 1974
3. Cillov, 1979
4. Cumhuriyet 29 June 1979
5. Cumhuriyet 29 July 1979
6. Cumhuriyet 12 August, 13 August 1979
7. Cumhuriyet 18 September 1979
8. Kafaoğlu, 1979
9. See State Planning Organisation, 1976
10. Avcıoğlu, 1968
11. Avcıoğlu, 1968, 440
12. Erdem, 1968
13. Yön Dergisi III
14. Mülayim, 1979
15. Selçuk, 1968
16. Milliyet, 7 October 1969
17. Hassan, 1970 and Çetiner, 1967
18. Diyarbakır Provincial Yearbook, 1973, 556
19. Ibid., 555
20. Ibid., 530
21. Ibid., 567

10. Patterns Of Migration

Permanent and seasonal out-migration from Eastern and Southeast Anatolia has a very long history. Rapid industrialisation and expansion of incomes in Europe promoted the demand for Turkish tobacco, cotton, raisins and other cash crops. During the second half of the nineteenth century, European capital and technology provided railways, ports, irrigation works, banks and assistance in the development of certain crops. (1) Cotton was one of the most important crops for export:

> In the twentieth century, Germany played a leading part in the development of cotton cultivation in Turkey, seeking to establish there a raw material base for its cotton textile industry. (2)

Novichev, writing in 1937, states that the Adana region attracted quite a number of seasonal workers:

> The majority of farm labourers were temporary workers who, especially during harvest time, left their villages in large crowds seeking work in the cotton areas. Often

whole groups went from one locality headed by their elders, who served as intermediaries between the labourers and the employers and received the whole wage fund for distribution among the individuals; taking advantage of their position, the elders thoroughly robbed their countrymen. The cotton region of Adana drew from 50,000 to 70,000 workers during harvest time. (3)

The rural masses were forced to seek additional income to pay their debts and to meet the needs of their families, not because the rapid development of capitalism proletarianised rural people who had to work as agricultural labourers, but because of the heavy taxation levied on the peasantry, coupled with merchant usury and landlord exploitation.

Today, cotton is not only exported as a raw material but is also used in Turkey's newly-developed textile industry. For this reason, cotton-growing regions have become even more important in drawing larger and larger numbers of labourers. In this chapter we shall attempt to give some particulars of out-migration from Gisgis and Kalhana.

Migration in Gisgis

Gisgis is affected mainly by out-migration. There are a number of families who have migrated into the village from other places, but this in-migration is generally insignificant: only eight families had moved into the village in the last ten years. Three of these were the families of the school-teacher, the nurse and the caretaker of the health centre, all of whom were appointed to their jobs in the village. Of the others, two families were from the neighbouring village, Sincik, who had no source of income in Sincik and had to come to Gisgis to sharecrop the lands of two teachers who were absentee landowners. Two families were from the villages of Dicle district, who bought land in the village through their relatives, and one family fled from their village because of a protracted blood feud which had claimed ten deaths to date. The head of this household works in Maden copper mine, which is about 40 kilometres away from the village, and he comes home at weekends.

Apart from the families who have come to settle in the village, there is a movement of individual women into the village through marriage. We noted that 20 heads of families had brought brides from other places. However, this movement of people through marriage is hardly significant in terms of migration.

In order to gauge the extent of emigration from Gisgis, household heads were asked whether or not they had any relatives outside the village. Table 32 is derived from the answers to this question:

TABLE 32 NUMBER OF RELATIVES LIVING OUTSIDE THE VILLAGE

NUMBER OF RELATIVES	HOUSEHOLDS	
	NUMBER	PERCENTAGE
None	24	14.7
1	64	39.0
2	31	18.9
3	21	12.8
4	13	7.9
9	11	6.7
Total	164	100.0

140 households have relatives living outside the village - 343 persons in all - and only 24 households have none. It should be noted, however, that most of the households in the village have kinship relations in common with other village households: thus two or more households might well have been referring to the same family or person when they identified their relatives living outside Gisgis, thus inflating the figure quoted above. Nevertheless, despite these possible ambiguities, it is certain that the level of migration from the village is very high.

Household heads were also asked to state to what destination their relations had migrated. It was evident from the answers (Table 33) that the Çukurova region, especially Tarsus and

Adana, was the most attractive place for rural migrants. As stated earlier, this is due to the rapid development of agriculture, labour-intensive cash crop production and import substitution industries in Adana and Tarsus.

TABLE 33 DESTINATIONS OF MIGRANTS FROM GISGIS

PLACE	PERSONS	
	NUMBER	PERCENTAGE
Ergani centre	72	21.0
Villages of Ergani	31	9.0
Diyarbakır	45	13.1
Tarsus/Adana	115	33.5
Elazığ/Maden	25	7.3
Ankara/Izmir/Istanbul etc.	42	12.3
West Germany (4)	13	3.8
Total	343	100.0

One of the older men of the village told us that fifty-two households had emigrated to Tarsus. The head of the first family to make this move had been there three summers before the emigration, working in the cotton fields as a hoer and cotton picker. Since he was offered a permanent job as an overseer in a capitalist farm in Tarsus, he took the opportunity and moved his family there, leaving his 10 <u>dönüms</u> of dry land for his relatives to sharecrop.

The mechanism of emigration to Tarsus and Adana is as follows: previously-emigrated families inform their relatives about job possibilities and, if the informed heads of households in the village are convinced that the job will increase their standard of living, they go to Tarsus or Adana to take the job and find accommodation. If they are satisfied with the new environment and the job they will come back and collect their families.

In addition to economic factors, social factors also force people to emigrate from the village. Blood feuds, whatever their cause, are very effective factors in making people emigrate from rural areas. Ali Çelen informed us that, in 1972, six families emigrated from the village because of a blood feud. The incident happened on a summer's day. Some straw had been left by the Alp family in a field near a place called Çay, after the harvest. Two oxen belonging to Bahri, of Mehmet Ağa's family, ate some of the straw while passing through the field, without his realising it. The wife of the owner of the field beat the oxen and then insulted and provoked Bahri, who, having first apologised to the woman, then began to reply to her insults in a similar vein. The woman went home and incited her husband and her father to action. The same evening, the father and the husband, mad with rage, went up to Bahri's house swearing and calling to him to come out. As soon as Bahri replied, they opened fire, in the dark, in the direction from which the voice was coming. One of the bullets hit Bahri's pregnant wife in the heart and she died instantly. In response to this, Bahri's nephew, the son of his brother Mehmet, shot down, with eight bullets, Kerim, the leader of the Alp family, in the market place in Ergani. Realising the impossibility of living in fear of reprisal, six households from Mehmet Ağa's family left the village for Adana to join other relatives there.

Ergani, as the nearest urban centre, attracts quite a number of people from the village. People migrating to Ergani, which is a commercial centre for the neighbouring villages and is in the process of rapid urbanisation, can find jobs in building construction and transportation. Those who emigrate to Ergani usually keep their ties with the village. They are provided with wheat and processed wheat (bulgur, döğme, cücük, etc.), grapes and products made from grapes (pestil, sucuk, pekmez, etc.). Apart from the job possibilities, the relatively easier life-style of the town, as well as educational reasons, are some of the other factors encouraging migrants to go to town centres. In the same way, those who emigrate to Ankara, Istanbul, Izmir, Diyarbakır and Elazığ also work more or less in the same sort of jobs in factories, building construction, transportation, etc.

From 1961 onwards, Turkey has been exporting workers to Western Europe, mainly to West Germany. The rapid development of capitalism in the West necessitated a labour force which could not be supplied by their own human resources as profitably as it would be by workers from less developed countries. (5) Quite a number of people of rural origin went to Western Europe before 1971, though the proportion of workers of rural origin declined during the decade 1961-71. (6)

Thirteen men from Gisgis were working in West Germany at the time of our survey - most of them between the ages of 20 and 30 - as brick-layers, carpenters, dustmen and street cleaners. Four of the workers were married before they went to Germany and left their wives and children with their parents. The families of these workers complained that they did not send money regularly from Germany. Some of them sent money to their parents and children a few times but irregularly, once in three or four months. As far as the families left behind were concerned, the workers in Germany were carried away with the attractions and bad habits of the West and were spending all their money there.

We asked the relatives of those people who had left the village why their relatives had left. The reasons given have been categorised in Table 34.

TABLE 34 REASONS FOR LEAVING THE VILLAGE

REASON CITED	NUMBER OF PEOPLE	PERCENTAGE
To seek work	210	61.2
Appointment as civil servant	33	9.6
Marriage	77	22.5
Blood feud	23	6.7
Total	343	100.0

It is clear that the majority of people who emigrated from the village did so for economic reasons. Those who left the village because of marriage were exclusively women. Bearing in mind the vagueness of the answer 'to seek work', we tried to obtain information on what sort of occupations were taken up by the emigrants (Table 35).

TABLE 35 OCCUPATIONS OF RELATIVES LIVING OUTSIDE THE VILLAGE

OCCUPATION	NUMBER OF PEOPLE	PERCENTAGE
Casual unskilled labourer	57	16.6
Agricultural labourer	23	6.7
Industrial labourer	46	13.4
Civil servant	33	9.6
Trader (including grocer, wholesaler etc.)	16	4.7
Artisan	9	2.6
Driver	13	3.8
Farmer	27	7.9
Housewife	70	20.4
Unknown	49	14.3
Total	343	100.0

The interviews also revealed that relatively rich farmers and usurers, as well as the rural poor and proletarians had left the village. Those who had accumulated some money capital from usury and those who had saved some money, either from agricultural production or from working somewhere for a period of time, or both, had either opened a grocery shop in the place where they had settled, or had invested their money in transportation. Some of them became grain merchants in Ergani town centre, giving credits to the farmers from their own or from other villages.

However, most of the people who left the village were those who either had no land, had lost their land because of indebtedness, or did not have enough land to sustain their family. Continuous land fragmentation, due to the population increase and the existing inheritance system, forces a part of the rural population to migrate to towns and cities. Moving to urban areas does not automatically solve all the unemployment problems, nor does it always alleviate the misery of the migrants. The very low level of industrialisation in urban areas does not allow the migrant population to be absorbed. After moving into a town centre, the migrants, if they have been unable to find a job, endeavour to create a business for themselves.

For example, in Ergani, male children of migrant families become shoe polishers and cold water or soft drink sellers in the streets from the age of 9 or 10 onwards. These drink sellers buy ice from housewives who have a refrigerator at home and are pleased to get a small amount of cash to help cover electricity costs, or to buy small items for themselves. The sellers then wander about in the market place with a decanter full of ice-cold water, ayran or lemonade, shouting 'Drink icy water' and the like, during the hot summer days. Female children may become beggars, going from house to house in the relatively rich areas of the town, asking for food, old clothes and money. Adult members of the family may become street vendors, selling all sorts of things, such as needles, cotton, plastic toys, household equipment, vegetables, fruit and nuts.

We have listed just some of the occupations in which the migrant workers may engage. Of course, this list is in no way exhaustive, nor representative of all the migrants in the urban areas of Turkey, since it is based on the declarations of the relatives of the migrants from Gisgis village. To what extent the figures given in this list are significant for the village, Ergani, or the whole of Turkey is arguable, but the main aim in giving these figures is not so much to derive any empiricist conclusion but rather to attempt to understand some tendencies in the employment of rural migrants in urban centres.

So far we have dealt with the question of permanent migration from Gisgis; however, this is only one side of the coin. We should also have a look at seasonal migration from the village. We have seen that peasant-based household economy predominates in the village and that households produce not only for home consumption but also for the market. However, all the economic activities of the household are geared to the reproduction of the household as an economic and social unit.

Being a part of a capitalist social formation, the household is inevitably involved in capitalist market relations, which pump out a part of the product produced by the household economic unit through the price mechanism. Coupled with this, usurous exploitation and the high rate of interest paid to banking capital, as well as ground rent in some cases, appropriated by landowners through various kinds of sharecropping arrangements, play important parts in the pauperisation of the peasants. In order to be able to reproduce itself, the household sends out some of its labour force to bring in supplementary income.

It is at this point that seasonal migration comes into existence. In addition to the low income of the household, the nature of agricultural work, the distribution of land, the division of labour within the household and population pressure are also effective in pushing out some of the labour force from the rural areas. For instance, in Gisgis, where vegetables and fruit (melons and grapes) are produced mainly for the market and grains for home consumption, the agricultural cycle leaves some of the work force unemployed. We asked the heads of households to state the number of months during which they had been unemployed in the past year (Table 36).

TABLE 36 UNEMPLOYMENT IN GISGIS

NUMBER OF MONTHS UNEMPLOYED	NUMBER OF UNEMPLOYED HOUSEHOLD HEADS	PERCENTAGE UNEMPLOYED
0	39	23.8
1-3	6	3.7
4-6	34	20.7
7-9	42	25.6
10-12	43	26.2
Total	164	100.0

Only 39 heads of household said that they were fully employed all through the year; all the rest had been unemployed at some time during each year. Considering the fact that some of these heads of households (teachers, caretakers, workers, drivers, etc.) do not derive their main income from agriculture, we can visualise the concealed form of unemployment within the village. Despite long periods of unemployment, not everybody would go out of the village for a seasonal job, owing to the uncertainties involved in finding one. For this reason, heads of households would sometimes send out their grown-up sons to earn a supplementary income, rather than going themselves. However, sixty heads of household had gone to work outside the village for a period of time in the year prior to our fieldwork in 1977.

The figures in Table 37 do not include those members of households who work outside the village for a period of time. However, this is not important for our purpose, which is to try to see the role of the household as an economic unit acting as a source for the labour requirements of developing rural and urban capitalism.

TABLE 37 SEASONAL LABOURERS OF GISGIS

NUMBER OF MONTHS WORKED OUTSIDE THE VILLAGE	NUMBER OF HOUSEHOLD HEADS WORKING OUTSIDE THE VILLAGE
1	3
2	17
3	12
4	4
5	8
6	10
12	6

Seasonal workers from Gisgis generally go to one of three areas: Diyarbakır province, Elazığ province, or the Çukurova region. Capitalist farms producing cotton in Adana in the Çukurova region, in Elazığ and, to a certain extent, in Diyarbakır, are the most important places in terms of seasonal wage labour recruitment. The development of capitalist agriculture and the production of cotton as a cash crop are, to a great degree, fairly new phenomena in both Diyarbakır and Elazığ, but they are well established in the Çukurova region. (7)

The proximity of the cities of Diyarbakır and Elazığ for the peasants of those provinces leads seasonal workers to prefer to seek work in their own provincial centres. However, the limited level of labour requirements in these two neighbouring provinces forces the seasonal migrant workers to go to other regions to seek employment. Building and road construction works are the two non-agricultural fields which offer job opportunities for seasonal migrants. The number of migrants who seek employment in construction work is very high. The competition among workers reduces the actual earnings of those who are employed in this sector, for there is no unionisation among such workers.

Migration in Kalhana

Unlike Gisgis, Kalhana attracts quite a number of migrant workers from the neighbouring villages, as well as from some more remote ones. A combination of several factors promoted the development of the production of cotton as a cash crop in the village and its vicinity. Commercial agriculture is a fairly new phenomenon in Southeast Anatolia, and is a result of the area becoming more integrated into the capitalist world economy. Such integration affects different areas at different times, and the time of integration is determined by various factors, such as the importance of the area for the capitalist world economy, the level of development of the productive forces in the area, the social formation of which the area is a part and the class formation within the social formation, etc.

Commercialisation of agriculture in Turkey has been intensified since the 1950s, as a result of a new policy adopted by the Democrat Party in accordance with the wishes of the West to direct Turkey towards becoming a source of food and raw materials. Industrialisation was doomed to be of the assembly type, and dependent. Without agriculture being commercialised, it was very difficult for the Turkish bourgeoisie (of a collaborative nature) to transfer resources from this sector. Also, the need for foreign currency for the importation of raw materials and intermediary goods intensified policies for the development of the prodúction of cash crops like cotton, tobacco and hazelnuts, which constitute most of Turkey's exports. New areas have been taken over for the production of these export crops. For example, the area under cotton production has risen from 297,761 hectares in 1948 to 674,419 hectares in 1980, and that devoted to tobacco from 106,099 to 290,000 over the same period. (8)

Farmers have been urged to produce commercial crops and have been provided with credits, seeds, fertilisers, etc. Short-term needs for foreign currency forced the government to provide these things to the farmers of suitable areas for the production of the desired crops. This was especially so in Southeast Anatolia, and in places like Kalhana, where natural resources allow the production of cotton. However, the construction of dams and canals is still under way in the area, in order to promote agricultural development. The nature of land distribution in the region, coupled with the mechanisation of agriculture in accordance with the new policy adopted in the 1950s, brought about huge marketable grain surpluses, which were paid for at higher than world market prices for political reasons, thus leading to the enrichment of the big landowners who produce for the market. In short, we can say that, as a result of the policy applied since the 1950s, some new areas were taken over for the production of cash crops like cotton. Kalhana is one of these places. It should also be emphasised that the nature of cotton production necessitates a large number of labourers, at least for a period of time during the production year.

Not only does a temporary labour force come to the village seasonally or daily to work in the cotton fields, but also some people come to the village to settle permanently, or at least for a few years. This is largely due to the big landlords' efforts to keep an easily-accessible labour source in the village in order to meet their labour requirements at peak seasons. In order to see the extent of migration for permanent, or at least for long-term, settlement in the village, we asked the heads of households to state whether they and their wives had been born in the village and, if not, where. We also asked when and why they had come to the village (Table 38).

TABLE 38 ORIGINS OF HOUSEHOLD HEADS AND THEIR WIVES IN KALHANA

ORIGINS	HUSBAND	WIFE/WIVES	TOTAL	PERCENTAGE
Born in the village	27	20	47	52.8
Born outside the village	16	26	42	47.2
Total	43+	46++	89	100.0

\+ One unmarried household head was excluded from the calculation.

++ Three of our respondents had two wives each, therefore the number of wives exceeds the number of husbands.

It is evident from Table 38 that quite a number of residents are not natives of the village. Given the patrilocal nature of the families, we can assume that some of the females came to the village for reasons other than the village's attraction as a place with work possibilities. This patrilocal nature of the families also excludes the possibility of the heads of households coming to the village because of marriage. More than one-third of the heads of resident families came from outside and have stayed in the village. Table 39 indicates the origins of the immigrants.

TABLE 39 ORIGINS OF HOUSEHOLD HEADS AND THEIR WIVES BORN OUTSIDE KALHANA

LOCATION OF ORIGIN	NUMBER	PERCENTAGE
Ergani centre	3	7.1
Villages of Ergani	36	85.7
Diyarbakır and its district other than Ergani	1	2.4
Other	2	4.8
Total	42	100.0

Most of the immigrants are from the villages of Ergani. They are mostly the poor of their village who could not survive there because they had neither land nor cattle, nor were there any job opportunities in their village. The majority of immigrant families live in houses or one- or two-roomed accommodation owned by the landlords in the village and pay very little or no rent for their accommodation. These arrangements satisfy both the landlords and immigrants. From the immigrants' point of view, finding a free, or at least cheap shelter and the prospect of work, seasonal though it may be, is better than nothing. From the landlords' point of view, having tied the immigrants to the village through the supply of free accommodation and assistance in case of difficulties, they will be able to meet at least a part of their labour requirements. Furthermore, the proximity of the village to Ergani town gives the immigrants the possibility of commuting between the village and town if they want to, and are able to find work there. Having stationed themselves in the village, one or two members of the family may go to town, working as porters, ameles, drivers and such like, while the rest of the family stays in the village and goes to work in the cotton fields whenever their labour is required.

The flow of immigrants into the village for employment does not mean that there is no out-flow of workers from the village. A number of people resident in the village leave for a period of time to seek employment either when their labour is not needed or when they find a better paying job outside. The nature of the village economy does not allow year-round employment for the poor, although a few of them may become personal servants of the landlord families.

Some members of households leave the village for a permanent job in urban centres and visit their families intermittently, the frequency of their visits depending on the distance of the place of work from the village, whether or not they are married and the amount of money they earn. If their earnings are not sufficient to meet their transport costs, they forego visits to the village. For instance, Hacı Gedikli works in the Sümerbank Yün Yıkama ve Şayak Fabrikası (Sumerbank Wool-washing and Serge

Factory) in Diyarbakır, earning about TL3,000 per month. He is married, with five children, the oldest being 15 years of age. His monthly income is not enough to enable him to take his family with him to Diyarbakır, where the cost of living is much higher than in the village. In the village, his family pays no rent, for they own their house. In order to repay his debts, Hacı Gedikli sold 20 dönüms of his land, and then sold the remaining 20 dönüms in order to bribe the officials so that he could get the job in Diyarbakır. Now he has no land, apart from a very small plot in front of his house, where they grow some vegetables, but these are far from sufficient to meet the family's needs. His wife and three older children work as cotton pickers in the village for a month or so in the autumn. His oldest son, Kemal, started to work for the first time in irrigating cotton for Fuat Bey, but he was paid a lower wage than the other men because he was younger. As a reason for employing him at a cheaper rate, Fuat Bey told him: 'Well, I am afraid I cannot employ you because you are very young and you cannot work as hard as the other workers. If you accept 10 liras per hour, as a favour I will employ you. If I did not like you and your father I would not take you on as a worker at this age'. So, although Kemal worked as hard as the others, he was paid less than the average worker. Hacı comes home fortnightly to see his family.

There are some other heads of households who have left their families in the village for permanent wage work. For example, Hüseyin Ergin works in Sivas and only comes to the village for a few days every three or four months. Whenever he comes home he brings money for his wife and children. Another example is Efrahim Kahraman, who works for Devlet Demir Yolları (The State Railways). He is able to visit his family in the village every week. He too has no land, and his family also works in the cotton fields.

These are only a few examples of the out-migration from the village. We asked the heads of households who were native to the village to state if they had any relations living outside the village (Table 40).

TABLE 40 NUMBER OF RELATIVES LIVING OUTSIDE KALHANA

NUMBER OF RELATIVES	NUMBER OF NATIVE HOUSEHOLDS	PERCENTAGE OF NATIVE HOUSEHOLDS
None	0	0.0
1	1	3.7
2	4	14.8
4	7	25.9
5	7	25.9
7	8	29.6
Total	27	100.0

Not a single native householder had no relative living outside the village. The declared number of relatives of native household heads was 126 in 1977, which shows the result of rapid depeasantisation of agriculture in the village as an aspect of general developments in Turkish agriculture. It was obvious from our interviews with the relatives of the emigrants remaining in the village that most of the people who had emigrated from the village had done so from the 1960s onwards.

Fehim Kaval's story seems to be relevant here. Fehim was born in Kalhana in 1920. His father owned about 50 <u>dönüms</u> of land. Around the 1940s, three successive crop failures due to bad weather conditions led his father to borrow a considerable amount of wheat and animal fodder from Şemsi Bey, in order to be able to alleviate the starvation conditions of his family and animals. Since he failed to repay his debt, he had to mortgage his land to Şemsi Bey for five years, on the condition that he would work the land on a sharecropping basis; Şemsi Bey would be considered the owner of the land and would provide the seed for cultivation. This meant, in fact, that Fehim's father had become a sharecropper on his own land, giving half of his products to his creditor. Eventually, Fehim's father was not able to repay his debt, and so he sold his land to Şemsi Bey, but he continued to work for both Şemsi Bey and Sami Bey as a sharecropper. On the death of Fehim's father in 1955, Fehim's two younger brothers left the village to seek work in the Çukurova, and later one of them found his way to West Germany in 1964.

Before the arrival of the first tractor in the village, land was cultivated by using oxen as draught animals, and the productivity of the soil for wheat did not exceed a return of 5 or 6 to one. When Sami Bey brought the first tractor into the village in 1960, most of his sharecroppers, previously landowning peasants, rebelled against him and his family, under the leadership of Şefik and Haci Gedikli, the descendants of Lobud Ağa. These men realised that the strength of the Aydoğan family had undermined their previous authority, which had stemmed from their grandparents' control over a vast amount of land, now mostly controlled by the Aydoğan family. The Gediklis provoked the peasants by saying that if the tractor was established as a means of production in the village, they would lose the usage of the land as sharecroppers. However, it was not too difficult for the Aydoğan family to suppress the rebellious peasants by calling in the military police (gendarmerie). Those who had occupied the Aydoğan lands in order to prevent the tractor being used in the village were not given any land by the Aydoğans to sharecrop for the following year. The instigators of the movement themselves did not have enough land to be able to let these people work as sharecroppers on their lands in order to compensate them for the loss incurred as a result of participating in the actions against the Aydoğans. Not only those people who had rebelled against the Aydoğans, but also some others, lost their access to land as a result of the machinery obtained by the Aydoğans with the credits supplied by the Agricultural Bank.

With the gradual enlargement of cotton production, which already existed in the village, from the 1960s onwards, the Aydoğans let some of the poor of other villages settle in Kalhana on condition that they would send one or two workers to work in the cotton fields. Of course, the amount of work and remuneration that cotton fields in the village can provide are not enough to sustain the growing number of village residents. Consequently, a part of the village population seeks work outside the village, seasonally or permanently. As a result, the mechanisation of agriculture increased the volume of migration into and out of the village. Seasonal migrants usually go to the nearby towns and cities to work in road and building construction. Some of them would even go to Adana, Istanbul or Izmir to work. The number of people declared by their relatives in the village to have emigrated, and the places to which they have migrated are given in Table 41.

TABLE 41 DESTINATIONS OF MIGRANTS FROM KALHANA

PLACE	NUMBER OF PERSONS	PERCENTAGE OF TOTAL
Ergani centre	31	24.6
Villages of Ergani	11	8.7
Diyarbakır	22	17.5
Tarsus/Adana	20	15.9
Elazığ/Maden	16	12.7
Ankara/Izmir/Istanbul etc.	21	16.7
West Germany	5	3.9
Total	126	100.0

It is obvious that, being the nearest urban centre, Ergani has attracted most of the migrants. As stated previously, Ergani is not an industrial centre to offer jobs to migrants. However, it is a commercial centre for a number of villages, as well as an administrative centre. (9) Rapid urbanisation of the town created new jobs in the service sector for the immigrants. Some of the migrants worked for others as <u>muavin</u> (assistant driver, helping the driver of a lorry or minibus, or coach), drivers, doorkeepers in government offices, porters for grain merchants, bakers in one of the several bakeries, and waiters in restaurants and coffee houses (which have mushroomed in the past 15 years). In 1977 there were 52 coffee houses in Ergani centre. Coffee houses in Turkey are the places where men gather together to play cards and drink tea and coffee. Some men would spend their whole day in these places. One of the native villagers told me: 'If you want to study the level of unemployment, have a look at the number of coffee houses per head in a place. Fifteen years ago there were only two or three coffee houses in this town, now their number is about a hundred'. He was exaggerating the number of coffee houses in Ergani, but he was right to use it as an indication of the level of unemployment. Men who are unable to find employment try to establish a business of their own, as street vendors selling things like çekirdek (roasted seeds of pumpkin, melon, water melon or sunflowers), nuts, leblebi (roasted chick peas), fruit, vegetables, plastic toys and so on.

Diyarbakır and Elazığ are two near and rapidly-developing provincial centres which can offer work for migrants. A number of state-owned factories, like the cement factory, sugar factory, the copper and chromium mine in Elazığ and the rakı (an alcoholic drink) factory, the wool-washing and serge factory in Diyarbakır, as well as hundreds of small privately owned workshops producing all sorts of things, are places where migrants can get work. The administrative apparatus and service are other sectors which offer work possibilities for migrants. However, the volume of migration is much higher than the number of jobs the cities can offer to migrants, because the development of industry cannot keep up with both the population explosion and the rapid proletarianisation of the rural masses. The most industrialised centres, like Istanbul, Izmir, Bursa, Ankara and Adana are also far from being able to absorb the rural masses released from their agricultural ties. The great distance between our study area and the more developed region of Western Turkey, coupled with uncertainties in finding work in the West, play a part in discouraging the choice of these distant destinations. Migrants prefer to go to the nearest urban centre, where they can keep their ties with the village community and relatives, and can seek help in case of difficulties. On the other hand, whenever they can overcome the uncertainties in finding work, they do not hesitate to travel 'to the other end of the world', in other words, to western Europe.

Finally, it might be added that those who stay in the village also seek to earn supplementary income by selling their labour to others. Apart from the peak season, however, the village economy is not capable of absorbing this labour force. Furthermore, the amount of land sharecropped by most of the sharecropping families does not absorb the whole labour force available in the family. This is in addition to the fact that the seasonal nature of agricultural production in the village, as well as the division of labour by sex within the household economy, leaves a part of the household labour force unused. Although all the heads of sharecropping families said that they were unemployed for a period of time each year, six of them said they had gone out of the village to seek work for two to five months of the year. On the other hand, those labourers with no access to land (there were twelve such families in the village) stated that at least one or two male members of their families would be out of the village seeking work of any sort while the women-folk and children would stay in the village, working in the cotton fields during the summer.

The exploitation of the peasant households by landlords, merchants, usurers and the state brings about a continuous impoverisation and even, in some cases, complete proletarianisation of the peasants.

Knowing the very limited job prospects outside agriculture, the peasant household tries as hard as possible to maintain their most important means of production: land. Seasonal work outside agriculture helps the peasant household to reproduce itself. On the other hand, capitalism takes advantage of the cheap seasonal labour, for which a part of the subsistence needs is met by the households in the village.

Notes to Chapter Ten

1. See Issawi, 1966, especially Part II Introduction; also the article by Von Pressel, and the extract from _Ziraat Tarihine Bir Bakış_ entitled 'The expansion of tobacco-growing in the nineteenth century, both _in_ Issawi
2. Novichev, 1937, 67-68
3. Novichev, 1937, 68-69

4. Although almost all respondents who had relations working in Europe stated that they were in Germany, we realised that some of these workers from the village were in fact in other Western European countries, and not only in Germany. The uniformity of the answers arose from the peasants' inability to differentiate West Germany from the rest of Europe. For example, they would ask where abouts in Germany was England. The same interpretation was evident among the peasants of Kalhana also.
5. See Paine, 1974 and Berger, 1975
6. Paine, 1974, 75-76
7. See Novichev, 1966
8. Varlier, 1978 and State Institute of Statistics
9. According to the village inventory surveys in 1962/63, carried out by the Ministry of Village Affairs, a total of 74 villages had direct economic relations with Ergani centre, 70 of which were also within the administrative boundaries of the town. See Köy Işleri Bakanlığı, 1966, 20-21

11. Conclusion

Turkish workers constitute a major part of the migrant labour force in Western European economies, especially in the case of West Germany, where they number approximately one million. This migrant labour force has played a central role in the rapid development of West European economies, particularly that of Germany, but has failed to generate any significant benefits for Turkey itself. This is so despite popular misconceptions about the benefits accruing from Turkish workers' hard currency earnings. For, as was shown in the preceding chapters, migration of Turkish workers is a concrete manifestation of Turkey's underdevelopment: an underdevelopment which is itself conditioned by Turkey's position within the capitalist world economy, in which countries such as Germany occupy hegemonic positions.

The mechanisms by which this combined and uneven development/underdevelopment relationship between Turkey and western capital were brought about are beyond the scope of this volume. The primary concern has been to highlight some aspects of this unequal relationship and, in particular, to focus on some of its manifestations at the level of the village and the household economy. It is for this reason that an attempt has been made to examine the changing structures of landownership, the nature of production relations, marketing and finance mechanisms, share-cropping arrangements, etc. as they appear at the village level. For it is suggested that such forces, relations and mechanisms are important in determining the nature and rate both of labour migration and underdevelopment in Turkey.

In the foregoing chapters, the following arguments have been made:

(i) The unequal landownership structures have not only persisted but have actually intensified, with large estates consolidating their positions while small owners have been forced to relinquish ownership and control over their plots.

(ii) Despite changing ownership structures, the historic relationship between large landlords and peasant households seems to have been maintained, albeit under different conditions.

(iii) The division of labour in the household has been an important factor in allowing it to persist, despite the emergence of forces which undermine its viability.

(iv) The role of merchant and usurer's capital has been significant, both in expropriating peasant surpluses and in articulating the household and village economy with national and international economies.

(v) The state has played an important role in generating the necessary structures within which merchant, finance and usurer's capital can operate in a manner which places peasant producers at a disadvantage.

(vi) An important consequence of these factors has been the process of labour migration from the village to centres in the national economy, and then to other countries.

Nevertheless, it should also be pointed out that an important theoretical concern of this work has been the role and the nature of the household unit of production at the village level. From the discussions in the preceding chapters, it is possible to conclude that, at least in Southeastern Anatolia, the household unit continues to constitute an important factor in the generation of surpluses (product and labour) from the rural economy. Of particular interest is the nature of the relationship between an expanding capitalism and the household unit. For it was observed that, although capital conditions the structures within which the household reproduces itself, the household is by no means a passive recipient. This was clearly seen in the manner in which the household division of labour, for example, adjusts itself both in order to meet the ever-increasing demands of capital and to guarantee the reproduction of the household itself. As such, it is hoped that this work can be seen as a contribution to the current debates, referred to in the introduction, that concern themselves with the role and the nature of the peasant household economy.

It is, of course, to be hoped that hasty political actions will not again be taken before a thorough understanding of social structures has been arrived at, since miscomprehension of the rural structures in Turkey on the part of the Turkish left proved to be fatal.

In the foregoing chapters, we have tried to indicate some of the mechanisms through which capital extracts surplus from household producers in Southeastern Anatolia, and this has the connotation that capital does not have to use wage labour in order to accumulate. In both small peasant household production and large landlord estates, peasant family labour plays an instrumental role for the accumulation of capital. Marketing, credit systems and price control by the state are the basic mechanisms of surplus extraction from the peasant household in Southeastern Anatolia. Retention of certain aspects, such as the use of family labour, and ownership of the means of production, may lead one to think that household production is a pre-capitalist survival for, despite its formal appearance, the conditions of household production have dramatically changed in the course of its life history. Although the formal appearances of a household production unit in the Ottoman Empire and in modern Turkey may reveal similarities, the relations of production engaged in by the household unit are totally different. In today's Turkey, the capitalist mode of production is dominant and the conditions of reproduction of the household as a unit of production are determined by this mode. The concepts of real and formal subsumption of labour by capital seem to be applicable in the transformation of Turkish agrarian structures. The concept of formal subsumption implies that capital can achieve effective control of the production process without undertaking its immediate organisation or dispossessing the direct producers. If this assumption is tenable, then the focus of attention becomes not the future proletarianisation of the peasantry under the dominance of capitalism, but the relationship between family-based household production and the activities of different forms of capital.

In foregoing chapters, we have shown that the existence of peasant household units is vitally important in the functioning of landlord farms that are basically aimed at profit maximisation. Given the concrete historical, political and economic conjuncture in Turkey, the subsistence-seeking mentality of the household as a unit of production and reproduction plays an instrumental role in the profit maximisation of large landlord farms. The existence of sharecropping families in landlord-dominated Southeastern Anatolian agriculture is not a sign of semi-feudalism, as some might claim, but a reflection of the landlords' strategy to take advantage of concrete conditions, making use of the destitution of the peasant households struggling to survive.

The important thing for the household is to be able to obtain that amount of product which is necessary for its reproduction. However, the amount of labour spent in obtaining this level is not assessed in monetary terms. It is this patriarchal way of cost calculation that marks the viability of the household under conditions where an enterprise based on rational calculations could not survive. In the profit maximisation process, large farms in Southeastern Anatolia internalise this non-rational calculation of labour cost by the household. Therefore, it is possible to argue that wage labour is not the only form of labour to increase profitability in agriculture. Accordingly, in suggesting political strategies, one has to be very careful, otherwise the consequences may be quite tragic.

Capitalism can dominate agriculture without actually establishing wage-labour capital relations. The capitalist domination of agriculture should not be confused with the existence of capitalist relations of exploitation. In the analysis of capitalist domination of agriculture, one has also to take into consideration the role of the state in determining the conditions of peasant production. Although it has not been our major concern here, the importance of the Turkish State becomes apparent in the way in which it conditions the structures, such as transportation, marketing and finance, for the process of capital accumulation, and in its effect on the household economy; for example, as in the case of state policies *vis-à-vis* agricultural credit, provision of improved agricultural inputs, and the marketing of certain crops. In such cases, state policies act as mediators, guaranteeing the expropriation of peasant surpluses by merchants and usurers.

The way in which the state acts in order to ensure a transfer of surplus from the rural sector is determined by its position in the World Capitalist System and by the requirement of the system from the Turkish social formation. Therefore, the analysis of the Turkish rural structure has to take into consideration the triple alliance of the state, local capital and international capital. In practice, this takes the form of the relationships between the state (through its institutions), the multinational concerns like the International Bank for Reconstruction and Development (IBRD), the International Monetary Fund (IMF), etc., and merchants, industrialists, landlords, etc. Unless the relations are seen from a global perspective, it is impossible to obtain a full comprehension of relations at regional, local and holding or production levels.

In recent years, it has become fashionable to analyse the capitalist transformation of agriculture at the level of the holdings or units of production, as exemplified by the Turkish agrarian debate discussed in the introduction. It must be stated, however, that the changes in Turkish rural structures cannot be fully understood unless treated as part of Turkey's industrialisation efforts after the Second World War and in the light of the state policies which intensified this process of a specific type of industrialisation. It may be recalled that the type of industrialisation followed by Turkey in her further integration into the World Capitalist Economy after the Second

World War was in the nature of import substitution. Import substitution industrialisation was supported by continuous transfer of resources from the agricultural to the industrial sector. Agricultural products are the traditional export goods. In other words, the export sector has made a large contribution by supplying much-needed foreign currency for the importation of capital goods. To ensure the involuntary financing of the accumulation in industry by the agricultural sector, the terms of trade were used against the agricultural sector. The industrial sector was protected through terms of trade, tariff walls, arbitrary import quotas and low foreign exchange rates.

The development of the agricultural sector is vital for the maintenance of import substitution industrialisation. An increase in agricultural production would further help industrialisation not only by bringing in foreign currency but also by lowering wage levels. Strategies adopted by the state in Turkey to increase productivity in agriculture have always excluded land reform policies. What has been supported in agricultural policies so far has been change in the productive basis of agriculture without touching the existing landownership structure. However, the occasional threats of land reform have been very instrumental in the commercialisation and capitalisation of large estates. The state has subsidised this process through improving the infrastructure and providing agricultural machinery and inputs. The provision of improved seeds, fertilisers, credits, in short modern technology, by the state has intensified class divisions in the countryside. As in many underdeveloped countries, the introduction of the Green Revolution has contributed to the inequalities in income distribution in rural areas, mostly benefiting large private farms. (1) The adoption of Green Revolution policies in the 1950s and 1960s and the implementation of rural development policies in the late 1970s and onwards by the Turkish State has gone hand in hand with the general rural development policies of USAID and the International Bank for Reconstruction and Development (IBRD). (2) Under the auspices of USAID, a new, highly-yielding Mexican Wheat variety was introduced (3) and it was mainly the large holdings, with their access to credits, fertilisers and agricultural extension services which benefitted from it. In Turkey, in accordance with changes in the World Bank's policies towards rural development, a shift has been made in rhetorics. Following severe criticism that the green revolution policies intensified inequalities in underdeveloped countries, the World Bank changed its policies in rural development. The new policy aimed to reduce poverty in underdeveloped countries through integrated rural development projects. McNamara, warning the governments of the underdeveloped countries, suggested that resources should be devoted to the bottom 40 per cent of the population and the projects should concentrate on small producers. It should be pointed out that the most poverty-stricken people of the underdeveloped countries are not small farmers but the landless proletariat and the poor of the shanty towns. Although the Bank talks about improving the living standards of the poorest 40 per cent of the population, it has no clear idea how to go about it. Poverty is seen as something isolated from its economic, cultural and sociological dimensions. But, in the Bank's rhetoric, there is no reference to the causes of poverty in underdeveloped countries. What happens in practice is that the World Bank gives credits to governments to implement rural development projects. Whether or not the poor in the underdeveloped countries will benefit from these projects depends upon the existing structures. In fact, despite the rhetoric, the World Bank is not very interested in the welfare of the rural poor in underdeveloped countries. What it is interested in is the intensification of the countries' dependence upon the centres of the World Capitalist System. Debt bondage is one way of achieving this. Another point of interest for the World Bank is an overall increase in agricultural marketable surplus. Therefore the commercialisation of small production units is important; whether or not this commercialisation of small farms benefits the rural poor is another matter.

Turkey has used World Bank credits to a great extent in rural development projects. In the 1950s, through a Junker type of capitalist transformation, large landlords were encouraged to produce for the market. From the early 1970s onwards, however, as cheap food and the foreign currency requirements of import substitution industrialisation could not be met with the existing network of relations and technology, a series of measures were taken to increase the marketable surpluses of small producers. It must be emphasised that the target group of people are not the poor, as consistently suggested in the rhetoric of the World Bank and of governments in Turkey, but the farmers who are able to produce a marketable surplus. This is substantiated by the World Bank's involvement in the establishment of agri-business industry in underdeveloped countries. (4)

In short, the rural development process in underdeveloped countries is not of an isolated nature. To the naked eye the involvement of the state and the multinational interests might not be clear if the study is confined to one production unit or a village in isolation from its regional, national and international context. It is hoped that the discussion of the state may present a contribution to debates concerning state involvement in the development of agricultural capitalism in Third World economies.

In conclusion, therefore, it may be said that this book has attempted to grasp some aspects of the historical and ongoing process of underdevelopment experienced by Third World societies. It has done so by focusing on particular manifestations of this process in the cases of Gisgis and Kalhana villages of Southeast Anatolia. As such, it does not claim to present an exhaustive study of the development of agricultural capitalism or the process of underdevelopment in Turkey. The limitations of available secondary sources, time and space have determined the scope and extent of the subject matter. It is for these reasons that the above can only be seen as the first step of an ongoing intellectual concern with the complex manifestations of the development of capitalism and the underdevelopment of Third World formations.

Notes to Chapter Eleven

1. For the impact of Green Revolution policies in various underdeveloped countries, see de Janvry, 1981; Feder, 1977a, 1977b; Griffin, 1979; Pearse, 1980
2. For a detailed treatment of the World Bank and USAID's activities in agriculture, see Aydın, forthcoming
3. For a sympathetic treatment of USAID's involvements in Mexican wheat production in Turkey, see Aresvik, 1975
4. For a concise treatment of how agribusiness industry operates in underdeveloped countries, see Feder, 1975, 1976

Bibliography

ABADAN-UNAT, Nemin (ed., 1979): Türk Toplumunda Kadın (Women in Turkish Society), Ankara: Türk Sosyal Bilimler Derneği Yayını

AKDAĞ, Mustafa (1945): 'Tımar rejiminin bozulusu' (Dissolution of the Tımar system), Ankara Üniversitesi Dil ve Tarih Coğrafya Fakültesi Dergisi IV

AKDAĞ, Mustafa (1971): Türkiye Iktisat Tarihi (Economic History of Turkey), Ankara: Ankara Universitesi Yayını

AKER, Ahmet (1975): 12 Mart Döneminde Dışa Bağlı Tekelleşme (Externally Dependent Monopolisation in the 12 March Period), Istanbul: Sander Yayınları

AKŞIT, Bahattin (1967): Türkiye' de Az Gelişmiş Kapitalizm ve Köylere Girişi (Underdeveloped Capitalism in Turkey and its Penetration into Villages), Ankara: DDTÜ Öğrenci Birliği Yayını

AKSOY, Suat (1969): 100 Soruda Türkiye' de Toprak Meselesi (The Land Problem in Turkey in 100 Questions), Istanbul: Gerçek Yayınevi

AKTAN, Reşat (1971): 'Analysis and evaluation of land reform activities in Turkey', Ankara Üniversitesi Siyasal Bilgiler Fakültesi Dergisi XXVI

AMIN, Semir (1976): Unequal Development, New York: Monthly Review Press

AMIN, Semir (1977): Imperialism and Unequal Development, Sussex: The Harvester Press

ARALOV, Semen Ivanoviç (1967): Bir Sovyet Diplomatının Türkiye Hatırları (A Soviet Diplomat's Memoirs of Turkey), Istanbul: Burçak Yayınevi

ARAS, Ali (1956): Güneydoğu Anadolu'da Arazi Mülkiyeti ve Işletme Şekilleri (Types of Landownership and Agricultural Management in Southeast Anatolia), Ankara: Ankara Universitesi Yayını

ARESVIK, Oddvar (1975): The Agricultural Development of Turkey, New York: Praeger

ARI, Oğuz (ed., 1977): Köy Sosyolojisi Okuma Kitabı (Rural Sociology Handbook), Istanbul: Boğaziçi Universitesi Yayınları

ASAD, Talal (ed., 1973): Anthropology and the Colonial Encounter, New York: Humanities Press

ATASAGUN, Yusuf Saim (1977): 'Türkiye'de teşkilatlı zirai kredi dağıtımının bugünkü durumu' (The current state of the distribution of organised agricultural credit in Turkey) in O. Ari (ed.): Köy Sosyolojisi Okumu Kitabı (Rural Sociology Handbook)

AVCIOĞLU, Dogan (1968): Türkiye'nin Düzeni: Dün - Bugün - Yarın (The Order of Turkey: Yesterday - Today - Tomorrow), Ankara: Bilgi Yayınevi

AYDEMIR, Şevket Süreyya (1966): Ikinci Adam, II (The Second Man, II), Istanbul: Remzi Kitabevi

AYDIN, Zülküf (forthcoming): Türkiye'de Azgelişmişlik ve Tarim Sorunu (Underdevelopment and the Agrarian Question), Ankara: Savaş Yayınları

AYNI ALI EFENDI (1964): Taksimat-ı Dar Livayı Ali Osman (Divisi of Ottoman Districts), Ankara: Gürsey Basımevi

BANAJI, Jairus (1976): 'Summary of selected parts of Kautsky's "The Agrarian Question"', Economy and Society 5(1)

BANAJI, Jairus (   ): 'Capitalist domination and the small peasantry: Deccan District in the late nineteenth century', Economic and Political Weekly XII (33-34)

BANAJI, Jairus (1977b): 'Modes of production in a materialist conception of history', Capital and Class 3

BARAN, Paul (1973): The Political Economy of Growth, Harmondsworth, Middlesex: Penguin Books

BARKAN, Ömer Lütfi (1937a): Osmanli Imparatorluğunun Kuruluş Devrinin Toprak Meseleleri (Land Problems of the Ottoman Empire in the Establishment Period), Ankara: Çiğir Matbaasi

BARKAN, Ömer Lütfi (1937b): 'Osmanli imparatorluğunda çiftçi sınıfların hukuki statusu' (Legal status of the farming classes in the Ottoman Empire), Ulku IX (50)

BARKAN, Ömer Lütfi (1938): 'Türkiye'de toprak meselelerinin tarihi esasları' (Historical principles of the land problem in Turkey), Ulku Dergisi XI (61, 63, 64)

BARKAN, Ömer Lütfi (1940): 'Türk toprak hukuku tarihinde Tanzimat ve 1274 (1858) arazi kanunnamesi' (The Tanzimat and the 1274 (1858) land law in the history of Turkish land law), Tanzimat I, Istanbul

BARKAN, Ömer Lütfi (1943): XV ve XVI Asırlarda Osmanli Imperatorluğunda Ziraı Ekonominin Hukuki ve Mali Esasları, C.I, Kanunlar (Legal and Financial Basis of the Agricultural Economy of the Ottoman Empire in the 15th and 16th Centuries, Vol I, Laws), Istanbul: Istanbul Üniversitesi Yayını

BAŞAR, Ahmet Hamdi (1966): 'Hatıralar: meşrutiyetten cumhuriyete kadar' (Memoirs: from constitutional monarchy to republic), Bariş Dünyası V(54)

BAYAR, Celal (1954): Celal Bayar'ın Söylev ve Demeçleri, 1920-1953 (Speeches and Statements of Celal Bayar, 1920-1953) collected by Özel Sahingiray, Ankara

BAYSAL, Ayşe (1979): 'Turk kadınının beslenme sorunları' (Nutritional problems of Turkish women) in Nermin Abadan-Unat (ed): Türk Toplumunda Kadın, 133-148, Ankara, Türk Sosyal Bilimler Derneği

BERGER, John (1975): A Seventh Man, Harmondsworth, Middlesex: Penguin Books

BERKES, Niyazi (1942): Ankara Köyleri Üzerinde bir Araştirma (Research on the Villages of Ankara), Ankara: Ankara Üniversitesi Yayını

BERKI, Şakir (1960): Toprak Hukuku (Land Law), Ankara: Ankara Üniversitesi Yayını

BERNSTEIN, Henry (1976): 'Capital and peasantry in the epoch of imperialism', Economic Research Bureau, University of Dar es Salam (mimeo)

BERNSTEIN, Henry (1977): 'Notes on capital and peasantry', Review of African Political Economy, 10, 60-73

BERNSTEIN, Henry (1979): 'African peasantries: a theoretical framework', Jnl. of Peasant Studies VI(4)

BEŞIKÇI, Ismail (1969): Doğu Anadolu'nun Düzeni: Sosyo-ekonomik ve Etnik Temeller (The Order of Eastern Anatolia: Socio-Economic and ethnic basis), Istanbul: E Yayınları

BEŞIKÇI, Ismail (1975): Bilim Yöntemi (Method of Science), Ankara: Komal Yayınları

BEŞIKÇI, Ismail (1977): Kürtlerin Mecburi Iskanı (The Enforced Settlement of the Kurds), Istanbul: Komal Yayınları

BETTELHEIM, Charles (1972): 'Theoretical comments' in A. Emmanuel: Unequal Exchange: A Study of the Imperialism of Trade, London: New Left Books

BEYSANOĞLU, Şevket (1962): Diyarbakır Coğrafyası (Geography of Diyarbakir), Istanbul

BEYSANOĞLU, Şevket (1963): Bütün Cepheleriyle Diyarbakır (Diyarbakir and all its Aspects), Istanbul: Şehir Matbaası

BIRTEK, Faruk and KEYDER, Çağkar (1968): 'Agriculture and the state', Jnl. of Peasant Studies II(4)

BORAN, Behice (1970): Türkiye ve Sosyalizm Sorunları (Turkey and the Problems of Socialism), Istanbul: Tekin Yayınevi

BORATAV, Korkut (1969a): Gelir Dağılımı (Income Distribution), Istanbul: Gerçek Yayınevi

BORATAV, Korkut (1969b): 'Tarımda feodal üretim ilişkileri, feodal kalıntılar ve basıt meta üretimi' (Feudal relations of production, feudal remnants and simple commodity production in agriculture), Emek 6

BORATAV, Korkut (1970a): 'Tarımda üretim ilişkileri üzerine' (On the relations of production in agriculture), Proleter Devrimci Aydınlık 1/15

BORATAV, Korkut (1970b): 'Gecikmiş bir uyarı' (A belated warning), Proleter Devrimci Aydınlık 20

BORATAV, Korkut (1973): 'Türkiye tarımının 1960lardakı yapısı ile ilgili bazı gözlemer' (Some observations on the structure of Turkish agriculture in the 1960s), Ankara: Siyasal Bilgiler Fakültesi Dergisi XXVII(3)

BORATAV, Korkut (1974): 100 Soruda Türkiye'de Devletçilik (Etatism in Turkey in 100 Questions), Istanbul: Gerçek Yayınevi

BOZARSLAN, Mehmet Emin (1964): Islamiyet Acısından Seyhlik ve Ağalık (Sheikhdom and Ağadom from an Islamic Point of View), Ankara: Toplum Yayınevi

BOZARSLAN, Mehmet Emin (1966): Dogunun Sorunları (Problems of the East), Ankara Iş Matbaası

BRENNER, Robert (1977): 'The origins of capitalist development: a critique of neo-Smithian Marxism', New Left Review 104

BRIEFING, 14 June 1977

BULUTOĞLU, Konan (1970): Türkiye'de Yabancı Sermaye (Foreign Capital in Turkey), Istanbul: Gerçek Yayınevi

CARDOSA, Ciro F.S. (1977): 'The formation of the coffee estate in nineteenth-century Costa Rica' in K. Duncan and I. Rutledge (eds.): Land and Labour in Latin America, London: Cambridge University Press

CARDOSO, Fernando Henrique (1972): Dependency and development in Latin America', New Left Review 74

ÇAVDAR, Tevfik (1970): Osmanlıların Yarı Sömürge Oluşu (The Transformation of the Ottoman Empire into a Semi-Colony), Istanbul: Ant Yayını

ÇAVDAR, Tevfik (1971): Milli Mücadeleye Başlarken Sayılarla Vaziyet ve Manzara-ı Umumiye (A Quantitative Analysis of the General Situation at the Beginning of the National Struggle), Istanbul: Milliyet Yayını

CEM, Ismail (1970): Türkiye'de Geri Kalmışlığın Tarihi (The History of Underdevelopment in Turkey), Istanbul: Gem Yayınevi

ÇETINER, Yılmaz (1969): 'Fındık tefecileri' (Hazelnut usurers), Cumhuriyet, Istanbul, 8 September

CHAYANOV, A.V. (1966): The Theory of Peasant Economy, Homewood, Illinois: Irwin

CILLOV, Halluk (1979) 'Buğday üretimi hakkinda' (On wheat production), Istanbul Ticaret, 17 August 1979

Cumhuriyet, Istanbul, 8 September 1967, 31 October 1968, 2 August 1978, 29 June 1979, 29 and 31 July 1979, 2, 12 and 13 August 1979, 8, 13 and 18 September 1979

Cumhuriyet (29 July 1979) 'TMO yetkilileri buğdaya zam yapılmayacağını bildirdiler' (The authorities of the Soil Products Office declare that there will not be a price rise for wheat)

Cumhuriyet (12 August 1979) 'Buğdaya ödenecek prim kiloda 50-100 kuruş arasında olacak, pancar taban fiatı 130 kuruş' (The premium to be paid for wheat will be between 50 and 100 kuruş per kilo, the floor price for sugar beet will be 130 kuruş)

Cumhuriyetin 50 Yılında Diyarbakir: 1973 Il Yıllığı (Diyarbakır in the 50th Anniversary of the Republic: 1973 Provincial Yearbook), Ankara: Iş Matbaacılık ve Ticaret

DARKOT, Besim (1958): Türkiye Iktisadi Coğrafyası (Economic Geography of Turkey), Istanbul: Sermet Matbaası

DINÇER, Nabi et al. (1969): Kooperatifçilik Sorunları Araştırması (Research on the Problems of Co-operativism), Ankara: DPT

DOBBS, Maurice (1963): Studies in the Development of Capitalism, London: Routledge and Kegan Paul

DOĞAN, Yalçın (1980): IMF Kıskacında Türkiye (Turkey in the Claws of the IMF), Ankara: Toplum Yayınevi

DOS SANTOS, Theotonio (1970): 'The concept of social classes', Science and Society, XXXIV(2)

DUNCAN, Kenneth and RUTLEDGE, Ian (eds., 1977): Land and Labour in Latin America: The Development of Agrarian Capitalism in the Nineteenth and Twentieth Centuries, London: Cambridge University Press

EMMANUEL, Arghiri (1972): Unequal Exchange: A Study of the Imperialism of Trade, London: New Left Books

ENNEW, Judith, HIRST, Paul and TRIBE, Keith (1977): '"Peasantry" as an economic category', Jnl. of Peasant Studies IV(4)

ERDEM, Azmi (1968): 'Müesseselesen tefecilik bölgemize soymaktadır' (Institutionalised usury is robbing our region), Yon Dergisi 113

ERDENTUĞ, Nermin (1956): Hal Köyünün Etnolojik Tetkiki (Ethnological Investigation of Hal Village), Ankara: Ankara Üniversitesi Yayını

ERDENTUĞ, Nermin (1959): Sün Köyünün Etnolojik Tetkiki (Ethnological Investigation of Sün Village), Ankara: Ankara Üniversitesi Yayını

ERDOST, Muzaffer (1969a): Türkiye Sosyalizmi ve Sosyalizm (Socialism and Turkish Socialism), Ankara: Sol Yayınları

ERDOST, Muzaffer (1969b): 'Türkiye'de feodalizmin bugünkü durumu üzerine bir taslak' (A sketch of the position of feudalism in Turkey today), Aydınlık Sosyalist Dergi 5

ERDOST, Muzaffer (1969c): 'Doğu Anadolu'da hayvancılığın feodal niteliği' (The feudal nature of animal husbandry in eastern Anatolia), Aydınlık Sosyalist Dergi 8

ERDOST, Muzaffer (1969d): 'Türkiye tarımında hakim üretim iliskisi üzerine' (On the dominant relation of production in Turkish agriculture), Aydınlık Sosyalist Dergi 13

ERDOST, Muzaffer (1970): 'Yeni opportunizmin eleştirisi' (Critique of the new opportunism), Aydınlık Sosyalist Dergi 19

ERDOST, Muzaffer (1971): 'Türkiye'de feodalizm var mi?' (Does feudalism exist in Turkey?), Türk Solu 80

FEDER, Ernest (1975): 'The new penetration of the agriculture of the underdeveloped countries by the industrial nations and their multinational concerns'

FEDER, Ernest (1976): 'How agribusiness operates in underdeveloped agriculture: Harvard Business School myths and reality', Development and Change 7

FEDER, Ernest (1977a): 'Macnamara's little Green Revolution: World Bank scheme for self-liquidation of Third World peasantry', Economic and Political Weekly, 3 April

FEDER, Ernest (1977b): 'The new World Bank program for the self-liquidation of the Third World peasantry', Journal of Peasant Studies III(3)

FIŞEK, Kurthan (1969): Türkiye'de Kapitalizmin Gelişmesi ve Işçi Sınıfı (The Development of Capitalism and the Working Class in Turkey), Ankara: Doğan Yayınları

FRANK, Andre Gunder (1969a): Capitalism and Under-development in Latin America, New York and London: Monthly Review Press

FRANK, Andre Gunder (1969b): Latin America: Underdevelopment or Revolution, New York and London: Monthly Review Press

GENC, M. (1975): 'Osmanlı maliyesinde malikane sistemi' (The tax-farming system in Ottoman finance) in Osman Okyar (ed.) Türkiye Iktisat Tarihi Semineri, Ankara: Hacettepe Üniversitesi Yayını

GLAVANIS, Kathy R.G. and GLAVANIS, Pandeli M. (1983): 'The sociology of agrarian relations in the Middle East: The persistence of household production', Current Sociology 31(2)

GÖKALP, Ziya (1975): Kürt Aşiretleri Hakkında Sosyolojik Inceleme (Sociological Investigations into the Kurdish Tribes), Ankara: Komal Yayını

GRIFFIN, Keith (1979): The Political Economy of Agrarian Change, London: Macmillan (2nd edn.)

GÜÇBILMEZ, Erdoğan (1972): Yenimahalle ve Kayadibi: Karşılaştırmalı bir Köy Araştırması (Yenimahalle and Kayadibi: A Comparative Village Study), Ankara: Ankara Üniversitesi Yayını

GÜLALP, Haldun (1980): 'Türkiye'de Ithal Ikamesi Bunalımı' (The crisis of import substitution in Turkey), METU Studies in Development 8(3/4)

GÜLALP, Haldun (1983): Gelişme Stratejileri ve Gelişme Ideolojileri (Development Strategies and Development Ideologies), Ankara: Yurt Yayınları

GÜNCE, Erol (1967): 'Early planning experiences in Turkey', Middle East Technical University: Planning in Turkey, Ankara

HALIL, Ali (1968): Atatürkçu Dışpolitika ve NATO ve Türkiye (Atatürkist Foreign Policy and NATO and Turkey), Istanbul: Gerçek Yayınevı

HARRISON, Mark (1977): 'The peasant mode of production in the work of A.V. Chayanov', Jnl. of Peasant Studies IV(4)

HASSAN, Ümit (1970): 'Tarımsal kredi sorunları - özellikle tefecelik' (Problems of agricultural credits, with special emphasis on usury), Ankara Üniversitesi Siyasal Bilgeler Fakültesi Dergisi XXV(4), 88-98

HATIPOĞLU, S.R. (1936): Türkiye'de Zirai Buhran (Agricultural Crisis in Turkey), Ankara: Yüksek Ziraat Enstitüsü Yayını

HERSHLAG, Z.Y. (1958): Turkey: An Economy in Transition, The Hague: Uitgeverij van Keulen

HERSHLAG, Z.Y. (1968): Turkey: The Challenge of Growth, Leiden: Brill

HINDERINK, Jan and KIRAY, Mübeccel Belik (1970): Social Stratification as an Obstacle to Development: A Study of Four Turkish Villages, New York: Praeger

HINDESS, Barry (ed., 1977): Sociological Theories of Economy, London: Macmillan

HINDESS, Barry (1973): The Use of Official Statistics in Sociology: A Critique of Positivism and Ethnomethodology, London: Macmillan

ILKIN, Selim and TEKELI, Ilhan (1977): 1929 Dünya Buhranında Türkiye'nin Iktisadi Politika Arayışları (Turkey's Search for Economic Policies in the 1929 World Depression), Ankara: ODTU

ILOĞLU, Asım Süreyya (1968): Memleketimizde Teşkilatlı Zirai Kredi (Organised Agricultural Credit in Our Country), Ankara: Ziraat Bankasi Matbaası

INALCIK, Halil (1955): 'Land problems in Turkish history', The Muslim World XLV

INALCIK, Halil (1959): 'Osmanlılarda raiyyet rusumu' (Ottoman taxes), Belleten XXIII(92)

INALCIK, Halil (1964): 'The nature of traditional society' in R.E. Ward and D.A. Rustow (eds.) Political Modernisation in Japan and Turkey, Princeton: Princeton University Press

INTERNATIONAL BANK FOR RECONSTRUCTION AND DEVELOPMENT (1951): The Economy of Turkey: An Analysis and Recommendations for a Development Program, London: John Hopkins

ISLAMOĞLU, Huri and KEYDER, Çağlar (1977): 'Agenda for Ottoman history', Review I(1) 42-53

ISSAWI, Charles (ed., 1966): The Economic History of the Middle East, 1800-1914, Chicago: University of Chicago Press

de JANVRY, Alain (1981): The Agrarian Question and Reformism in Latin America, Baltimore and London: John Hopkins

KAFAOĞLU, Aslan Başer (1979): 'Tarımsal fiyatlar' (Agricultural prices), Cumhuriyet, 2 August

KANBOLAT, Yahya (1963): Türkiye Ziraatinde Bünye Değişikliği (Structural Change in Turkish Agriculture), Ankara: Siyasal Bilgiler Fakültesi Maliye Enstitüsü

KARAOSMANOĞLU, Yakup Kadri (1968): Politikada 45 Yil (45 Years in Politics), Ankara: Bilgi Yayınevi

KARDAM, Ahmet (1970): 'Milli demokratik devrim ve köylü meselesi' (National democratic revolution and the peasant question), Aydınlık Sosyalist Dergi 24

KARPAT, Kemal (1959): Turkey's Politics: The Transition to a Multi-Party System, Princeton University Press

KARPAT, Kemal (1967): Türk Demokrasi Tarihi (History of Turkish Democracy), Istanbul: Istanbul Matbaasi

KAY, Cristobal (1977): 'The development of the Chilean hacienda system' in K. Duncan and I. Rutledge (eds.): Land and Labour in Latin America, London: Cambridge University Press

KELEŞ, Ruşen (1964): 'Regional disparities in Turkey', Yedinci Iskan ve Sehircilik Haftası Konferensları: 11-13 Haziran 1963 Ankara (Conferences of the Seventh Settlement and Urbanisation Week, 11-13 June, 1963, Ankara), Ankara: Iskan ve Şehircilik Derneği Yayını

KEYDER, Çağlar (1976): 'The dissolution of the Asiatic mode of production', Economy and Society II, 178-196

KEYDER, Çağlar (1981): The Definition of a Peripheral Economy: Turkey 1923-1929, Cambridge: Cambridge University Press

KIRAY, Mübeccel Belik (1964): Ereğli: Ağır Sanayiden Önce Bir Sahil Kasabası (Ereğli: A Coastal Town before Heavy Industry), Ankara: T.C. Başbakanlık, D.P.T.

KOÇ, Mehmet Şükrü (1969): Ulus 27 September

Koçi Bey Risalesi (Koçi Bey's Essay) (1939), Istanbul, Vakit Matbaası

KÖY IŞLERI BAKANLIĞI (1966): Köy Enventer Etüdlerine Göre Diyarbakır (Diyarbakır According to the Village Inventory Surveys), Ankara

KÖYLÜ, Kazım (1947): Türkiye'de Büyük Arazi Mülkleri ve Bunların Işletme Şekilleri (Large Landed Estates and their Management in Turkey), Ankara: Yüksek Ziraat Enstitüsü Yayını

KROEBER, Alfred Louis (1948): Anthropology, New York: Harcourt, Brace and World

KÜÇÜK, Yalçın (1971): 100 Soruda Planlama, Kalkınma ve Türkiye (Planning, Development and Turkey in 100 Questions), Istanbul: Gerçek Yayinevi

KURMUŞ, Orhan (1974): Emperyalizmin Türkiye'ye Girişi (The Penetration of Imperialism into Turkey), Istanbul: Bilim Yayınları

KURUÇ, Bilsay (ed., 1963): Iktisat Politikasının Resmi Belgeleri (Official Documents on Economic Policy)

KUTLAY, M. (1970a): 'Geri kapitalizm' (Backward capitalism), Emek III(2)

KUTLAY, M. (1970b): 'Türkiye'de geriliğin gelişmesi' (The development of backwardness in Turkey), Emek III(3)

LENIN, V.I. (1964): The Development of Capitalism in Russia, Moscow: Progress Publishers

LEWIS, Bernard (1968): The Emergence of Modern Turkey, London: Oxford University Press

LITTLEJOHN, Gary (1977): 'Chayanov and the theory of the peasant economy' in Barry Hindess (ed.): Sociological Theories of Economy, London: Macmillan

LONG, Norman (1975): 'Structural dependency, modes of production and economic brokerage in rural Peru' in I. Oxaal, T. Barnett, D. Booth (eds.): Beyond the Sociology of Development, 270-271, London and Boston: Routledge and Kegan Paul

LONG, Norman (1977): An Introduction to the Sociology of Rural Development, London: Tavistock

LONG, Norman and ROBERTS, Bryan R. (1978): Peasant Cooperation and Capitalist Expansion in Peru, Austin, Texas: University of Texas Press

LUXEMBURG, Rosa (1951): The Accumulation of Capital, London: Routledge and Kegan Paul
MANDEL, Ernest (n.d.): 'Capitalism and regional disparities' - translation of his article in Socialisme (17) April, May, June 1969
MANDEL, Ernest (1974): Marxist Economic Theory, London: Merlin Press
MARDIN, Şerif (n.d.): Jon Türklerin Iktisadi Fikirleri (Economic Ideas of the Young Turks), mimeo
MARTINEZ-ALIER, Juan (1977): 'Relations of production in Andean Haciendas: Peru' in K. Duncan and I. Rutledge (eds.): Land and Labour in Latin America, London: Cambridge University Press
MARX, Karl (1973): Surveys from Exile, Harmondsworth, Middlesex: Penguin Books
MARX, Karl (1974): Capital, London: Lawrence and Wishart
MEILLASSOUX, Claude (1972): 'From reproduction to production', Economy and Society I(1)
MEILLASSOUX, Claude (1975): Femmes, Greniers et Capitaux, Paris: Maspero
Milliyet, Istanbul, 7 October 1969, 24 July 1979, 16 September 1979
MÜLAYIM, Ziya Gökalp (1967): Tarımsal Kooperatifçilik (Agricultural Co-operativism), Ankara: Ankara Üniversitesi Yayını
MÜLAYIM, Ziya Gökalp (1968): 'Tarımda tefecilik sorunu' (The usury problem in agriculture), Ulus VII(1)
MÜLAYIM, Ziya Gökalp (1979): 'Pamuk ve tefeciler' (Cotton and usurers), Milliyet, 16 September
MYRDAL, Gunnar (1957): Economic Theory and Underdeveloped Regions, London: Duckworth
NICHOLLS, William H. (1955): 'Investment in agriculture in underdeveloped countries', American Economic Review, May
NOVICHEV, A.D. (1937): 'The development of commodity-money and capitalistic relations in Turkish agriculture' in C. Issawi (ed.): The Economic History of the Middle East 1800-1914, Chicago: University of Chicago Press
NOVICHEV, A.D. (1966): 'The development of agriculture in Anatolia' in C. Issawi (ed.): The Economic History of the

Middle East, 1800-1914, Chicago: University of Chicago Press
ÖKÇÜN, Gündüz (ed. 1968): Türkiye Iktisat Kongresi, 1923, Izmir: Haberler, Belgeler, Yorumlar (Economic Congress of Turkey, 1923, Izmir: News, Documents and Commentaries), Ankara: Ankara Üniversitesi Yayını

ÖKÇÜN, Gündüz (1971): 1920-1930 Yılları Arasında Kurulan Türk Anonim Şirketlerinde Yabancı Sermaye Sorunu (The Issue of Foreign Capital in Turkish Incorporated Companies Established in the 1920-1930 Period), Ankara: Ankara Üniversitesi Yayını

OKYAR, Osman (n.d.): Zirai Fiyat Politikası: Türk Tecrubesi (Agricultural Price Policy: The Turkish Experience) mimeo

O'LAUGHLIN, B. (1978): 'Meillassoux's "Femmes, Greniers et Capitaux"', Critique of Anthropology II

OXAAL, Ivor, BARNETT, Tony and BOOTH, David (eds., 1975): Beyond the Sociology of Development, London and Boston: Routledge and Kegan Paul

OZANKAYA, Özer (1969): 'Doğu Anadolu Sorunu' (The question of Eastern Anatolia), Ankara Üniversitesi Siyasal Bilgiler Fakültesi Dergisi XXIV(3)

ÖZGÜR, Özlem (1975): 100 Soruda Türkiye'de Kapitalizmin Gelismesi (The Development of Capitalism in Turkey in 100 Questions), Istanbul: Gerçek Yayınevi

ÖZGÜR, Özlem (1976): 100 Soruda Sanayilesme ve Türkiye (Industrialisation and Turkey in 100 Questions), Istanbul: Gerçek Yayınevi

PAINE, Susan (1974): Exporting Workers, London: Cambridge University Press

PATNAIK, Utsa (1979): 'Neo-populism and Marxism: the Chayanovian view of the agrarian question and its fundamental fallacy', Jnl. of Peasant Studies IV(4)

PEARSE, Andrew (1980): Seeds of Plenty, Seeds of Want: A Critical Analysis of the Green Revolution, London: Oxford University Press

RAMACHANDRAN, Nadaraja (1974): Agricultural and Industrial Development Policies in Turkey: A Review, Paris: OECD Development Centre

REDFIELD, Robert (1956): Peasant Society and Culture, Chicago: University of Chicago Press
SAHLINS, Marshall (1974): Stone Age Economics, London: Tavistock
ŞANDA, Huseyin Avni (1970): Reaya ve Köylü (Subjects and Peasants), Istanbul: Habora Kitabevi
SAYIN, Tahir (1969): Zirai Krediden Istifade Şartları (Conditions for Obtaining Agricultural Credit), Ankara: Şark Matbaası
SELÇUK, Ilhan, Cumhuriyet, 31 October 1968
SELIK, Mehmet (1961): Türkiye'de Yabancı Özel Sermaye, 1923-1960 (Foreign Private Capital in Turkey, 1923-1960), Istanbul: Boğazici Üniversitesi
SENCER, Muzaffer (n.d.): Osmanli Toplum Yapısı (Ottoman Social Structure), Yöntem Yayını
SHANIN, Teodor (1971a): 'Peasantry: delineation of a sociological concept and a field of study', European Jnl. of Sociology XII
SHANIN, Teodor (ed., 1971b): Peasants and Peasant Societies, Harmondsworth, Middlesex: Penguin Books
SHANIN, Teodor (1973-74): 'The nature and logic of peasant economy', Jnl. of Peasant Studies 1 and 2
SILIER, Oya (1981): Türkiye'de Tarımsal Yapının Gelişmesi: 1923-1938 (Development of the Rural Structure in Turkey: 1923-1938), Istanbul: Boğazici Üniversitesi
SÖZER, Ahmet Necdet (1969): Diyarbakır Havzası (The Diyarbakır Basin), Ankara: Iş Matbaacılık ve Ticaret
STATE INSTITUTE OF STATISTICS (1963): Köyler Istatistiği: 1960 Sayımına Göre (Village Statistics According to the 1960 Census), Ankara
STATE INSTITUTE OF STATISTICS (1977a): 1975 Annual Survey of Manufacturing Industry: Preliminary Results, Ankara
STATE INSTITUTE OF STATISTICS (1980): 1980 Census of Agriculture: Results of Household Survey, Ankara
STATE INSTITUTE OF STATISTICS (1984a): 1980 Census of Population: Social and Economic Characteristics, Ankara
STATE INSTITUTE OF STATISTICS (1984b): Agricultural Structure and Production, 1981, Ankara

STATE PLANNING ORGANISATION (1963): First Five Year Development Plan, 1963-1967, Ankara

STATE PLANNING ORGANISATION, CO-ORDINATION DEPARTMENT (1972): Unbalanced Development between Regions in Turkey, Ankara

TANKUT, Hasan Reşit (1939): Köylerimiz: Bugün Nasıldır, Dün Nasıldı, Yarın Nasıl Olmalıdır (Our Villages: How they are Today, How they were Yesterday, How they should be Tomorrow), Istanbul: Kenan Basımevi

TANZIMAT, I, Istanbul, 1940

TAUSSIG, Michael (1977): 'The evolution of rural wage labour in the Cauca Valley of Columbia, 1700-1970' in K. Duncan and I. Rutledge (eds.): Land and Labour in Latin America, London: Cambridge University Press

TAYANÇ, Tunç (1973): Sanayileşme Sürecinde 50 Yıl (50 Years in the Process of Industrialisation), Istanbul: Milliyet Yayınları

TEZCAN, Sabahat (1979): 'Turk kadınının sağlık sorunları' (Health problems of Turkish women) in Nermin Abadan-Unat (ed.): Türk Toplumunda Kadın, 73-88, Ankara: Türk Sosyal Bilimler Derneği

TEZEL, Yahya (1971): 'Cumhuriyetin devraldığı tarım yapısının oluşumu hakkında bazı düşünceler' (Some reflections on the historical evolution of the agricultural structure inherited by the Republic), Siyasal Bilgiler Fakültesi Dergisi XXVI(4), 270-275

THORNBURG, M.W. et al. (1949): Turkey: An Economic Appraisal, New York: Twentieth Century Fund

TIKKU, G.L. (ed. 1971): Islam and its Cultural Divergence, Urbana, Illinois: University of Illinois Press

TIMUR, Taner (1971): Türk Devrimi ve Sonrası (The Turkish Revolution and its Aftermath), Ankara: Ankara Üniversitesi Yayını

TIP Bilim Kurulu Raporu (1968), Ankara, mimeo

TÖKIN, Ismail Hüsrev (1934): Türkiye Köy Iktisadiyatı (Village Economics of Turkey), Istanbul: Kadro Mecmuası Yayını

TÖKIN, Ismail Hüsrev (1932): 'Türkiye'de derebeylik rejimi' (The feudal system in Turkey), Kadro Mecmuası, August

TONGUÇ, Ismail Hakki (1938): 'Köy eğitim meselesi' (The problem of village education), Ülkü 65

TÜM IKTISATÇILAR BIRLIĞI (1974): Türkiye'de Işçi Ücretleri ve Enflasyon (Wages and Inflation in Turkey), Ankara TIB Yayını

TÜMERTEKIN, Erol (1968): Türkiye'de Iç Göcler (Internal Migrations in Turkey), Istanbul: Istanbul Üniversitesi Coğrafya Enstitüsü Yayını

TUNÇDILEK, Necdet (1967): Türkiye Iskan Coğrafyası: Kır Iskanı (The Geography of Settlement in Turkey: Rural Settlement), Istanbul: Istanbul Üniversitesi Coğrafya Enstitüsü Yayını

TURKISH INDUSTRIALISTS' AND BUSINESSMEN'S ASSOCIATION (1978): The Turkish Economy: Prospects for Growth with Stability, Istanbul: TUSAID

TÜRKIYE IŞÇI PARTISI (1968): Bilim Kurulu Raporu (Report of the Science Commission of the Turkish Workers' Party)

TÜRKIYE TICARET ODALARI, SANAYI ODALARI ve BORSALAR BIRLIĞI (1978): Iktisati Rapor (Economic Report)

TÜTENGIL, Cavit Orhan (1975): 100 Soruda Kirsal Türkiye'nin Yapisi ve Sorunları (Structure and Problems of Rural Turkey in 100 Questions), Istanbul: Gerçek Yayınevi

ÜSTÜNEL, Besim (1965): Kalkınmanın Finansmanı: Karma Ekonomide Planlama ve Gelişme (The Finance of Development: Planning and Progress in a Mixed Economy), Istanbul: Ekonomik ve Sosyal Etüdlar Konferans Keyeti Yayını

UZUNÇARSILI, Ismail Hakki (1964): Osmanlı Tarihi (Ottoman History) II, Ankara: Türk Tarih Kurumu Yayını

VARLIER, Oktay (1978): Türkiye Tarımında Yapısal Degişme Teknoloji ve Toprak Bölüşümü (Structural Change, Technology and Land Distribution in Turkish Agriculture), Ankara: Başbakanlık Devlet Planlama Teşkilati Yayını

VON PRESSEL, W. (1966): 'Railway projects in Turkey, 1872-1900' in Charles Issawi (ed.): Economic History of the Middle East, 1800-1914, Chicago: University of Chicago Press

WALLERSTEIN, Immanuel (1974a): The Modern World System: Capitalist Agriculture and the Origins of the European World Economy in the Sixteenth Century, New York: Academic Press

WALLERSTEIN, Immanuel (1974b): 'The rise and future demise of the world capitalist system: concepts for comparative analysis', Comparative Studies in Society and History XVI

WARD, Robert and RUSTOW, Dankwart A. (1964): Political Modernisation in Japan and Turkey, Princeton: Princeton University Press

WOLF, Eric (1955): 'Types of Latin American peasantry: a preliminary discussion', American Anthropologist LVII(3) Pt I

WOLF, Eric (1956): Peasants, New Jersey: Prentice-Hall

WOLPE, Harold (1975): 'The theory of internal colonialism: the South African case' in Ivar Oxaal et al. (eds.): Beyond the Sociology of Development, 229-252, London and Boston: Routledge and Kegan Paul

YALMAN, Nur (1971): 'On land disputes in Eastern Turkey' in G.L. Tikku (ed.): Islam and its Cultural Divergence, Urbana, Illinois: University of Illinois Press

YASA, Ibrahim (1954): Hasanoğlan Köyü (Hasanoğlan Village), Ankara: TODAIE Yayını

YASA, Ibrahim (1961): Sindel Köyü (Sindel Village), Ankara: TODAIE Yayini

YASA, Ibrahim (1966): 25 Yıl Sonra Hasanoğlan Köyü: Karşılaştırmalı Toplumbilimsel Araştırma (Hasanoğlan Village after 25 Years: A Comparative Sociological Research), Ankara: Ankara Üniversitesi Yayını

YASA, Ibrahim (1970): Türkiye'nin Toplumsal Yapısı ve Temel (Social Structure and Basic Problems of Turkey), Ankara: Turkiye ve Orta Doğu Amme İdaresi Enstitüsü Yayınları no 119

YERASIMOS, Stefanos (1975): Azgelişmişlik Sürecinde Türkiye (Turkey in the Process of Underdevelopment), I, II, III, Istanbul: Gözlem Yayınları

Yon Dergisi 111 and 113, Ankara

ZHUKOVSKY, P. (1951): Türkiye'nin Zirai Bünyesi (Rural Structure of Turkey), Istanbul: Türkiye Şeker Fabrikası Yayını

GOVERNMENT PUBLICATIONS

Including those specifically mentioned in the bibliography, the following government publications were consulted:-

Düstür : Üçüncü Kitap (Code of Law : Third Book)

EKONOMI VE TARIM BAKANLIĞI (1938) *Orta Anadolu Zirai Işletme Hesapları* (Agricultural Management Accounts of Central Anatolia)

KÖY IŞLERI BAKANLIĞI *Village Inventory Surveys* of the provinces of Adiyaman, Bitlis, Diyarbakır, Gaziantep, Hakkari, Mardin, Siirt, Urfa and Van

STATE INSTITUTE OF STATISTICS

Agricultural Censuses of 1927, 1950, 1963, 1970 and 1980

Agricultural Structure and Production, 1981

Annual Foreign Trade Statistics

Annual Industrial Surveys

Annual Survey of Manufacturing Industry, 1975

Censuses of Population: 1955, 1960, 1965, 1970, 1975, 1980

Industrial Census of 1963

Köyler Istatistiği, 1963

Statistical Yearbook of Turkey, 1950, 1960-62, 1973, 1977, 1983

Summary of Agricultural Statistics (annual)

Türkiye'de Toplumsal ve Ekonomik Gelişmenin 50 Yili: 1973 (1973: 50 years of Social and Economic Development in Turkey), 1977

Türkiye Milli Geliri 1948-1973 (National Income of Turkey: 1948-1973), 1973

STATE PLANNING ORGANISATION

Destekleme Politikası Uygulamasının Çay Şeker Pancarı, Pamuk ve Findik Üreticileri Üzerindeki Etkileri (The Effects of Price Support Policy on the Producers of Tea, Sugar Beet, Cotton and Hazelnuts), 1976

First Five-Year Development Plan: 1963-1967, 1963

Second Five-Year Development Plan: 1968-1972, 1967

Third Five-Year Development Plan: 1973-1977, 1973

Dördüncü Beş Yıllık Kalkinma Planı: 1979-1983 (Fourth

Five-Year Development Plan: 1979-1983), T.C. Resmi Gazete, 12 December 1978

STATE PLANNING ORGANISATION, COORDINATION DEPARTMENT (1972); Unbalanced Development Between Regions in Turkey

TABLE A.1 NATIONAL PRODUCT 1973-1982

(TL. billions)

A. At current prices	1973	1974	1975	1976	1977	1978	1979	1980	1981	1982
Agriculture, forestry, fishing	73.2	105.5	136.1	177.3	219.8	301.3	465.8	925.4	1,328.2	1,669.1
Industry	53.4	76.7	93.5	115.0	158.0	273.4	479.9	1,026.7	1,581.1	2,173.6
Construction	14.8	18.8	24.6	31.0	42.1	64.0	103.9	213.0	285.2	357.0
Wholesale and retail trade	35.1	52.3	64.8	81.6	107.0	165.9	301.8	642.7	1,010.7	1,352.6
Transport and communications	25.3	35.5	43.3	54.8	72.2	110.1	199.6	409.2	623.3	808.5
Financial institutions	6.6	10.1	12.6	16.8	20.2	25.9	36.4	71.9	132.5	181.0
Ownership of dwellings	10.9	13.3	17.9	24.6	34.1	53.7	86.0	191.9	263.6	352.7
Private professions and services	14.1	19.3	25.0	31.9	41.2	62.6	106.8	222.4	331.3	443.5
Government, health, education	32.3	38.2	50.5	66.5	101.5	133.1	235.2	377.7	481.2	686.6
Gross domestic product at factor cost	265.7	369.8	468.4	599.6	796.1	1,190.1	2,015.3	4,080.5	6,037.1	8,024.6
Net income from abroad	14.3	17.4	16.6	11.0	9.9	15.9	43.6	107.2	140.0	138.3
Indirect taxes	31.8	42.1	53.3	69.3	79.5	102.2	165.3	279.6	453.5	565.3
Subsidies	- 1.9	- 2.2	- 2.5	- 5.0	-12.6	-17.5	-24.7	-32.1	-75.1	-71.2
Gross national product at market prices	309.8	427.1	535.8	675.0	872.9	1,290.7	2,199.5	4,435.2	6,555.5	8,656.9
B. At constant (1968) prices	**1973**	**1974**	**1975**	**1976**	**1977**	**1978**	**1979**	**1980**	**1981**	**1982**
Agriculture, forestry, fishing	32.4	35.8	39.7	42.7	42.2	43.3	44.5	45.3	45.4	48.5
Industry	30.2	32.7	35.6	39.2	43.1	46.0	43.4	40.9	43.8	45.2
Construction	9.0	9.5	10.3	11.2	11.8	12.3	12.8	12.9	12.9	13.0
Wholesale and retail trade	18.9	21.0	23.0	25.2	26.4	27.4	26.8	25.7	28.2	29.9
Transport and communications	13.9	15.1	16.3	17.8	19.0	19.5	18.6	18.0	18.7	18.9
Financial institutions	3.3	3.6	3.9	4.2	4.6	4.8	4.9	5.0	5.1	5.3
Ownership of dwellings	6.6	7.0	7.5	8.5	8.8	9.2	9.5	9.9	10.2	10.4
Private professions and services	7.0	7.6	8.3	8.9	9.2	9.5	9.4	9.3	9.8	10.2
Government, health, education	13.7	14.6	15.5	16.6	17.5	18.6	19.4	20.5	21.4	22.5
Gross domestic product at factor cost	135.0	146.9	159.9	174.1	182.7	190.6	189.5	187.6	195.5	203.9
Net income from abroad	6.0	4.8	3.6	2.5	1.8	1.9	2.8	2.1	1.8	1.3
Indirect taxes	16.4	17.5	19.0	20.8	21.8	21.4	19.5	18.9	19.9	20.9
Subsidies	- 1.0	- 1.1	- 1.1	- 1.6	- 2.9	- 4.7	- 3.5	- 2.4	- 2.5	- 1.9
Gross national product at market prices	156.5	168.0	181.4	195.8	203.4	209.2	208.3	206.1	214.7	224.2

TABLE A.2 INDUSTRIAL PRODUCTION 1973–1981

	Unit	1973	1974	1975	1976	1977	1978	1979	1980	1981
Mining, fuel, energy:										
selected products	1,000 tonnes									
Coals		7,848	8,546	8,360	8,068	7,672	7,740	7,020	6,598	7,223
Lignite (ungraded product)		10,670	11,160	11,850	13,720	14,870	18,030	15,170	15,700	17,400
Chrome ore		574	734	947	949	949	670	540	447	507
Iron ore		2,570	2,284	2,347	3,629	3,469	4,200	2,920	2,716	2,856
Copper		26	29	27	28	31	32	33	32	45
Crude petroleum		3,511	3,309	3,095	2,595	2,713	2,736	2,831	2,330	2,100
Petroleum products		12,532	12,715	12,784	13,115	14,414	12,815	10,818	12,475	12,606
Electric power	billion kWh	12	14	16	18	21	22	23	23	25
Manufacturing:										
selected products:	1,000 tonnes									
Pig iron		896	1,200	1,197	1,518	1,396	1,569	1,966	1,876	1,830
Steel ingots		1,163	1,458	1,458	1,457	1,397	1,628	1,892	1,845	1,830
Sheets and pipes		311	401	259	287	377	360	290	270	219
Cement		8,946	8,939	10,855	12,342	13,833	15,344	13,812	12,875	15,008
Coke		1,432	1,396	1,401	1,821	1,751	1,865	2,044	1,937	2,019
Superphosphate		479	586	962	854	916	820	952	..	..
Glass		101	108	115	131	156	154	168	106	208
Paper and cardboard		304	321	328	373	363	304	301	301	368
Sugar		677	767	907	1,182	995	1,009	983	1,042	1,270
Olive oil		53	130	90	150	60	142	40	70	165
Woollen and cotton yarns (million metres)		55	53	47	50	42	42	48	45	46
Woollen and cotton fabrics		223	216	220	212	185	210	196	182	228

Source: State Institute of Statistics

TABLE A.3 AGRICULTURAL PRODUCTION 1973-1982

	Unit	1973	1974	1975	1976	1977	1978	1979	1980	1981	1982
	1,000 tonnes										
Cereals:											
Wheat		10,000	11,000	14,750	16,500	16,650	16,700	17,550	16,500	17,000	17,500
Barley		2,900	3,330	4,500	4,900	4,750	4,750	5,240	5,300	5,900	6,300
Maize		1,100	1,200	1,200	1,310	1,265	1,300	1,350	1,240	1,200	1,360
Rye		690	560	750	740	690	620	620	525	530	420
Other		913	877	911	905	857	867	817	849	780	841
Pulses		589	665	675	752	813	729	762	810	868	1,206
Potatoes		2,200	2,275	2,490	2,850	2,800	2,750	2,870	3,000	2,988	3,000
Sugar beet		5,095	5,707	6,949	9,406	8,995	8,837	8,760	6,766	11,165	11,500
Tobacco		149	203	200	324	248	297	217	234	177	206
Cotton		513	598	480	470	575	475	476	500	458	481
Oilseeds		1,469	1,472	1,355	1,430	1,517	1,374	1,511	1,653	1,507	1,381
Wool		61	76	78	54	55	57	59	62	64	62
Fruit and nuts:											
Grapes		3,344	3,347	3,247	3,080	3,180	3,496	3,500	3,600	3,700	3,500
Figs		190	156	175	188	175	185	200	205	250	250
Hazelnuts		251	244	317	245	290	310	300	250	350	218
Citrus Fruits		691	900	958	975	1,147	1,081	1,147	1,182	1,225	1,201
	Thousands										
Livestock											
Cattle goats		14,259	14,410	14,802	15,158	15,552	15,964	16,580	17,017	16,983	
Sheep and goats		58,793	59,285	60,129	60,012	60,984	62,389	64,801	64,222	68,524	
Poultry		40,677	41,006	41,736	48,203	50,964	54,711	58,941	60,240	58,834	

Source: State Institute of Statistics and State Planning Organisation

	1973	1974	1975	1976	1977	1978	1979	1980	1981	1982
I. Agricultural products	832	852	793	1,254	1,041	1,542	1,344	1,672	2,219	2,141
Cereals	64	27	28	70	120	262	167	181	326	337
Fruit and vegetables	259	294	276	375	440	561	647	754	795	649
Hazelnuts	122	173	154	203	251	331	353	395	302	241
Dried fruit	83	68	76	68	100	145	166	212	208	168
Citrus fruit	25	26	29	87	77	44	53	87	125	77
Others	29	27	17	17	12	41	75	60	160	163
Industrial crops and forestry products	457	460	434	734	432	617	446	606	813	741
Cotton	306	244	230	438	210	348	227	323	348	297
Tobacco	133	205	183	251	176	225	176	234	395	348
Others	18	11	21	45	46	44	43	49	70	96
Live animals and Sea products	52	71	55	75	49	102	84	131	285	414
II. Mining and quarrying products	42	80	105	110	126	124	132	191	194	175
III. Processed and manufactured products	443	600	503	596	586	622	785	1,047	2,290	3,430
Processed agricultural products	149	130	128	98	137	110	151	209	412	569
Manufactured products	294	470	375	498	449	512	634	838	1,878	2,861
Textiles and clothing	106	147	128	263	260	309	378	424	803	1,056
Hides and leather industry	45	75	65	50	52	40	44	50	82	111
Forestry industry	8	24	2	7	1	1	2	4	20	33
Chemical industry	18	37	33	47	34	24	23	76	94	148
Rubber and plastic industry	1	1	5	3	3	2	3	16	72	60
Petroleum products	49	86	36	16	-	-	-	39	107	343
Glass and ceramics	7	12	18	20	27	30	37	36	102	104
Cement	15	8	24	16	9	41	45	40	198	207
Iron and steel industry	2	1	20	22	14	21	31	34	100	362
Non-ferrous metal industry	22	40	21	17	20	12	15	18	30	45
Metal products and mac.	9	16	18	16	14	18	18	30	85	143
Electrical equipment and products	1	1	1	2	3	4	4	11	26	75
Others	11	22	4	19	12	10	34	60	159	174
Total	1,317	1,532	1,401	1,960	1,753	2,288	2,261	2,910	4,703	5,746

Source: State Planning Organisation

TABLE A.5 IMPORTS BY COMMODITIES 1973–1982

(US $ millions)

	1973	1974	1975	1976	1977	1978	1979	1980	1981	1982
I. Agriculture and livestock	14	306	202	77	112	50	36	50	125	176
II. Mining and quarrying	243	806	882	1,191	1,546	1,486	1,818	4,006	4,098	3,852
Oil	222	752	806	1,106	1,436	1,396	1,712	3,862	3,878	3,640
Crude oil	201	694	718	1,002	1,152	1,044	962	2,952	3,258	3,419
Oil products	21	58	88	104	284	352	750	910	620	221
Others	21	54	76	85	110	90	106	144	220	212
III. Industrial products	1,779	2,607	3,555	3,725	4,037	2,943	3,092	3,759	4,641	4,657
Agriculture-based processed products	9	150	227	147	58	50	115	301	229	176
Industrial products	1,770	2,458	3,329	3,578	3,978	2,893	2,977	3,458	4,412	4,482
Chemicals	426	338	531	554	555	476	524	727	946	839
Fertilizer		100	48	98	214	283	356	395	254	51
Rubber and plastics		135	176	183	266	154	145	181	240	237
Leather and hide	0	1	1	0	0	0	0	0	1	0
Forestry products	2	1	2	2	2	2	1	3	2	6
Textiles	40	46	66	58	51	50	46	79	78	103
Glass and ceramics	21	21	26	25	25	18	28	35	40	34
Iron and steel	248	531	679	546	690	408	345	462	605	591
Non-ferrous metal industry	67	131	102	89	97	42	55	87	141	122
Metal products	516	14	15	27	15	20	14	23	23	37
Machinery		637	984	1,070	1,060	761	903	843	1,223	1,309
Electrical appliances	146	174	273	274	291	218	251	270	336	374
Motor vehicles	234	246	332	518	572	378	221	223	356	594
Other industrial products	6	82	93	134	141	83	88	130	167	185
IV. Imports with waiver	50	58	99	136	102	120	123	94	69	49
Total	2,086	3,777	4,738	5,129	5,797	4,599	5,069	7,909	8,933	8,734

Source: State Planning Organisation

TABLE A.6 PRICES 1973-1982

Indices 1963 = 100 (Annual averages)

	1973	1974	1975	1976	1977	1978	1979	1980	1981	1982
Wholesale prices:										
Total	240	312	343	397	492	751	1.231	2,551	3,488	4,369
Food and feeding stuffs	225	305	358	412	506	734	1,093	2,190	3,101	3,759
Cereals	201	318	337	365	430	545	774	1,638	2,819	3,373
Livestock	349	371	444	621	891	1,323	1,959	3,806	4,437	5,673
Livestock products	226	297	432	453	577	981	1,473	2,625	3,245	4,205
Raw materials and semi-finished products	265	323	319	372	470	779	1,461	3,152	4,135	5,387
Fuel	327	356	378	393	457	960	1,717	4,630	6,142	7,911
Minerals	201	301	305	319	386	645	1,353	2,735	3,302	4,585
Building materials	208	253	275	383	642	963	1,676	3,157	3,700	4,802
Textiles	276	341	300	398	490	681	1,190	2,135	2,613	3,464
The cost of living:										
Ankara, total	241	278	331	386	473	725	1,174	2,365	3,168	4,067
Istanbul, total	244	302	366	430	541	876	1,433	2,784	3,831	5,083
Food	243	297	378	459	565	864	1,333	2,554	3,503	4,702
Heating and lighting	268	339	374	461	611	1,096	2,122	4,404	5,302	6,454
Clothing	239	309	323	341	453	775	1,515	2,814	4,052	5,504
Other	245	308	352	371	495	958	1,616	3,386	4,802	6,113

Source: Ministry of Commerce

TABLE A.7 SELECTED STATISTICS ON SOUTHEASTERN ANATOLIA, 1980

PROVINCES	POPULATION			ECONOMICALLY ACTIVE POPULATION (12 years of age and over)		LITERACY (among people 6 years of age and over)		UNIVERSITY GRADUATES	
	Total	Urban	Rural	Working in agriculture	Working in other activities	Illiterate	Literate	Male	Female
Adıyaman	367,595	116,986	250,609	25,021	18,744	59,273	124,877	1,877	383
Bitlis	257,908	93,757	164,151	79,529	19,247	122,249	75,055	1,142	145
Diyarbakır	778,150	374,264	403,886	194,232	75,979	358,480	250,940	5,682	1,059
Gaziantep	808,697	512,745	295,952	117,130	159,130	276,225	372,429	6,157	2,016
Hakkari	38,534	18,009	20,525	56,182	11,897	81,090	37,523	777	112
Mardin	564,967	192,004	372,963	167,996	48,087	276,505	157,078	3,201	570
Siirt	445,483	183,808	261,679	125,877	37,888	216,500	122,134	2,391	386
Urfa	602,736	282,419	320,317	151,309	62,753	291,709	178,799	3,472	605
Van	468,646	156,852	311,794	147,679	41,194	227,476	132,312	2,545	448
S.E. Total	4,002,716	1,930,840	2,401,871	1,164,955	475,622	1,909,507	1,451,312	27,271	5,724
Other Regions	40,734,241	17,714,167	22,690,079	9,939,546	6,942,209	10,287,816	23,860,064	601,478	209,315
Turkey Total	44,736,957	19,645,007	25,091,950	11,104,501	7,417,831	12,197,323	25,311,211	628,749	215,039

Source: State Institute of Statistics, 1980 Census of Population: Social and Economic Characteristics, Ankara, 1984

TABLE A.8 AGRICULTURAL LANDS IN TURKEY, 1927-1981 (000 hectares)

Year	Cultivated	Fallow	Vineyards and Olive Groves	Fruit and Vegetables	Forests
1927	7,600	n.a.	n.a.	n.a.	n.a.
1938	8,463	3,674	660	650	10,386
1946	8,413	4,680	n.a.	n.a.	n.a.
1956	15,572	7,881	1,195	682	10,418
1962	15,167	8,048	1,401	816	10,584
1966	15,454	8,528	1,496	888	10,584
1970	15,591	8,705	1,576	1,467	18,273
1974	16,154	8,506	1,580	1,688	20,170
1978	16,349	8,200	1,601	1,892	20,155
1981	16,687	8,204	1,633	1,965	20,199

Source: State Institute of Statistics

TABLE A.9 CHANGES IN THE DISTRIBUTION OF HOLDINGS BETWEEN 1950 AND 1980

	TURKEY						EASTERN ANATOLIA					
Size of Holdings (Decares)	1950 Agricultural Census		1973 State Planning Organisation		1980 Agricultural Census		1950 Agricultural Census		1973 State Planning Organisation		1980 Agricultural Census+	
	% of total h'hlds	% of total land	% of total h'hlds	% of total land	% of total h'hlds	% of total land	% of total h'hlds	% of total land	% of total h'hlds	% of total land	% of total h'hlds	% of total land
1-50	61.7	18.9	70.5	21.3	20	20.1	58.5	18.4	66.2	15.9	56.0	8.7
51-100	21.8	18.8	16.2	18.9	20.2	21.2	21.7	20.4	15.8	13.1	17.6	11.8
101-200	10.5	19.1	8.5	19.8	11.5	23.8	11.4	21.2	12.4	21.6	14.8	19.6
201-500	4.4	16.9	3.7	18.6	5.3	22.7	7.2	18.9	3.6	11.1	8.0	23.5
500+	1.6	26.3	1.1	21.4	0.9	12.2	1.2	21.2	2.0	38.3	3.6	26.4

+ S.E. Anatolia only

Sources: State Institute of Statistics
Agricultural Census of 1950 and 1980, and
Oktay Varlier, Türkiye Tarımında Yapısal Değişme Teknoloji ve Toprak Bölüşümü (Structural Change, Technology and Land Distribution in Turkish Agriculture), Ankara, Başbakanlık Devlet Planlama Teşkilatı, 1978

TABLE A.10 AGRICULTURAL CREDITS IN SELECTED YEARS, 1950-1981

	SOURCE				TL millions
Years	Agricultural Bank	Agricultural Bank through credit Co-operatives	Sales Co-operatives and Unions	General Directorate of Agricultural Supplies	Total
1950					2,032
1951					2,712
1952					3,753
1953					4,252
1954					5,640
1955					7,190
1971	2,068	1,825	2,269	-	6,191
1972	2,797	2,391	4,572	-	9,811
1973	3,833	2,778	9,433	-	16,247
1974	4,107	3,143	14,900	-	22,716
1975	5,152	4,454	22,939	4,207	36,835
1976	7,166	6,036	21,875	4,382	39,565
1977	9,018	7,854	29,253	1,479	47,701
1978	12,284	10,678	35,091	5,934	64,178
1979	17,909	17,752	61,717	22,111	119,643
1980	36,377	36,440	95,131	16,873	184,958
1981	50,561	47,243	132,731	55,260	267,207

Source: State Institute of Statistics and Turkish Agricultural Bank

TABLE A.11 SUPPORT PRICES FOR SELECTED CROPS (Turkish lira per kilo) 1974-1982

Crop	1974	1975	1976	1977	1978	1979	1980	1981	1982
Cotton	7.83	8.00	10.08	10.75	13.75	25.00	50.00	63.00	78.00
Raisins	10.00	10.00	10.50	12.00	17.50	40.00	85.00	110.00	132.00
Sugarbeet	0.40	0.50	0.58	0.62	0.90	1.42	3.08	4.50	5.86
Tea	6.25	7.50	8.50	10.00	12.00	14.50	26.05	41.00	55.00
Figs	5.50	6.00	7.00	8.00	10.50	22.00	50.00	65.00	78.00
Wheat	2.12	2.34	2.58	2.86	3.20	4.72	9.00	17.41	22.86
Sunflowers	3.75	5.50	5.75	6.50	8.50	12.00	30.00	40.00	50.00
Hazelnuts	13.50	14.00	14.50	16.50	21.50	37.50	110.00	125.00	150.00
Tobacco	23.15	31.29	39.13	44.39	50.10	60.91	112.23	160.00	211.84

Source: State Institute of Statistics

TABLE A.12 CURRENT AND REAL SUPPORT PRICES FOR SELECTED CROPS, 1963-1982+

	WHEAT			COTTON			HAZELNUTS			WHOLESALE PRICE INDEX
	Current prices (kuruş)	Real++ prices (kuruş)	Real Price Index	Current prices (kuruş)	Real++ prices (kuruş)	Real Price Index	Current prices (kuruş)	Real++ prices (kuruş)	Real Price Index	
1963	73	73.0	100.0	200	200.0	100.0	535	535.0	100.0	100.0
1964	73	72.1	98.8	208	205.5	102.8	440	434.8	81.3	101.2
1965	78	71.3	97.7	199	181.9	91.0	520	475.3	88.8	109.4
1966	78	68.0	93.2	202	176.1	88.1	500	435.9	81.5	114.7
1967	78	63.2	86.6	218	176.7	88.4	525	425.4	79.5	123.4
1968	78	61.3	84.0	228	179.1	90.0	525	412.4	77.1	127.3
1969	80	58.6	80.3	227	166.3	83.2	570	417.6	78.1	136.5
1970	85	58.3	79.9	267	183.3	91.7	730	501.0	93.6	145.7
1971	100	59.2	81.1	312	184.7	92.4	800	473.7	88.5	168.9
1972	100	50.2	68.8	344	172.6	86.3	800	401.4	75.0	199.3
1973	120	50.0	68.5	544	226.6	113.3	940	391.5	73.2	240.1
1974	214	68.9	94.4	800	256.6	128.3	1,350	433.0	80.9	311.8
1975	234	68.2	93.4	800	233.1	116.6	1,400	407.9	76.2	343.2
1976	258	65.1	89.2	1,075	271.1	135.6	1,450	365.0	68.3	396.6
1977	286	58.1	79.6	1,075	218.5	109.3	1,650	335.3	62.7	492.1
1978	325	43.3	59.3	1,375	183.1	91.6	2,150	286.4	53.5	750.8
1979	490	39.8	54.5	2,500	203.1	101.6	3,750	304.7	57.0	1,230.7
1980	1,025	40.2	55.1	5,000	196.0	98.0	11,000	431.2	80.6	2,551.0
1981	1,741	49.9	68.3	6,300	180.6	90.3	12,500	362.5	67.8	3,488.0
1982	2,286	52.3	71.6	7,800	178.5	89.25	15,000	343.3	64.2	4,369.0

+ In computing the real prices, wholesale prices published by the Ministry of Commerce have been used

++ 1963 = 100

Index

Abdülkerim Üney 117, 205, 206, 207
Adana 80, 132, 173, 174, 177, 179, 222, 233, 234, 236, 237, 242, 250, 251
Adıyaman 51, 64
Afyon 215
Ağa, see Landlord
Ağri 5
Agricultural Bank 32, 33, 99, 111, 153, 191-196, 199, 200, 201, 202, 204, 205, 207, 219, 220, 249
Agricultural Census 1963 6, 214
Agricultural Credits 32, 33, 41, 61, 99, 111, 133, 137, 143, 153, 188, 191-209, 219, 220, 222, 229, 231, 239, 244, 249, 256, 258, 259, 260
Agriculture 3, 5, 6, 7, 8, 10, 11, 13, 17, 26, 31, 32, 39, 40, 44, 45, 51, 53, 56, 57, 59, 76, 89-
Ali Çelen 237
Alp family 237
Animals 32, 34, 44, 64, 71, 74, 87, 94, 97, 98, 99, 104, 106, 107, 117, 118, 120, 121, 123, 129, 130, 132, 133, 134, 135, 140, 147, 149, 156, 157, 158, 159, 174, 175, 179, 183, 185, 186, 187, 192, 197, 198, 200, 205, 222, 225, 228, 229, 230, 237, 246, 248, 249
Ankara 62, 69, 204, 215, 227, 231, 237, 251
Arif Başdemir 130, 132, 133, 135
Armenians 125
Artisans 60, 109

Aşağı Balahur 103, 126, 127, 206, 207
Hüseyin Aslanoğlu 105, 106, 155
Aşar 31, 33, 34
Ayans 15, 16
Aydoğan family 103, 104, 105, 111, 122, 125, 126, 132, 204, 231, 247, 249
Başlık 77, 79, 84, 132, 165, 208
Bitlis 15, 51, 58, 64, 222
Blood feuds 234, 236, 237
Boğaz 74
Bourgeoisie 28, 30, 37, 38, 40, 61, 62, 193, 243
Bursa 251
Cadastral surveys 32, 230
Çapakçur Sancak 16
Capital accumulation 17, 23, 24, 28, 34, 38, 143, 144, 168, 170, 171, 190, 213, 256, 258
Capitalism 1, 2, 3, 5-13, 17, 18, 25-30, 32, 36, 45, 58, 65, 150, 161, 162, 167, 183, 188, 190, 191, 234, 238, 242, 252, 257, 261
Çayirdere 70
Celal Pala 117, 205, 206
Cemal Okan 107, 108
Central Bank 218
Çermik 16, 69, 70, 74, 87, 121
Christians 30
Cizre 15
Class 2, 3, 4, 10, 12, 14, 24-28, 31, 38, 39, 40, 118, 129, 162, 259
Colonialist exploitation 3, 24, 26, 27, 37
Commodity production 5, 8, 11, 36, 129, 130, 135, 191, 209
Contraceptives 82, 88
Co-operatives 33, 65, 98, 191, 195, 196, 212, 219, 220, 221, 229, 230
Corvée 34, 133, 134, 138, 170
Cotton 29, 30, 32, 80, 97-99, 101-106, 111, 125, 130, 151, 152, 156, 173, 174, 182, 193, 205, 207, 212, 217-221, 229, 230, 233, 236, 240, 242-244, 246, 247, 249, 252
Crops 13, 44, 45, 63, 80, 93, 98, 99, 101, 106, 107, 108, 112, 121, 132, 143, 147, 150, 151, 181, 182, 187, 188, 192, 193, 197, 200, 203, 207, 208, 212, 217, 218, 219, 225, 227, 229, 230, 232, 236, 243, 244, 248
Çukobirlik 212, 221, 229, 230
Çukurova 29, 80, 101, 150, 173, 174, 177, 179, 182, 205, 235, 242, 243, 249
Cumhuriyet Newspaper 215, 216
Çüngüş 97, 125
Dağarası 70
Demirtepe 70
Dibektaşı 70
Dicle district 234
Dirlik 14, 15
Diyarbakır 5, 16, 17, 51, 58, 61, 64, 69, 86, 93, 109, 117, 139, 140, 141, 157, 162, 184, 191, 200, 204, 205, 216, 222, 225, 228, 231, 237, 242, 243, 247, 251

Doctors 22, 55, 80, 82, 86, 87
Education 26, 34, 54, 65, 82, 88, 237
Efrahim Çatal 171, 172, 173, 174, 175, 176, 177, 180, 181, 182, 183
Efrahim Kahraman 247
Elazığ 132, 152, 156, 162, 163, 184, 204, 229, 230, 237, 242, 243, 251
Electricity 29, 39
Emek journal 5, 10
Ergani 17, 63, 69, 70, 74, 86, 87, 97, 109, 112, 115, 117, 121, 125, 126, 133, 145, 162, 172, 178, 181, 184, 191, 199, 200, 202-207, 226, 228, 231, 237, 239, 240, 246, 250, 251
Erzurum 5
Etatism, see State capitalism
Euphrates River 97
Europe 29, 30, 193, 233, 238, 251, 254
Fahim Güçlü 155
Family farms 11, 44, 76, 144, 169
Farmers' Union 221
Fehim Kaval 248
Fertilisers 13, 44, 56, 61, 62, 102, 104, 105, 108, 111, 112, 153, 154, 192, 201, 202, 203, 204, 205, 207, 244, 259, 260
Feudal relations 3, 5, 6, 7, 8, 10, 15
Fruit 63, 64, 93, 98, 101, 107, 108, 118, 130, 206, 212, 217, 218, 225, 226, 228, 233, 237, 240, 241, 251
Fuat Bey, see Aydoğan family
Gaziantep 5, 51
Gedikli family 122, 123, 124, 125, 126, 246, 249
Genç 15
Germany 29, 111, 233, 238, 249, 254
Gisgis 1, 14, 17, 22, 50, 65, 69-188, 191, 199, 204-207, 213, 226-232, 234, 235, 238, 240, 241, 242, 261
Gözlü 203
Grains 30, 39, 42, 44, 63, 93, 99, 101-108, 117, 125, 130, 132, 139, 140, 151, 153, 172, 174, 178, 179, 180, 181, 182, 184, 185, 186, 187, 193, 200, 207, 212, 213, 214, 216, 218, 225-229, 237, 239, 241, 244, 248, 249, 250, 259
Greece 30, 31
Güclü cousins 111, 112
Güldoğan family 124
Hakki Ağa, see Gedikli family
Hakkari 51, 64
Halil Ergin 155
Halil Yoldaş 155
Hamdi Bey 105, 111
Handicraft industry 34
Has 14
Hasip Ağa 172

Hatay 5
Health 55, 65, 71, 80, 86, 87, 88, 173, 231, 234
Hospitals 22, 55
Household economy 1, 2, 11, 12, 13, 17, 18, 22, 65, 76, 77, 137, 143, 144, 161, 162, 165, 184, 188, 190, 240, 241, 252, 254, 255, 256, 258
Hükumet 15
Hüseyin Ergin 247
IBRD 42, 258, 259
Illiteracy 54
Iltizam 15, 115
Imadiye 15
IMF 42, 43, 214, 258
Industry 7, 10, 17, 29, 30, 31, 34, 35, 37, 39, 41, 42, 43, 44, 45, 53, 57, 58, 60, 64, 65, 80, 167, 211, 212, 250, 251, 259, 261
Independence, War of 29, 30
Inflation 40, 43, 213, 214
Infrastructure 22, 29, 39, 41, 50, 97
Inheritance 16, 110, 118, 239
Iran 16, 64
Irrigation 56, 91, 93, 95, 97, 99, 101, 102, 103, 104, 105, 106, 107, 133, 172, 175, 176, 177, 183, 184, 220, 229, 233, 247
Iş Bankası 35
Iskenderun 215, 225
Ismet Pasha 36
Istanbul 29, 36, 40, 62, 204, 215, 222, 231, 237, 250, 251
Itah Sancak 16
Izmir 36, 62, 194, 237, 250, 251
Izzet Güçlü 155
Kabile 81, 82
Kahya 61
Kalhana 1, 14, 17, 22, 50, 65, 72-188, 191, 204, 206, 207, 213, 226, 229, 230, 231, 232, 234, 243, 244, 248, 261
Kautsky 3, 7
Kemalists 27, 29
Kemertepe 70
Kermukan 132
Kerpiç 71, 74, 156
Kesentaş 86, 87
Keydanevleri 72, 74, 103, 129
Kezin 230
Kenya 94, 215
Kulub Sancak 16
Land, control of 13, 31, 44, 56, 59, 91, 111, 129
Land reform 32, 62, 193, 259
Landless peasants 5, 6, 32, 44, 59, 60, 61, 80, 87, 89, 104, 111, 116, 117, 124, 129, 130, 134, 135, 146, 148, 151, 152, 153, 156, 169, 170, 197, 204, 231, 260
Landlords 2, 5, 7, 14, 25, 31, 32, 33, 36, 37, 40, 53, 61, 62, 65, 74, 80, 88, 98, 102, 106, 107, 110, 111, 112, 122, 123, 126, 127, 129, 130, 132-135, 137-144, 147, 149, 151-156, 172, 179, 181, 193, 198-201, 204, 205, 211, 217, 218, 219, 229,

230, 231, 244, 246, 252, 255, 256, 258
Landownership 1, 6, 9, 14, 15, 16, 17, 32, 38, 45, 59, 60, 62, 69, 89, 91, 94, 95, 97, 110, 112, 115, 118, 120, 122, 126, 127, 129, 138, 147, 148, 155, 170, 179, 195, 199, 204, 229, 255, 259
Large estates 16, 17, 60, 127, 135, 142, 144, 159, 255, 256, 259
Lentils 63, 93, 97, 101-108, 130, 132, 151, 174, 175, 179, 180, 226, 229
Lobud Ağa 122, 123, 249
Maden district 132, 234
Mahmudiya 15
Malen (Pinarkaya) 72, 103, 129, 206, 207
Mardin 5, 51, 64, 222
Market gardening 63, 64, 97, 98
Marketing 13, 93, 97, 98, 101, 111, 112, 121, 137, 143, 178, 187, 192, 211-232, 256, 258
Marmara 29
Marriage 77, 79, 84, 85, 132, 162, 165, 208, 235, 238, 239, 245
Marshall Aid 40, 193
Mechanisation 2, 26, 31, 32, 41, 42, 51, 58, 62, 76, 104, 109, 110, 111, 133, 142, 143, 153, 180, 181, 193, 244, 250
Mecit Güzey 200
Mehmet Çok 163
Mehmet Şerif Ece 183, 184, 185
Merchant capital 5, 6, 13, 30, 32, 37, 38, 191, 207, 212, 255
Merchants 25, 30, 31, 32, 33, 36, 37, 38, 40, 60, 65, 102, 112, 125, 129, 152, 194-199, 202, 203, 205-209, 211, 214-219, 222, 227, 228, 230, 232, 234, 250, 252, 258
Mersin 36
Migo 132
Migration 13, 23, 26, 58, 76, 79, 80, 82, 84, 85, 156, 166, 168, 232, 233-252, 254, 255
Mihrani Sancak 16
Military, the 4, 39, 43, 132, 165 171, 208, 249
Milliyet Newspaper 215, 221
Ministry of Commerce 35, 218
Ministry of Monopolies 218
Ministry of Village Affairs 5, 60
Miri lands 14, 15
Muhtar Seydo 153, 154
Mülk 16
Mürit 26
Muş 58
Mustafa Çetin 155
NATO 43
Nobility 30
Nokta magazine 43
Notables 15, 16, 60, 122, 123, 193
OECD 42, 43
OEEC 41
Oil 222, 225
Ömer Civelek 155
Öşr 15
Ottomans 14, 15, 16, 29, 30, 35,

60, 122, 123, 125, 138, 256
Paraffin 34, 142, 178, 198, 206, 230
Pasture lands 42, 94, 98, 142, 143, 192
Peasant holdings 1, 2, 11, 16, 17, 44
Peasantry 2, 3, 4, 10, 12, 13, 14, 25, 26, 31, 33, 37, 45, 118, 127, 137, 138, 159, 167, 168, 220, 234, 256
Pertek Sancak 16
Political parties 25, 26, 56, 80, 193, 212, 243
Private sector 35, 39, 42, 53, 57
Production, means of 13, 44, 65, 122, 123, 127, 129, 137, 138, 141, 143, 144, 190, 207, 229, 232, 256
Production, modes of 7, 8, 9, 10, 12, 13, 27, 29, 256
Production, relations of 1, 2, 5-11, 13, 14, 26, 27, 28, 59, 65, 69, 88, 112, 118, 122, 127, 133, 135, 137, 138, 139, 141, 144, 145, 159, 162, 167, 211, 217, 255, 256
Production, units of 7, 9, 10, 12, 17, 65, 76, 103, 137, 141, 143, 144, 159, 161, 255, 260, 261
Proletariat 3, 12, 156, 167, 197
Provincial councils 34
Railways 29, 39, 142, 225, 230, 233, 247
Ramazan Kaval 155
Reaya 14-17
Recep Ergin 155
Religious leaders 30, 165
Roads 34, 54, 132, 225
Rural structure 1, 2, 3, 4, 10, 16, 26, 44, 256, 258
Sakizli 101
Salt 34, 36, 178, 198, 206, 230
Schools 22, 54, 55, 71, 72, 74, 132, 165, 174, 234
Seeds 13, 44, 62, 111, 112, 132, 139, 140, 141, 150, 154, 192, 197, 198, 203, 205, 207, 244, 248, 259
Sehrizar Sancak 16
Semi-feudal relations 3, 5, 6, 7, 8, 10, 257
Seydi Kaval 155
Share cropping 5-10, 41, 59-61, 80, 89, 98, 103-106, 110, 112, 116, 117, 120-122, 125, 126, 129, 130, 132-134, 139-159, 170, 172-174, 179, 183, 197, 201, 203, 204, 206, 229, 234, 236, 241, 248, 249, 252, 255, 257
Sheikhs 25, 26, 87
Shell Oil Company 222, 225
Siirt 5, 29, 51, 64, 222
Sincik (Çayirdere) 70, 234
Sipahis 14, 15, 17
Sivas 247
Small holdings 5, 8, 11, 16, 17, 60, 76, 107, 117, 127, 135,

142, 194
Social formation 18, 22, 27, 137, 143, 211, 241, 243, 258
Socialism 4, 9, 10
Söke 219, 220
Sokman sancak 16
South Africa 26, 27, 28
Standard Oil Co. 36
State capitalism 29, 38, 39, 41
State Institute of Statistics 53, 54, 55, 64
State Planning Organisation 62
Sugar 34, 37, 38, 39, 97, 98, 103, 104, 105, 142, 198, 206, 218, 229, 230, 231, 251
Sultan Selim 16
Tarsus 80, 220, 235, 236
Taurus mountains 70, 72
Taxes 14, 15, 17, 31, 32, 33, 34, 35, 37, 38, 39, 40, 117, 126, 127, 141, 167, 219, 234
Telephones 35, 54
Tercil Sancak 16
Tevekli 70
Textiles 37, 39, 43, 80, 233, 234
Tigris river 93
Timar 14, 16
Tobacco 29, 30, 32, 212, 217, 218, 219, 231, 233, 244
Toprak Mahsulleri Ofisi 154, 212-217, 226, 227
Trabzon 36
Tractors 41, 56, 95, 104-107, 109-112, 120, 124, 125, 126, 132, 134, 135, 142, 153, 155, 193, 207, 249
Trakya 216
Transportation 26, 29, 31, 41, 54 62, 65, 87, 102, 107, 110, 111 117, 118, 121, 147, 152, 154, 173, 178, 179, 181, 185, 203, 205, 221, 225, 226, 227, 228, 230, 237, 239, 246, 258
Tribal leaders 25, 26, 30, 60, 61 122, 138
Tunceli 5
Turkish Left, the 4, 256
Turkish Match Monopoly 36
Turkish Petroleum 222
Turkish Republic 16, 17, 24, 25, 31, 32, 33, 62, 115, 137, 138, 142, 258, 259
Turkish Workers' Party 5, 9, 24, 194
Underdevelopment 17, 18, 22, 23, 24, 25, 26, 27, 28, 29, 30, 45, 254, 255, 261
Unemployment 23, 43, 76, 143, 165 167, 241, 242, 251, 252
Universities 55
Urfa 5, 51, 64, 139
USA 36, 40, 41, 42, 259
Usurer capital 5, 6, 32, 191, 255
Usurers 32, 33, 34, 117, 125, 129, 194-197, 199, 200, 204, 205, 207, 208, 209, 219-222, 232, 234, 239, 252, 258
Van 16, 51, 64, 222
Vegetables 32, 63, 64, 70, 91,

93, 97, 98, 107, 108, 118,
118, 130, 171, 172, 174,
175, 177, 178, 180, 182-185,
203, 206, 207, 212, 226,
228, 231, 240, 241, 247,
251
Village Inventory Surveys 5,
6, 60
Vineyards 70, 93, 97, 98, 118
Wage labour 3, 7, 8, 9, 10,
11, 60, 76, 98, 105, 110,
112, 129, 130, 133, 135,
139, 144, 145, 150, 153,
159, 162, 167, 168, 169,
170, 173, 183, 190, 191,
207, 226, 242, 256, 257
Women 76, 77, 79, 82, 84, 85,
104, 152, 161, 162, 166,
167, 168, 170, 171, 175,
178, 181-186, 188, 235,
237, 239, 252
World Bank 41, 193, 260
Yozgat Province 105, 179
Yukarı Balahur 72
Yunusoğlu 101
Zakir Bey 123 see Aydoğan
family
<u>Zeamet</u> 14, 16
Zengetil 172
Zimoyik (Dibektaşı) 70
Zirkiilyan (Dağarası) 70
Ziyarek (Tevekli) 70
Zülfü Ağa 203